Confessions of a Heroin Addict's Mother

Confessions of a Heroin Addict's Mother

A Memoir of Self-Reflection

Eva Summerhill

Surrogate Press®

Photos and Text Copyright ©2020 Eva Summerhill

All rights reserved.

No part of this publication may be reproduced, stored in a retrieval system, or transmitted in any form or by any means, electronic, mechanical, photocopying, recording, or otherwise, without written permission of the author.

evasummerhill@gmail.com
evasummerhill.com
confessionsofaheroinaddictsmother.com

Published in the United States by
Surrogate Press®
an imprint of Faceted Press®
Park City, Utah

Surrogate Press, LLC
SurrogatePress.com

ISBN: 978-1-947459-28-1

Library of Congress Control Number: 2019913371

Book cover and interior design by: Katie Mullaly, Surrogate Press®

Dear Reader,

This book, born out of both pain and self-reflection, is my attempt to offer hope to the countless families who have suffered, or are still suffering, amidst a national crisis that took 63,632 lives in 2016, and 70,200 lives in 2017, according to the Center for Disease Control and Prevention. To put those numbers in perspective: 57,939 U.S. soldiers lost their lives during the entire Vietnam War. This is my story, from my perspective. There are others who might have seen or remembered events differently than I. It is up to them to tell their own story, if and when they are ready.

I wanted to keep things as real and raw as when it happened, to eventually help lift the stigma around this very important discussion. I wanted to keep the real names of people and places. I wanted to include photos. But alas, the stigma persists, and I have had to change all of the names, including my own, to protect my son's future, for I still hold on to hope for all of us for a peaceful, normal, healthy life. My intention was to find answers and help others, not to point fingers.

If you acquired this book because you are experiencing a similar story, my heart aches for you. You are not alone. You did not cause this. May your pain be lessened by following my journey, and may you find peace.

Sincerely,

A Mom

Table of Contents

Chapter 1: Graduation...1

Chapter 2: Second Chances...24

Chapter 3: A New Year 98

Chapter 4: Homeward Bound 128

Chapter 5: New Beginnings... 132

Chapter 6: Let God and Let Go 155

Chapter 7: The Ideal Mother......................................182

Chapter 8: To Help or Not to Help 191

Chapter 9: A New Year 196

Chapter 10: The Trip.. 217

Chapter 11: One Voice Recovery 230

Chapter 12: Harm Reduction.....................................235

Chapter 13: Jail 246

Chapter 14: Home 251

Chapter 15: Turning Point 254

Credits...257

Acknowledgments...259

About the Author 261

Graduation
CHAPTER 1

Spring, 2016

One after another they came. A Senior Rite of Passage. Yale. Made the rowing team. A banner stretched between two tanned hands. Dartmouth. I wonder if he's playing cello there? For eleven years, he played with Tyler. I hold onto memories of the two on a chamber orchestra summer trip to Ireland. It would be a shame if at least one wasn't playing. Such talents. A few are going to USC. The young entrepreneur was accepted to the USC Lovine and Young Academy, rooming with his big brother who is already in drama school there. A few are going on church missions, proving their conviction to a god I haven't found. I can't avoid any of it as I scroll down the page. A reminder of my son's failure. My failure. I'm sincerely happy for them. My son's friends that I have watched through years of school functions, cello recitals, soccer games, sleepovers, carpool rides, and birthdays. I guess I'll like the posts. Posts of proud parents I haven't seen much of in the last couple of years. I am too ashamed to reach out. Too pained to field the questions. Their students, fitting into their neat little plans.

John said not to get competitive about it. Tyler has chosen a different path. He will get there in his own time. In his own way. It doesn't help me to hear that, even from my therapist. I'm still anxious to answer the phone, yet afraid that he won't answer his. I pay for the damn phone. The phone that makes the deals. The phone that makes him the money for his next fix. I pay. How can I know he's alive without his phone? I pay. Our umbilical cord.

First my friends withdrew because of embarrassment. They didn't know what to say. Then, they could feel sympathy but not empathy. With sympathy you can pity, but empathy requires one to put oneself in another's shoes. For another mother, that is just too painful, even for a minute.

1

Then, it was out of fear. Fear of associating themselves with me, or for their kids to associate with him.

November, 2015

Real Boys, Simple Abundance, The Tao of Motherhood, Utah Family Adventure Guide. I scan through the bookcase to find it; journal of a plan gone awry cowering behind books of other authors' plans for me. Authors who only know their experience, their child, their area of expertise. Not mine. It's always helped me to write about it. It helps me organize my thoughts as they scamper around my brain waiting to be put into neat little lines. If I say it in person, the scattered thoughts might be misunderstood, come out wrong, or in a rush of anger spewing pain all over the listener. Disappointment is difficult to mask verbally. It's much easier on paper. If it's on paper, it appears to be part of my Grand Plan. Notes to live by or learn from. Even a side note scribbled on the margin of an outline makes it somehow a legitimate part of the story. Something that was meant to happen but was somehow left out.

Journal Entry, August 2, 1998

"...The contractions showed no signs of slowing and I could see from the look on the nurse's face that I was going to have a baby today....They had a neonatal nurse come in and talk to me about pre-term deliveries. They hurried Chris through a tour of the Neonatal Intensive Care Unit so he knew what to expect....It wasn't exactly the birth experience we had planned."

Beyond the journal entry documenting a rocky entry into the world, our life, to me, had seemed fairly normal. Not mundane, or boring, but generally happy, at least from my perspective. When Tyler arrived, we lived in a small post war brick rambler in Millcreek, a suburb of Salt Lake, with a massive yard and a short walk to Tanner Park, where we would frequently walk our dog. The one unusual thing about our family was that Tyler arrived with a brother, Weston, already thirteen years older than him. Weston was quiet, while Tyler would never be described as such. I would consider them close though, and their age difference was such that they seemed to arrive at milestones at the same time. The first day of kindergarten for Tyler was the first day of college for Weston. I really did feel like I had parenting down with Weston. He was agreeable and quiet. He was the child of a previous marriage and, young as I was when he was born, my confidence in being a mother was nurtured tremendously and I really never expected anything different in my second child.

As with most families, I suppose, there was always the balancing act on holidays of trying to somehow get to both Chris's and my parents for their celebrations, but we did, and had some wonderful, as well as a few drama-filled holidays. Chris was terribly close to his family which was both great and also difficult for this sometimes-thin-skinned outsider, who would rather walk home seven miles in the rain than be yelled at by her Mother-in-law. But mostly we had joyous times together and Tyler grew extremely close to Chris's parents.

Our days were occupied with the typical activities of a young, suburban family. I had been lucky enough to inherit a little bit of money that allowed me to pay off my student loans, invest some, and be a stay-at-home mom for the first two years of his life. It was a rare day that I did not take him to the park, on a play date, to the zoo, the aviary, or on some other activity. We had a wonderful playgroup of "older" mothers, which by Utah standards is over thirty. I had met someone at the Jewish Community Center swimming pool who had invited us into the group and we have all continued to be friends. At least the moms have. A few of the kids in the group still do things together, but Tyler now shuns these kids, as he does all of his friends that are not heavily involved in drugs.

Tyler's recollections of his early years were that they were filled with what he now describes as dysfunction. I really never saw it that way. He was always supported and loved by many, so this completely baffles me.

New Year's Eve, 2003

It was a strange night to help move friends, but there we were, kids playing together in the basement while the adults tried to create a party out of one of the most laborious of life's chores. The details, now vague, around the reason our friends needed to move that particular night, had something to do with a builder misusing construction loan funds, which had turned into some sort of legal action, which then resulted in a long wait for them to finally get into the home they had built. I don't remember the rest, because the fight overshadowed my memory of the specifics. This was our social group. Friends that we camped with, spent Halloweens trick-or-treating with. There were Easter egg hunts and birthday parties together. Tyler had practiced riding bikes in the circle near their house because our street was too steep for a training-wheel sporting five-year-old.

As sometimes happens with a bunch of unsupervised kids in a basement, someone came upstairs crying. From what I gathered, Tyler had been mean to someone. Chris misheard the story, or didn't want to hear it, and blamed the other kids. He had already been on edge because he didn't want to be there. He had felt like our friend Samuel, who we were helping move, and to whom we were giving up our New Year's Eve, was spending more time drinking beer and directing everyone than helping. Chris kind of just went along with social situations that I had arranged most of the time and tonight was no exception. Reluctant and awkward. Self-righteous and defensive. My understanding was that Tyler had been in the wrong and should be reprimanded. We left, and drove over Traverse Mountain toward my Dads' in Utah County to spend the midnight hour with my siblings who had come into town for the holidays. I couldn't contain my anger as I yelled.

"If you always defend him when he's wrong you will turn him into your Uncle Roger!" He yelled back, "How dare you compare him to my Uncle!"

Roger was the infamous uncle. The talk of all of the family parties, eyes rolling in unison. In his early fifties, he had not yet worked a day in his life. Enabled, entitled, bailed out, excused. Everyone else in the family was successful, hardworking and driven. Roger's father, Chris's grandfather, was the owner of a large company and he took pride in his solid reputation as an asshole. He was ruthless and controlling. His funeral gathering of family and acquaintances seemed to be a competition on who could tell the best story that exemplified his meanness. Roger's brother, Don, who was Chris's father, had been everything Roger was not; a physician, musician, and outdoorsman.

A comparison to Roger was no compliment, but I felt that Roger might have been different if he had ever been taught to own his behavior. If the family would not have stepped in to cushion his falls and pay all of his expenses, he might have had a chance. All of this, while "protecting" him, by rationing his cigarettes and alcohol and distributing them to him, when they felt the time was right. Roger died at the age of fifty-three, in a nursing home, from the complications of a lifetime of drug and alcohol abuse.

The rest of the drive over the mountain was icy and silent. At my dad's, Chris blasted in and announced to everyone that he was leaving me, that he couldn't take it anymore. He did leave me there that night and drove to wherever...he was gone for days. My dad drove me back over the mountain to our home in Draper after the ball had dropped on Time Square and the curtain had dropped on my marriage.

The divorce would happen. Not immediately, however. We limped along for years, resentment and unrest replacing respect and hope. Tyler was eight. I buried myself in work and tried to settle into the rhythm of week-on week-off parenting. I worked to numb my brain, numb the hurt. This was the arrangement for years. Tyler, the two Jack Russell terriers, a cello, activity stuff like skis or soccer equipment were all packed up and sent from house to house. Our cars were more like gypsy wagons. The beginning of the week off would be so jarring, with a silence so deafening I would long for the dogs and kid noise to permeate the empty spaces. I retreated away from friends, inward toward the quiet, into that safe place inside myself.

I don't want to make it sound like Chris was to blame for all of our difficulties. We always played a strange game of trading places in enabling Tyler. We all took turns being the rescuer, the victim, or the perpetrator. This became apparent after the divorce, and even more pronounced when the cycle of addiction sucked us all in. Our relationship triangle became a circle as the corners were eventually worn off, as it was hurled over the addiction cliff, confusing who was playing which role on any given day.

Books are typically written about how to deal with the "family disease" of addiction, when your family is "intact." Damn it I hate that word. It denotes something dismembered. In a very strange way though, the addiction made our split-up family tangled in unexplainable ways. It was as though someone had glued something that was irreparably broken together, like a teapot broken in too many pieces to be functional, but glued together nonetheless. Our family seemed like the greatest oxymoron of all; broken, yet enmeshed.

Tyler said that he hadn't minded the divorce. He sensed the unrest and tension and early on said he was glad to have each parent to enjoy separately for who they were, and at different times. He later came to say that he hated the week-on week-off schedule and blamed the schedule, and us, for ruining his life. He wanted to live predominantly at one house, though he could never really say which, and I didn't feel like pushing him to choose. It seemed to change with his feeling toward one or the other at the moment. He talked with me, or Chris about the other parent to try and drive us apart; to control situations. He started to manipulate us over it. He was always bothered when Chris and I spoke and frequently asked why we could not be like "normal" divorced families and never speak to one another. I didn't feel like it should be a child's choice to choose which parent he wanted to live with, that a situation like that would lead him into believing he could manipulate everything. I also don't always think that a kid knows what's best for them. Or I guess it was possible that I was not humble enough to believe that I was not the parent that was best for him.

I waited about a year to start dating, too emotionally raw to open myself up to the vulnerability inherent in the process. I didn't really even get out and do much that first year. I just worked and regrouped. The first person I dated wasn't even someone I sought out, but a man I had met at my step-father's birthday party. A decent man, but he, and a few others that I dated over the next few years, were not quite "it" for me. Not that I knew what "it" was.

Then I met Rick. I guess Tyler was twelve or so. On paper, and for the most part in real life, he was "it." He was a physician in Salt Lake. He had a Harvard chemistry degree and went to Columbia Medical School. He was an impressive athlete, winning the title of National Champion in men's endurance mountain biking when he was in his early fifties in the expert class. He was a serious outdoor enthusiast, naturalist, classical pianist, and music lover. And, to top it off, he had two fantastic kids that Tyler and I loved dearly. The only problem was that he was an addict. I knew going in. He made it clear from our first date that he had waited until he had been clean and sober a year before he started dating, that I

Chapter 1: Graduation

was his first date since his divorce, and that staying clean and sober was his primary goal at the moment. I figured that I would support his sobriety in any way that I could, and that we would be fine. We had four rocky years of alternating joy and despair, and finally, a relapse that cost us our relationship. We had ridden the roller coaster long enough. How could I have been arrogant enough to think that an addiction that cost him his wife of twenty years, and nearly his medical license, was something that he would give up for me? I had sacrificed mine and Tyler's stability to try and save a relationship that never should have been. I had hoped we would be the family that I dreamed of being part of. In trying to keep our mish-mashed family together, I had ignored Tyler's retreat into himself.

Though nobody can say if it would have started, even if we had been paying attention, by the time we noticed, it was already out of control. I had found rolling papers on his bed-stand at Rick's right after we moved in with him, two years into the relationship. Then, a frantic call from Chris came one day when he had found something like forty-five homemade pipes and bongs in Tyler's closet. He wanted me to come right away and witness it. I could barely understand him through his sobs. Pictures were taken. We had marveled at the ingenuity and questioned why that much effort had not been applied to his school work. We had a sort of pipe building fifteen-year-old MacGyver on our hands. Fishing gear from his grandpas, sockets from my tool box, a bunch of different sized plastic bottles nestled inside each other, double bongs, paper towel rolls stuffed with dryer sheets to mask the exhaled smoke. I could kind of understand if a pipe had been found in his pocket, a sneak-peak of what it was like to feel high. But this was an obsession. Something he did by himself in the darkness of his room. Some serious thought and time had gone into creating these things, and he was clearly spending a lot of

7

time high. This wasn't just a joint getting passed around in a crowd of teenagers at a party.

The drug testing started when he turned sixteen so that he could drive his car. He resisted. He wanted to argue the merits of smoking pot and called the arguments against using recreational pot conspiracies. He wanted to debunk the collection of medical reviews that Rick had printed off for him in his office as lies. He redlined the reviews and wrote his counter-argument in the margins, arrogant enough to say he knew better than the collection of doctors that had compiled all of the reports written on marijuana use in the medical journals over the years. He wanted me to read article after article that he would find on the nefarious sites that he visited touting the virtues of marijuana. He wanted to write for *Vice Magazine* when he was older, so that he could contribute to the drivel that he was trying to shove my way. He wanted to know if I had ever smoked pot so he could call me a hypocrite if I was honest. What could I say to this line of questioning? If I had never smoked it, I just didn't understand. If I had, how could I blame him? There was no right answer.

When Rick and I broke up, I moved into what was immediately available, affordable, and month-to-month, while I figured out a more permanent living situation. My realtor and good friend owned a rental that was immediately available. The Victorian we moved into behind the capitol building was tiny, quaint, and funky, but it would have to do for a while. The location was spectacular in some respects, and the views over the downtown area were breath-taking. I could also ride my mountain bike out my front door and climb to the radio towers behind town, then down into City Creek Park and back home. I called it the Chicken Ride because the GPS track of the ride was shaped like a chicken. There aren't many places that I could do that; hardly see a soul

after leaving my neighborhood in the foothills, though I was overlooking a major city. I could ride through the hillside above town, through two parks and past the State Capitol Building, and be back home in forty-five minutes. From our rental it was about the same distance for Tyler to get to school as it was from Rick's house in Emigration Canyon, and he had a good reliable Toyota Highlander that his dad had bought for him from his grandmother Carolyn. As long as he was testing clean, he could still drive it to school, as he finished up his Senior year at Eastland, the college prep school he had been attending since first grade.

Eastland had been a wonderful school but I don't know at this point if his peer group influenced him, or, as he said, he influenced them. He was with lots of kids with lots of money, and often little supervision. I always counseled him not to BE the kid I "warned him about."

After a dispute between Tyler and Chris, Tyler would finally get what he wanted, to stay at one home, all of the time. Mine. We trudged through the beginning of the school year battling it out with grades, moods, and outbursts that I knew were not normal. I just hoped this was some kind of phase or hormone surge and that Tyler would eventually understand that he had to get it together to finish school so that he could finally leave for college; a goal he had always had. Leaving home was as important to him as going to college. I just wanted the year to be over, to know that he had graduated and was going on to live his adult life, and hopefully gain some much-needed maturity and wisdom in his last year of high school.

Highland Ridge, October 2015

I got a call from Tyler's friend. They had Tyler and he was suicidal. It was a school day but she had called her mom who gave her permission to help him out instead of going. She wasn't the only one though. His entourage from Skyline High, his social group outside of his school, took him to Primary Children's Hospital and I met them there. Chris was already there. Tyler had already filled out a questionnaire that indicated that he was depressed and suicidal. Drug tests were done. A nurse was placed outside his door. What I felt was attention seeking behavior with his friends turned into about ten hours at the ER, a drug test that gave him up, and a ride in an ambulance to Highland Ridge, which was a short-term behavioral hospital.

The ER doc told us there was benzodiazepine in his blood as well as THC. When I spoke with his friend Zoe via text the next day, I told her drugs were found in his system. After I pushed her a little, she said she wasn't surprised that there were benzos, as he was doing large quantities of Xanax. I had no idea he was doing this, and no idea where he was getting them. This explained the rage. My research online, a scary prospect for any parent, told me that benzos like Xanax were horrible to get off. The rage would come from chasing the high. His blood pressure was ridiculous, and I learned that the withdrawals could be deadly.

I jotted down notes from my reading online of the symptoms onto a writing pad.

-Sleep disturbance

-irritability,

-increased tension and anxiety,

-panic attacks

-hand tremor

-sweating

-difficulty with concentration

-confusion and cognitive difficulty

-memory problems

-dry retching and nausea

-weight loss

-palpitation

-a host of perceptual changes

-hallucinations

-may provoke life threatening seizures

Chapter 1: Graduation

Text Conversation with Zoe, October 13, 2015:

What happened?

> Tyler is at Highland Ridge. He is not supposed to talk to friends or have visitors. We don't know how long he will be there…my guess is a couple weeks??? He was so angry he attacked me in the intake room and hurt me. He really needs this. I really appreciate your help in this. He is such an awesome kid I'm sure he'll get better with some work.

What is Highland Ridge?

> It is a mental health hospital. It's in Midvale. The docs will assess him today. They just wanted him to get some sleep last night"

Can we visit him?

> They won't allow friend visits or calls. I will certainly keep you updated. He knows you guys love him though he's gonna act pissed you took him to the ER. Don't take it personally. It is for his own good. Trying to help him understand that a break from everything is good and he really needs to concentrate on changing patterns.

I'm sure it will help. He should never hurt you like that. He loves you so much. He just doesn't know how to show it. I think that Highland Ridge is a good place for him. Let me know what happens. Thank you so much.

> Thank you! I will let you know.

Later that day:

> Hey Zoe, Tyler clearly had THC in his system but tests aren't good at finding stuff like spice. They need to find out where the anger is coming from. You don't know if he was doing anything else that wouldn't show up do you?

I knew about the benzo's already but I wanted to see what she knew.

As far as I know Tyler never did spice. He didn't really talk about the drugs he did.
Did you give him a urine test for all drugs?

> Yes, urine and blood. He did consent to that. Positive for THC and cannabinoids. We had found an entire duffle bag of other shit a couple months ago. Experimental stuff from a smoke shop like kratom (sp?). A lot of stuff where the docs just don't know what it could do to you.

I'm surprised that they didn't find Xanax. He was doing an unusually large amount of that

> Yes that too. Do you know where he has been getting that stuff?

I was hoping that I could gain her trust, and out of concern for Tyler, she might give us more information, but she stopped answering my texts.

He was released from Highland Ridge after a week. No cure. No resolution. No relief. Just the space to dwell for a week. There was some sort of plan put together upon his release to continue counseling and a psychiatrist was recommended, though their waiting list was months long.

I couldn't see that this stay had done much to help, and had cost a significant amount of money, but Tyler did get a little rest, and so did we. He then went back to school, a week further behind, and mad as hell.

A Division of Child and Family Services counsellor showed up at Eastland shortly after Tyler's stay at Highland Ridge. The counsellor wanted to question Tyler's school counselor about some reported abuse of Tyler by Chris. I knew that Zoe had called and reported Tyler's dad, probably based on something Tyler said to her. Tyler's school counselor, Carrie, was not a stranger to our family's issues and quickly ended their investigation with her knowledge of what we were up against with Tyler. Tyler may have considered his dad an ass at times but he was far from abusive. Chris was crushed and humiliated by the insinuation that he was abusive.

Accident(s), Senior Year, Fall, 2015

It was his first accident, in his life and that day. Hurrying, he was late to school, took the turn too quickly, and slid into someone. A police report was written up; it had been his fault. I had received the call from his dad. Everyone was fine, just minor car damage (though the driver of the other car would later make huge, false, medical claims).

I had plans to go to a concert with my friend Shonna that night. A rare night out, and Tyler had plans with friends, anyway. I was to meet him at home later.

At this point in time, things were really crazy at home. Tyler was not doing well in school and seemed more concerned about friends than anything else. He was still wearing a boot from breaking his foot skateboarding before he went to Highland Ridge and he was nearly impossible to get along with. His rage was often uncontrollable in a way I couldn't comprehend. What could he possibly be so angry about? I was looking forward to a break with a friend, even if it was to a dive bar to see a band I was only vaguely familiar with.

We waited in line to get into the show. Two middle-age moms looking sheepishly at the young-ones and bar dwellers we were joining for the evening. We had about twenty minutes before they would let us in so we caught up with each other and made small talk with people in line. I hated bothering my friends with my stressful situation with Tyler but I needed to talk to someone. I just wished that I could talk sometimes to someone going through the same kinds of things. I'm glad my friends' kids are doing well, though slightly envious. It's so difficult when fear for your child permeates most of your thoughts. I knew I had become a real downer to be around socially.

    The call came in while we were in line. Tyler had been in a second accident in the same day! This time, the car was totaled but he was fine. Excessive speed on his part as well as the guy who pulled in front of him. Who has two accidents in the same day? His sturdy Toyota Highlander that his dad had bought him from his grandma was gone. His freedom... gone. Our freedom...gone. The last tiny bit of trust in his ability to be independent and trustworthy...gone. His dad picked him up at the scene, the car was towed away. I was sent unbelievable pictures of the destruction. The first of many close calls and near-death experiences we would all live through. A practice round of sorts. He was in such a rage when his dad picked him up from the scene he could not be calmed. I wanted to go find them and see for myself that he was alive. I don't know why I couldn't just believe Chris. He just got out of Chris's car and ran away on his broken foot, as though Chris had anything to do with the accidents. We didn't know, but assumed he was high on something...otherwise why would the accidents have happened? Why would he not have been more careful after the first? Why was he in such a rage?

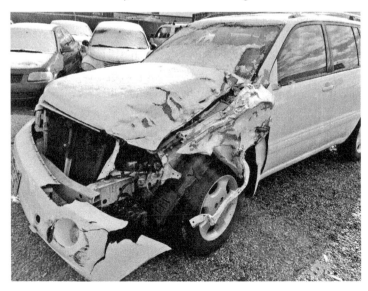

There would be no more car. The insurance company questioned if he had something they should know about that would help them understand why he was so reckless. Chris would claim later that an investigation was done and they somehow found out he was in Highland Ridge. They would use their suggestion of problems to deny much payment on the car. I didn't believe him. Neither did Tyler. It seemed like a fear tactic but I understood his intent even if I didn't believe his story.

It was now up to me to get Tyler from downtown Salt Lake, near the Capitol, to Sandy for school and get him home, a forty to sixty-minute drive round trip, twice a day. Me who would have to take him to all lessons, appointments, counseling and everything else. It seemed so ridiculous to be driving him during his Senior year. There is nothing worse than someone losing a freedom after enjoying it for a while...Tyler lost his freedom in having a car, and I lost my freedom in his not having a car. Pure hell, considering the distance and the impact on my work schedule. It seemed that Tyler tried to make it more difficult, probably hoping that we would break down and get him another vehicle. I was constantly waiting for him to be ready, and begging for him to hurry.

Doctor Bloodstone

It was my turn to take him to be tested, though Chris never actually did. Instead, Chris liked directing me to implement the rules. The kits at Walgreens only tested for pot and we needed a full ten-panel test. I got the name of a physician that ran a mobile drug testing business from Rick, because he was in a diversion program to keep his medical license and was required by the state to submit to random testing, which he usually had done at his office, by the mobile testing guy, in the patient restroom. For Rick, his addiction had forced upon him the humiliation of pissing in a cup, in front of someone, in his workplace public restroom.

Dr. Bloodstone happened to have an office near school, so it was convenient. If one could paint an image of a creepy, bizarre doctor's office, it would look like this. There were dated magazines and books, furniture that looked like it had come from a thrift store, and dim lighting. There was a fountain that bubbled over with something that looked like fog that sent a mist around the room, creating a questionable mood for a medical office. A frail looking woman in a dingy house dress and tube socks slouching down around her ankles shuffled out of a back room mumbling incoherently. Her thinning, greasy hair was combed nicely, I had guessed by someone else. I asked her name, feeling awkward, like I needed to make conversation to fill the uneasy air. She stared, unblinking, drooling a little, and shuffled toward the door. I was fairly certain that she was not supposed to be out wandering around, as she was, without a doubt, seriously disabled. Tyler was clearly shaken by the scene. As the woman tried to open the heavy door, I called back into the back room to get help in dealing with her. Dr. Bloodstone came out of the back and tenderly led her back to a chair and asked her, like a grandparent would speak to a young child, to sit quietly.

Dr. Bloodstone took Tyler back to administer the test and the two came back, everything negative, but he made it clear that he did not test for Ecstasy, acid, or alcohol. An open invitation for Tyler to try every drug not listed. As we settled up the thirty-dollar payment, Dr. Bloodstone looked sternly at Tyler, but spoke to him in the same grandparent - like way that he had spoken to the lady.

"Your last name is Watkins, do you know Don Watkins?"

"Yes, he's my grandpa."

"Good man, I used to work with him when we were ER doctors. That was before my wife over there fried her brain with drugs. Now, I do what I can to take care of her. You kids have no idea what you are doing to yourself. How old do you think she is?" he asked with her sitting right in the chair next to us, incoherent to the fact that we were talking about her, talking over her. Tyler knew better than to venture a guess so he said that he didn't know. She looked like she was at least seventy to me. She was fifty-three.

We left, both shaken by the experience, but I was filled with gratitude to him for his pointed, yet caring lecture. I wanted to write him a note expressing my thanks for taking the time to talk to Tyler but I did not, for some reason. Perhaps because things were to get outrageously busy in the next couple months and I would soon learn that while Tyler appeared to have listened to and heard what the good doctor had said, it would not change the course of his actions. The invincibility of youth, or the illness of addiction, or both, would reign over all logic.

Chapter 1: Graduation

Every day seemed to be filled with anxiety for all of us. Tyler was charming and apologetic and intensely likable at times. Full of hugs. The insanely popular kid that everybody loved. Champion of the underdog but still cool to the cool kids. The kid, about whom I got a "Plaudit" letter from his math teacher, telling me that he comes up after class every single day to tell her "thank you." At other times, he was so filled with rage that he would fly into a tirade that would scare me. Breaking things, kicking in my door to grab the phone I took away. There were times when he wanted to stay up late talking and telling me how everything would be all right. That he felt really close to me at that moment, and that he was optimistic about his future. Then, I would wake, hearing him up in our small house near the Capitol, the back door creaking open. I would go out at two a.m. to see him doing something in his car. He had just told me a few hours before that he felt optimistic.

Police Visits

On one particular day, he was too depressed to go to school. How many times had I heard that you must listen to someone who threatens suicide? He had said it a hundred times. We had been told by counsellors that Tyler had told them that he just said that to manipulate us; that he was depressed, but not really suicidal. I had no choice but to go to work that day. I had to leave him home. I couldn't force him to go to school physically and no amount of cajoling would, or ever did work.

I started heading over to my remodel project in Holladay. A new bathroom for some neighbors from a neighborhood that we had lived

Confessions of a Heroin Addict's Mother

and worked in a few years' prior on an investment house that I got caught holding, unable to sell during the recession of '08. Though it was tough, both financially and on my ego, to not sell the house as quickly as I expected, it was such a wonderful neighborhood, that at least we had that. It provided a solid, consistent home for us where we felt connected and we quickly established many dear, lasting friendships. We became known in this little "Mayberry" neighborhood as that gal who remodels houses with the son who was obsessed with soccer. In the two years that we lived there, I would work on the house while Tyler would dribble his soccer ball and shoot goals on our large corner lot, greeting and talking to all of the neighbors as they strolled by, or as they walked their kids to school. His persistence with that soccer ball lead him to be the Real Salt Lake dribbling champion for his competitive soccer league when he dribbled (with me recording it) five hundred and thirteen dribbles. He was awarded a signed ball by the team for his effort. The focus he was able to muster up in that regard was awesome. I would work on numerous projects in the neighborhood for the next couple years that I got through connections and friendships.

I really had not wanted to leave him that morning. It hadn't seemed right to let him skip school when he was already so behind and was having difficulty catching up. Chris was out of town, as he was frequently, as a freelance camera operator and film producer, and he had Tyler's grandmother, Carolyn, calling to check up on him. They had argued for some reason. My guess was that she was angry that he wasn't at school as she knew he was behind. She and Tyler's grandfather, Don, had set up an education trust from inheritance to pay for his school and they were understandably distraught that he was not doing well. We really could not have sent him to that school without their help.

He threatened suicide to her on the phone. That is something that causes panic in a parent, even on the hundredth time it is spoken, even after you are told by his counsellors that they don't think he really means it, their opinion derived from the countless times that he told them he was only bluffing. This was Carolyn's first time to hear it from him. She called Chris and he had called the police. They were on the way; I was told in a frantic phone call from Chris. This stuff always happened when he was gone. (Not that I wouldn't have turned around to be there even if Chris were around.) I got off on the next freeway exit, turned around, and headed back toward the Capitol and home. Like so many other work days this year, work would have to wait.

Carolyn spoke with officer Burgess and gave him a detailed background on Tyler. They spoke at length as the officers were parked around the corner waiting for me to get back home. I pulled into the driveway and they pulled in right behind me. Before the three of us walked in the house he asked if we had any weapons at the house. I told him I knew better than that, considering the constant suicide threats. I didn't believe in having guns around anyway. I went in ahead of the police. He was in the shower. I called into the bathroom and told him he had visitors and needed to grab a towel. He had a confused and reluctant tone as he replied,"OK, who is it?" as he came out of the bathroom wrapped in just a towel. He looked incredulously at the officers standing in our living room.

Unlike so many times before, today we did not have empty threats. Action was taken. Threats in our family would typically happen on both sides, Tyler's and ours. We would threaten to take things away. Chris would start a countdown of how much time Tyler had to comply, or I had to make him comply as the enforcer. Tyler would threaten to end it all. Or if he didn't like how something was going, he would make everyone miserable until he got his way.

I had picked him up after school a month or so before this police visit, after he lost his car in the accident and we headed to his cello lesson. In the good days, from the time he started playing in second grade until recently, this was never a problem, but on this particular day he was in a rage when I picked him up. My hope was that Evan, his cello teacher, would take him to a place musically that I had seen in him before. Get him wrapped up and lost in the music until whatever rage he was feeling was calmed. He had so much respect for Evan, and in Tyler's typical polite form, he had always thanked him after each and every lesson. I had felt that his gratitude was sincere. We were nearing Evan's house when Tyler declared that he was not going. He wasn't in the mood. He would not have disrespected Evan before. But that day, he disrespected everyone. I thought maybe if I just kept driving, he would surely come to his senses. But here, instead, every stop sign that I came to in this residential

Confessions of a Heroin Addict's Mother

neighborhood was an opportunity to try and open his car door and jump out. I rolled through three stops, not pausing long enough for him to get out. He still had his cast on so I hoped he wouldn't try. I couldn't roll through the stop near the grocery store because it was a four way and there were other cars. I had to let him bolt.

This time, with the police standing in our living room, bolting wasn't an option. Tyler had asked if he could put some clothing on. There was no exit to the outside from his room, so the officers stood outside his door while he changed. He came back out with just pants and no shirt, his muscular seventeen-year-old chest bare, as he puffed it out with more bravado than the moment called for. These two were no threat. They were kind and understanding, and Tyler settled down and spoke to them respectfully. Officer Burgess asked Tyler if it was alright if he called in a crisis counselor from Uni, the University of Utah Psychiatric Hospital. The officers would be right outside sitting in the squad car until we were done meeting with the counselor. This was the new protocol for suicide crisis calls such as this. Tyler consented.

The counselor knocked and I let him in, and the officers out. Tyler turned on the charm as he sat and spoke to him in our dining room. I do not recall his name, as so many counselors' and therapists' names have floated in and out of my brain over the last couple of years. It always seems that the crisis at hand muddles formalities such as name recall. He said he had a long history of employment in crisis situations, and held a private practice, but worked for Uni on call for those times that the police needed assistance on psychiatric matters beyond their expertise.

We sat in our tiny, funky Victorian rental filled with things that represented who we were. A music stand near the window, a massive bookshelf taking up the entire dining room wall. Books on art, music, good literature, lots of small art pieces created by me, by family, or curated. I watched him scan the shelves, eyes fixating on one, then another item. It must be interesting to be able to get a snapshot of a family's life in a crisis moment, unprepared for guests as well as unprepared for another crisis. He inquired a bit about some of the books. A book on classical music had caught his eye. I told him that Tyler was a fabulous musician, my go-to brag about a child who truly was a gifted musician, more so than he probably recognized in himself. He was one of those kids who could

20

hear a song and pick out the notes without much effort. He was that way on the guitar as well. I couldn't resist sharing with people this wonderful thing about Tyler. It was part of my denial that he had slipped into an unrecognizable person. My cover-up for him. My private school going, soccer playing, cellist son's secrets were hidden underneath his exceptional talents and likable persona.

The counselor probed further about what Tyler's interests were. Did he want to go to college? What did he want to study? Without hesitation, Tyler said that he wanted to go to the University of Utah and get a business/marketing degree. Then probably go on to get an MBA. He could see himself being an entrepreneur of some kind. He was convincing. He spoke of his future with optimism and excitement in his voice, like he wasn't just winging it. Like he had a plan.

The counselor concluded, after talking to us for about forty-five minutes, that Tyler was not suicidal. He had no specific plan to carry out a suicide. He spoke with optimism. Yeah, so he had experimented with some drugs...who hadn't? No big deal there. "He sounds like someone with a bright future ahead of him." Even I was convinced. He left and motioned for the cops to drive away. After he left, Tyler said, "I was only trying to get him to leave...I didn't mean any of that. I was manipulating him. I learned that from the best of them." I could only guess who he was referring to. He always called his dad a manipulator so I believe he was talking about him, but I suppose it could have been directed at me.

Sparky

Sparky was the Jack Russell Terrier who had been a part of our family for sixteen years, and who was so neurotic that he had chewed the hair off of the back of his tail, which was never to grow back. We had bought him from a breeder on Ninth East about a year after Tyler was born and the two had been raised together. They were partners in crime with photos to prove it. The two of them, sitting inside the bottom kitchen drawer that I kept snacks in, eating cookies. The two of them, digging dirt out of a planter and emptying it onto the living room floor, Tyler with his shovel in hand. The two of them in the bathtub together, after Sparky decided to jump in while I was bathing Tyler.

In the divorce, Sparky and Chester, our other Jack Russell, travelled back and forth between houses in the custody arrangement. They were always with Tyler. Sparky had a way of sensing the mood of the house and either responding with a knowing look and comforting nuzzle or, in really tense situations, hiding or shaking uncontrollably. He was so ugly that you couldn't help but love him, even if he was often times difficult. I ran with the dogs frequently on the trails near the house, the two of them darting back and forth, returning often enough to make sure that they knew where I was, then scampering off to dig for animals or chase other dogs. In the winter, we would hike, and I would just see their little tails sticking up above the snow as they walked on the path where the snow had been trampled down earlier, not minding the cold if it meant getting out.

At fifteen, Sparky was attacked by an Airedale Terrier while we were hiking, and it was nearly his demise. Forty-six stitches and many little drains had been placed to get the infection out from under his skin. We nursed him back to health by feeding him egg yolks and yogurt that we had dipped our finger in and stuck in his mouth, essentially force feeding him. I took him to work with me at one of my project houses and kept him warm with a sock filled with barley that I heated in the microwave, laying it next to him in his bed as I worked. His recovery was a miracle, and despite his age, he made an almost full recovery. Old age would catch up with him, but not for another year.

Though he was mostly deaf and had obvious cataracts, he was still able to get around fairly well, though he now needed to be lifted on and off the bed. Chris and I disagreed on the date to take him to be euthanized. "He's still running with me." He could only go a mile or so and then I would need to carry him, but I didn't really feel like he was having a bad

Chapter 1: Graduation

life yet, or that he was in any real pain. It was only an inconvenience to accommodate his disabilities and I didn't want to be put in a position of playing God. Besides, I couldn't bear to actually do it.

This all went down before we knew about any serious drug use, though we knew that Tyler was definitely struggling with something. We should have known that it would set him off to lose his dog. We took Sparky on his last hike, at Corner Canyon, near the vet in Draper. We had hiked and run here so many times before when we were together as a family. Sparky knew these scrub oak covered trails well. Chris brought him his last meal of French fries, his favorite, though he refused them. He preferred McDonalds to Burger King but that's all that was available nearby. He took off to chase a rabbit, only making me doubt our decision even more.

Driving down to the vet in separate cars, we were led into the room where they explained how the procedure would work and then asked multiple times if we were sure that this was what we wanted. I wasn't sure. I was sure it wasn't what I wanted. I felt manipulated by Chris again, and I felt like he was being selfish about the inconvenience that the dog had become. It was so strange to be detached from Chris and still have to make decisions together. Never truly divorced, I guess. I have never cried as hard as I did when he went lifeless in my arms, though I requested that I be the one to hold him as he went limp, trying to own the decision.

Tyler would say later that losing Sparky was the beginning of a depression that really sent him into a horrible time period. He blamed the loss for turning him to drugs, though many things would be blamed along the way, everything but himself, until much later in his recovery.

Second Chances
CHAPTER 2

Second Nature, November, 2015

Carrie had done all that she could. As a school counselor, she had been there like nobody else for Tyler. He trusted her when he trusted no other adults. She had told us that she knew that they were getting the best of him at school. Chris and I had both opened up to her about our struggles at home, and she had a fairly good picture of what our dynamics were, from dealing with and observing our family over the previous couple of years. She knew details and quirks few others ever would. Tyler had even made appointments with her on his own when he needed to check in, though, really, I think that he was trying to convince another adult that his parents were crazy, and further drive a wedge between Chris and myself.

Carrie had walked the fine line of counseling him on his depression and serious drug problem while trying to keep him in a school that had a zero-tolerance drug policy. Even one of the most beloved teacher's children had been expelled for smoking pot outside a school dance, off the school property. Carrie started laying the ground-work to ease us into the idea that Tyler might not graduate. She suggested outside help from an educational consultant named James, who helped struggling kids and their families by assisting them in the daunting task of finding treatment programs or schools that might be appropriate for their needs.

Chris and I held out hope that we would not need James' help, and that Tyler would somehow be motivated by the rest of the seniors' mutual and growing anticipation of graduation. There were so many senior luncheons, trips, and activities to enjoy. Certainly that would motivate Tyler to get back on track.

In addition to losing his dog, Tyler had also blamed his recent depression and his inability to concentrate and get back into the swing of his classes on his week-long stay at Highland Ridge. The holidays were fast approaching, and he was seriously behind in most of his classes. We had all hoped, Carrie included, that Tyler would be able focus on school after the brief stay at Highland. Though we were now aware of his addiction to Xanax, we never did find out where he got it. Drug testing would be consistent but random. We would be more vigilant about who he was with and what he was doing. The phone would be tracked. We had a meeting with the school administration, including Carrie, the Upper School Dean, The Grade Twelve Dean, and other administrators who all, at one time or another, had taught Tyler over his twelve years at Eastland. They were all present to help us understand the gravity of the situation. We knew. Tyler seemed oblivious still. He wanted to turn the meeting into an opportunity to blame everyone else for everything he could dig up. He seemed unable to feel remorse, shame, or be contrite. We didn't have the financial resources of most of the families at Eastland and grasping for an excuse for his behavior, he cited that he didn't have his own computer, and that caused him to be behind. As though he didn't have access at any time to either Chris's or mine. Poor, underprivileged Tyler. He tried to slay me in front of everyone. Chris was unable to attend, so I took the brunt of it. He had horrible parents. He had to travel back and forth between houses. All of the lame excuses. No personal responsibility.

I really had wondered if attending Eastland as a kid from a middle-class family had affected him in ways we couldn't see. I wondered if he had been embarrassed to bring people to the house, when his best friend had his own wing in a mansion. Maybe he had to set himself apart in a different way, like playing the badass. I guess if you don't have money you can hide behind a larger than life personality and get away with it. As though you've got to bring something to the table, and if it isn't money, it's a big personality.

Carrie called us and told us that things were not improving at school. It's not like we didn't already know. She suggested that we have a meeting with the educational consultant that she had told us about and discuss options for graduating. He wouldn't charge us for the meeting, unless he placed him somewhere. The thought of him not finishing at a school that we had all been so invested in was crushing. All of that work, money, and time, and he might get a diploma from a public school, or worse yet, something like a GED. Twelve years at the same school, all of our community and social life cut short. An education squandered. A good future now limited. Arrangements were made for Chris and me to meet James at Einstein's Bagles off of Wasatch Drive. Tyler would be going to his friend Alex's house after school, and we would pick him up later and discuss what happened at our meeting with James.

I was thirty minutes early to the meeting. I thought I could read a few emails and have a cup of coffee before James and Chris arrived, though concentrating on anything besides the question of whether Tyler would graduate from Eastland would be difficult.

I ordered my coffee and sat down at my laptop, which Tyler had been borrowing the night before to chat with a friend. He was typically pretty secretive and good at covering his tracks. I don't know what made him so careless as to leave the screen open to a letter to his friend that he had met at Highland Ridge. Panic set in as I read the letter. I was mortified. I saw it as a loud cry for help.

Tyler's Skype message to friend he met at Highland Ridge, early November, 2015

Zoe told my parents about me doing Xanax and stuff and that I overdosed the day after I left. so I was so mad at her when I got back. but before I got sent off she was the one that took me to the hospital, so I had her take my backpack that was full of various drugs to my friends house who I trust a lot. So when I got back I went to my friends and checked my backpack and a shit ton of stuff was missing, like a bag of shrooms, a really good molly pill, and a bunch of my Xanax. And to be honest I'm kinda a drug dealer ... and its fucked up kinda lol, but I make way too much money to stop. So she told my parents about that shit and then took my drugs. So I called her out when I found out, and she's denied it completely for weeks, but she wouldn't leave me alone about wanting to hang out again, so she told me she'd admit to it even though she didn't do it, and I have been hanging with her again. And she's like the prettiest chick I even know. But now she's like half dating this other guy and she keeps leading me on. And last night we hung out and she brought like 20 people over to my house, and I took 5 tabs of acid and 300 mg of molly and she did too. But since she's like dating that motherfucker, I couldn't do anything. And so I hooked up with her best friend.

Sent a little later

Sunday

But its not as bad as it seems, cuz Zoe told me her friend had just gotten out of a shitty breakup, so she said she was lonely and thought I was cute. And I was on so much acid and didn't give a fuck. But I dunno, I just can't stay mad at Zoe. During the summer we dropped acid together and we were like, on the border of dating, and she told me that she was so into me a bunch, and it seemed so truthful, and then later that day we went to a concert and did molly, and then her ex boyfriend who's 24 was there and she got back with him, like a day after seeing him, and I saw them talking during the concert. And she is 16 so that is kinda fucked up. So I went to a concert with her the week after and did 14 mg of Xanax, and she invited her boyfriend and they met up. Which kinda pissed me off, so I ended up hooking up with like 8 random chicks like right in front of her.

Yeah I get super protective over girls too. And my standards ever since being with Zoe have gone through the roof, so I just have like no interest in a lot of girls. Like I can't date most girls, and girls always get attached after like brief hook ups. And at my school there are literally 2 girls I would date. It's super lame, and I really need a girl right now, but the only one I want is taken and keeps hurting me.

I just lost all motivation after Highland Ridge, and now I can't even function doing school work. So I might get kicked out of the school i've gone to for 11 years because I'm so damn depressed. I'm still getting visuals from all the acid last night kinda lol. I do way too much drugs ;(My dad GPS tracks my phone too. And he's on it all the time. So every time I go somewhere, he calls and asks what I''m doing. So it makes it really sketch with the whole drugs thing. My mom just got so

Confessions of a Heroin Addict's Mother

pissed at me. I need to get out of this fucking house so bad.

She got mad at me for skyping too.

I'm so sorry Summer. Relationships are so fucking hard always :(I only have one friend who I enjoy hangin out with, and I used to hang out with him all the time, until last week when he got caught using my prescription Adderall by his mom, and now they think I got him on drugs. But all my other friends, especially the girl I really like I feel like just use me for my drugs. I can get like everything, and I'm kinda a total drug addict, and I can't find a way to stop cuz it's the only thing that makes me happy, but it just seems like people just hit me up all the time about smoking weed or doing shit like that. Which I enjoy but I kinda want a real friendship that doesn't revolve mostly around doing drugs. its my fault though, I feel like, cuz I can't stop, really. :(

I mean I've pretty much done everything but meth and heroin. And I overdosed on 3x the lethal dose of Xanax and Oxycontin by myself in my room. And woke up the next morning and snorted more Oxy., forgot about what happened the night before, then remembered later that night and it scared me so bad because I just remember what it felt like, and I felt amazing which is bad, but I couldn't see anything and I was trying to text my best friend but I couldn't type. and the only thing that came through to him was like "ithinkkknk oime overdosingog" and then I told him that I was alright with it. so the next night I freaked myself out so bad being so close to death, that I almost did 3X what I had done the night before just to end it all.

Like I had the pills out and I was getting ready to do em, but I convinced myself not to.

I'm so fucking depressed right now girl
:(
honestly I thought about doing all my drugs today and killing myself
;(

Chapter 2: Second Chances

I felt like I was being crushed by something. Hyperventilating, I knew I was in a public place and I must have been obviously distraught, but it didn't matter. Nothing mattered but the scene that just kept spinning through my head. My child dealing drugs. My child admitting to being a total addict. My child trying to text someone while overdosing. My child doing all of his drugs today to kill himself. He had to have wanted me to see the letter.

I called Chris,

"Come quicker...I need you to see this."

"Just tell me damn it." In a rush, I told him, "I really don't know how to explain it. He was using my computer last night to message a friend and left the letter open on the screen saying he was going to end it all by taking all of his pills."

"I'll be right there."

Chris arrived a couple minutes before James. He had just enough time to get the idea that our meeting would be much more than just getting Tyler into the right counselor or holding him back a year before James walked into Einstein Bros. Bagels. We called him to tell him we found the letter and to make sure he was still coming. He must have known who we were by the panic in our faces. We skipped the niceties of formal introductions and handshakes and cut straight to the chase. We had met previously via email and James knew that I didn't want to waste a second. I was too anxious to pretend like I cared about anything except helping Tyler immediately. Like a mother lion ready to rip someone apart.

"You need to read this," I said as I shoved my laptop toward him. He took it and sat down at the table. Chris and I joined him, reading it again over his shoulder, as though something might have changed, or maybe we had misunderstood something. He looked up.

"We have to do something right now, not later."

James suggested Second Nature, in the mountains in Duchesne. It was a wilderness therapy program. I had heard about it before from my counsellor John, who Tyler had gone to with me a number of times. James knew the owner, and had placed a lot of kids there that had done well. He always checked in with the kids that he sent there, by visiting the remote mountain camp. It was brutal and cold, but the counseling was top-notch. There weren't a lot of options that we could see besides this.

29

Confessions of a Heroin Addict's Mother

We needed to get him away from his life here and push the "reset" button. We needed to buy Tyler some time to contemplate his situation, his life, and where he was headed. We knew he wouldn't willingly agree to it. James said that was alright, he had people that could "escort" him there.

"You mean like kidnap him?"

"Yeah, most kids won't go willingly. We have big college football players that you pay to get them up there."

"You must be kidding."

"No, sometimes we fly them to another state to get the kids and bring them to Utah. They show up in their rooms when they are sleeping so they can't resist."

I couldn't believe we were even considering this. What else could we have done? We would have been complicit in his suicide if we had done nothing. He had not responded to counseling or anything else we had tried, and once he was eighteen, we would not be able to do anything.

So, we had our own child kidnapped. An hour and a half after making the decision, a meeting had been planned between James and Tyler. They were to meet at Starbucks to discuss some ideas for graduating. Tyler's friend Alex would drop him off, and we told him that we would be picking him up after he and James had talked. We didn't though. Tyler walked into Starbucks and sat down to chat with James, who suggested they walk and talk. The football players were waiting in the parking lot. I didn't see them take him. I didn't want to. Guilt and anxiety paralyzed me as I tried to fill out the paperwork in the Kinkos across the street from Starbucks, while my child was being placed in a car by two really big guys. We faxed the financial information up to Second Nature, and paid the transport company to kidnap him, like weird backwards ransom.

I went back to my quiet house. Peace, guilt, and worry accompanied me. I had one important job to do in my life and I had failed miserably. I didn't even want the holidays to come. My child was not there. My first child, Weston, was grown, gone, and doing his thing. Successfully launched. I went up to my boyfriend, Matt's house in the little rural town of Oakley, a fifty-minutes-drive from Salt Lake, to spend the holidays with his family. I tried to pretend like I belonged somewhere. We had been dating since last spring so it was still a fairly new relationship, but it was nice to have somewhere to go.

Chapter 2: Second Chances

Letter from Tyler to Chris and me, November 23, 2015

Dear Mom and Dad,

I made it up to camp, and I can already tell that I'll get much more out of this than Highland Ridge. A much better vibe. I'm not too happy about the whole Starbucks experience, but we'll talk later. I love you guys no matter what, and I hope you feel the same way!

Love,
Tyler Watkins

    The letter that I'm to write needs to portray my anger, my disappointment; how his behavior has impacted me. His dad has been asked to do the same. Tyler will write his own life story. What has gotten him to this point, placed in the middle of the mountains, in the middle of nowhere, in the middle of winter. His life story will be read aloud, around the campfire to his group, their first introduction after a week of solitude and meditation on their circumstances. Impact letters from family will then be read for the group to compare and contrast. Bullshit will be called on most of his story, and the others know, because they had to do it themselves when they were new. Vindication and revenge for having been put on the spot. A teenager's nightmare.

Tyler's Life Story, November 24, 2015

I was born August 1st, 1998, in Salt Lake City, Utah. My mother was seven months pregnant with me, and she and my father knew they must fly back from a small city in Canada in order to safely birth their 2 month premature son. I was a day away from having citizenship as a Canadian.

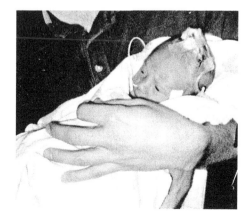

For the first years of my life, I was not accelerating at the same level as others my age and this was a big worry to my

31

Confessions of a Heroin Addict's Mother

parents. I had a very difficult time learning to walk, speak, and develop as a normal child would. I even had a lazy eye.

My parents got over their initial concern about my development as I quickly grew out of my issues. The doctor even fixed my lazy eye. Yet, growing up did not always come so easily, and my phase of acting out had begun.

I was one to never take no for an answer, and always got the things I wanted if tantrums were thrown. My mother took me to a tap dancing performance at a very young age, as she thought it would provide solid entertainment for a youngster like myself. I could care less about tap dancing, but on stage, in the back, sat a bottle of Coca Cola on a table. My focus went straight to getting what I wanted and I began to continuously ask for my own bottle of Coca Cola. The answer was no, but as I continued to ask, the anger built, causing me to begin screaming, "I want Coke! I want Coke." I was dragged out by my mother after those around us gave unhappy glares for ruining the tap dancing performance.

These times of acting out continued throughout my early years. I even became aggressive if I didn't get the thing I yearned for. This anger transferred to acting out, if I even got in trouble or did something wrong, because I could never accept that I was wrong. In one instance, I was locked in my room for acting up at the dinner table and not eating my food. This led me to slam my toy chest into the wall, making a hole in the drywall. I proceeded to take a plastic baseball bat to the door because my parents wouldn't let me out.

My parents still saw a bright future for me, and decided to apply me to the Eastland School, which is an intensive private school that preps for college from grades kindergarten-12. I was able to make it into school there, but it took a lot of tutoring to get up to the same level as the other first grade students, who had started at Eastland in kindergarten. At the beginning I was hiding under my desk, and making noises, but after a couple years, I was at a 5th grade reading level in the third grade.

Third grade was the year my parents divorced, after years of yelling and fighting. The fighting happened throughout my growing up, but I knew

Chapter 2: Second Chances

nothing other than that is what family did, and I had been raised in a very high anxiety household, with both my parents living there.

The decision was that I would stay week on week off with each of my parents, taking my two Jack Russell Terriers with me each time, along with most of my belongs, including my cello, which I had played since the second grade.

The divorce truly was not very upsetting to me for very long, because I knew the intensity of the household would decrease immensely, and I could get to have Christmas twice. However, trouble started when it began to become a big pain to continue to travel back and forth constantly between both my parents, who each had their own style of raising me.

This problem continued throughout middle school and into upper school, but I was never given a choice to stay at either household. I just had to do what my parents told me to do and go where they wanted. It was always a battle who got me on the holidays, and it resulted in the continuation of high anxiety within both households and in my life.

I had never truly realized the level of strictness that my family held until my social life became a priority. I was not allowed a cell phone until eighth grade, and texting was not a part of my life for a year. Once I got texting, it was quickly taken away when my girlfriend, (who had been kept a secret due to the strictness of my family) had sent me a text about making out and my mom had caught a glance of it.

At this point in my life, this was the worst thing I had ever been caught for, and I was in a huge amount of trouble. My parents would never have expected me to do something bad.

I quickly learned that I only could get away with things, with my parents, if I made them think I was always doing good things. This is when I leaned that manipulation and lying were ways to get my freedom.

At the age of 14 I had a feeling of emptiness growing inside me. This is something I later learned to be depression. The way I began to compensate for this feeling was to get out of the house as much as I

*could. I had taken up skateboarding for a couple years, and I would
always use the excuse to go out and skate, to go out and smoke weed.
At first it was just on occasion, but then it turned into frequent use,
after it became readily available to me at most times. It turned into a
habit that took up my time, I built lots of new devices for smoking. I had
a bag filled with various illegal and very engineered things that was at
the count of about 40+ different items. I had left it all in my closet, and I
was completely content with that, because my parents never thought I
would be doing something like that.*

*It was when my mom caught me (by finding rolling papers on the night
stand while we were living in her boyfriend's house) that it went to hell.
My dad was told what happened, and it lead him to check my room.
What he had found was so shocking to him because he had always
seen me as such a great person, but his opinions quickly changed when
he opened up the closet to find my creations. He dubbed my room the
"doobie dungeon."*

*Trust was lost, for months, but it rose back up quickly, due to the "act"
that I would constantly put up with my dad, and always told him what
he wanted to hear.*

*I never trusted telling my parents my feelings because I was afraid I
would get in trouble. This is when I realized that I was almost living two
separate lives; one when I was in the house, and one when I was out
with friends. Once I got my license to drive, this became a much bigger
deal than before, because it allowed me to go where I chose to, and I
could get away with whatever I wanted. I was never once caught lying,
but lied basically every day.*

*My level of drug use went from just pot, to hallucinogens, and then
later to pills. The problem I had, is not that I was addicted to one drug,
but that I knew I could always handle myself no matter how doped up in
front of my parents, or others, who I could not let know. This caused me
to use various drugs at any point I wanted, because even if I knew I had
to be at family dinner in an hour, I still wanted the challenge of seeing if
I could get away with it.*

Drug use was a way for me to get out of the deep depression that I

Chapter 2: Second Chances

faced day to day. As far as I could tell, it was just a coping mechanism, and it wasn't affecting my schoolwork or social life.

The heavy use of Xanax is what truly got me into the trouble I face today, and is what caused so much worry within my family.

For so long I had struggled with the constant change in households, the differences between them, and the constant checking in by both parents. I decided to speak with my mom about backing off on the constant parenting, and allowing me some level of freedom, where I knew I wouldn't have to lie, because I was only months away from turning 18 and being an adult. She agreed with me, and things were working out.

However, my father was not allowing me the same freedom as my mom. Every day, even when I wasn't at his house, he would call to see what I was up to, and to tell me about his day. I felt like I was being treated like a little kid all the time, but I knew I needed to have a sense of independence in order to survive once I turned 18. I did things that demonstrated my growing up; I made calls for insurance, got good deals on windshield replacements when a lady kicked a soccer ball into my car, and I even attempted to get the emissions test done on my car. But that is when things went bad with my dad once again. I was searching the laptop for information on my emissions. For some reason, my dad had expected me to grab a magnet off of the fridge with the phone number for my emissions. He came over to where I was sitting and began to call me a dumb ass, about six times, and he pushed me after each time he said it. So I stood up and got in his face, and asked him if he was going to hit me. He grabbed the collar of my shirt with a lot of force. I decided that I would defend myself in the safest way possible without hurting him, so I whipped him into a head lock. He flipped out, and I decided to let him go. He then proceeded to take the keys to my car and run out to my Toyota. I followed, and tried to hop in, but he began flooring it while I was stepping in. I ran along side the car in socks as fast as I could, bruising my feet, and almost falling underneath the car and getting run over. This is when I lost all trust for my dad, and reflected on other past incidences where he had betrayed my trust. When I was 15, he made a contract with a list of things for me to complete that was about two pages long. He told me that if I did not sign the contract, he would place a bag of something he had found back in my room months before, and call the cops on me. At this time I was completely clean, and felt as though he was blackmailing me. On various other occasions he had threatened to take away all of my belongings if I did not do what he wanted. All trust was gone in my mind, and my mother even agreed that his actions were not the right thing to do as a parent.

As I started my senior year, I felt that the depression got deeper and deeper. That's when the use of Xanax became a part of my daily life. I began to attempt to reach my father and let him realize that I had emotions, and I wanted to open up to him, but his rules and regulations could never allow it. I decided that in order to get their attention and realize I was serious, I would threaten suicide. This caused my dad to call the cops to my mom's house. I walked out of the shower in a towel to two cops in my living room. I explained to them that things were fine, and told them my plans for the future such as graduating high school, getting a business degree, and going to graduate school in marketing. They left without a worry. Then later that week, my mom took away my phone in an attempt to look through my phone due to my suicide threats. I knew I would not hurt myself, but they took it very seriously. My mom locked herself in her room with my phone. I knew if she opened up my phone, she would see texts from friends and realize my drug use. I acted immediately to ensure that she did not see these things. After she said no to opening the door, I took a swift kick into the door and shattered the frame, breaking the lock. I walked in and grabbed my phone. My mother saw this as very threatening, and her view of me changed right in front of my eyes. I was no longer that little Tyler, but now I was thought to be threatening and much stronger than even I knew. The next day, she saw a large black knife sitting next to the pillow on my bed. Her first thought was that I would hurt myself with it, so she took it away. I had just bought it because I thought it looked cool, and had no bad intentions. I proceeded to show her that I had another knife, and it was useless to take it away. So I flipped it out and then back in. With her new perception of me being a dangerous human being, she saw me switching out the knife as me brandishing it

Chapter 2: Second Chances

at her in a threatening manner. I would never do that, especially to my own mother. She decided to call the cops on me and told them that I had threatened her with a knife. I told my side of the story, and one of the cops believed me, but the other was belligerent, and got up in my face. This was all during a school day, and I was already two hours late to school because of the conflict. I was so unhappy with my situation. I called the girl who I had been going back and forth with for months, and I went to her school and picked up her and her best friend. Both of them had spent time in treatment centers, suffered from depression, and her friend had even been in wilderness camp. They had also had a friend commit suicide a year before, and they were much closer to me, than they were to him. So when my mom called and asked what I was doing, she asked to talk to them on the phone and they told her of my suicidal threats. My mom wanted me to go to the hospital, and that caused my friends to agree. I decided that I would agree to it, because I thought I would be able to get out in a couple hours when I explained myself. We went to the hospital and my parents met us. I was taken into a room with no idea what to expect. My parents explained their side of the situation to the doctors, while I sat waiting in a gown, stuck in a room where a nurse sat outside, with a constant watch on me. I spoke about my symptoms of depression, but not about my suicidal thoughts. I was forced into a drug test which came up positive for THC and Xanax. Before the results had come back from the test, a woman from University of Michigan came into my hospital room offering a 15 dollar Amazon gift card if I could take a quick quiz on an I-pad. That sounded pretty damn cool to me, so I signed a form without even a glance at what it said. I took the quiz which confirmed that I was showing signs of depression and suicidal thoughts, on top of testing positive for unprescribed drugs. The form I had signed stated that they had the right to put me in treatment if any red flags came up. After 10 hours of sitting in the hospital, they decide to tell me that they were taking me to a mental treatment rehab center. They forced me to be strapped to a gurney, and wheeled out to an ambulance where they took me to the hospital. They took me through a single set of doors and into a room with various paintings of bears. I was told I could put my regular clothes back on and change out of the gown. I put my pants back on, slid my shoes back on, and laced em up. My mom, dad, and I sat around a table, and a woman came in and began to tell us the rules of the treatment center. This is when I realized things were even more serious than I ever could have imagined. Complete lockdown. No touching anyone. And nothing that could potentially be used to harm oneself. I had to place my phone, necklaces, bracelets, and shoes in a bag that I would get back at the end of my stay. I was not happy at all, and I didn't expect any of this to be happening. After her explanation of the rules, the woman left the room. Now it was just me and my parents. I figured this was my last chance at salvation. All my belongings sat in a bag that rested under the leg of my mom's chair. There was a single unlocked door. I attempted to grab the bag, pulling up with all my force, accidentally flipping my mom out of her chair. She hit her arm on the table and fell to the ground. I stopped my run for glory because I couldn't leave my mom like that.

I was taken upstairs, through what seemed like a million locked doors. I was taken to my room, where my roommate lay in bed. After the staff person left me, I asked him what he was in here for. He replied,

"Cannibalistic thoughts and homicidal thoughts." I immediately knew I didn't belong there, but somehow slept fairly well that night. Everyone was watched basically all the time. After days of sitting through pointless and very un-useful information, except a few groups, everybody was assigned a counselor. I was "lucky" enough to be assigned the counselor who was out of town on a business trip. The first time I met him was on the day where I was assigned my family meeting with him, so I ended up having to try to explain myself to my counselor for the first time in front of my parents. That caused me to have to stay another night, because I couldn't fully explain my situation in the presence of my dad, especially. The next day, I had a meeting with just the counselor, allowing me to get let out later in the day.

When I got back, my problems with my parents got nothing but worse. They lost all trust in me, and they had so little in the first place. My depression only worsened, now that I had no freedom at all. My car was taken away and I was drug tested weekly. All faith in my dad was lost, and he lost all faith in me, causing him to kick me out of the house.

Chapter 2: Second Chances

I then lived at my mom's house, but she didn't trust me either. I was still unable to express my emotions for fear that if I did she would send me off somewhere.

We had to make the tough choice to put down our 16 year old dog, who grew up with me basically my entire life. My best friend was no longer allowed to hang out with me. Then, I lost all of my freedom when somebody turned left in front of me and totaled my car. My dad told me that I wouldn't be able to use the insurance money to buy a new car. I became deeply depressed. I expressed my emotions with my mom. I worked hard on my final exams for the term that ended on the 23rd of November. I was very happy to be on break, and finally a glimmer of hope had risen from my depression. After my last exam, I hung with my friends until I got a text from my mom that said I had a meeting with a therapist at Starbucks to talk about how I could proceed with my schoolwork, given the depression I had been dealing with since I left rehab. I told him my story, and he asked me to take a quick walk with him outside. I agreed, and before I knew it, two cops had me in their arms and were leading me to a truck, where they told me I was being sent to a wilderness camp. Now, I'm missing my entire break from intense schooling, but I'm afraid that when I get back I will be thrown out of school. I also am missing what seems to be the final months of my high school years and my final year of being a kid. I'm missing my friends and my last winter's dance at school, all because of the depression I was left with, after what was supposed to be a rehabilitation treatment center. I'm just trying to keep my head up high....

His letter roughly resembled the pages of my birth experience journal, only exaggerated and formed into his own narrative of being an outsider, being different, not being normal. How in the hell did he get the idea that he had a lazy eye? Where did that even come from? He wasn't "normal" because his parents got divorced, was forced to go to private school, was forced to go back and forth between parents in their custody arrangement...

Impact letter from me to Tyler, written November 24, 2015, read ??

Dear Tyler,

I hope that this letter finds you well and optimistic about your future. I take responsibility for sending you to Second Nature, and I did so when I came to the realization that you had allowed yourself to spin so completely out of control that I did not think you, or I, or anyone else, could bring you back from the free fall that you were in. I fully understand how angry you must feel toward me for doing this. I know it must have been terribly embarrassing and somewhat frightening to have some big guys escort you out of Starbucks, and into the mountains, after I had told you we were having a meeting about your education options if you could not continue at Eastland.

The events that led to my decision are numerous these days, but I know that your problems did not start a couple of months ago. The incident that I recall that first made me realize that your behavior was beyond ordinary and acceptable occurred when I tried to take your skateboard away, when you were fourteen or fifteen, because you refused to wear your helmet. Your reaction to my punishment was to wrestle me to the ground, and pin me down for nearly 10 minutes. Had my phone been near, and if I were able to dial, I would have certainly called the police as it would have been called an assault. I regret that I did not make a much bigger deal of it at the time. I don't know if you were abusing drugs at this time, but I did not deserve the response that I got from you. I was so disappointed and hurt that you would harm me in such a manner. I wondered how I could have raised a child that would physically harm a woman, especially his own mother. I wondered how you would treat your wife and kids in the future, when you had little respect for me. Your only defense of yourself after this incident was to tell me that you got physical with me because you had a right to have your skateboard. You seemed almost proud of your physical strength, and you seemed satisfied at the realization that you could overpower me.

After the skateboard incident, you became more and more withdrawn. It was difficult to get you to come out of your room and engage with me or anyone else. Family vacations, if you did go, were under great protest and

Chapter 2: Second Chances

discussion. Even asking you to come out to watch a movie or eat with me took a major effort and would often turn into protests from you.

The next big event that led me to bringing you here was the frantic call from your dad, a couple of years ago, that I needed to get to his house and see all of the pipes and bongs that you had crafted and stashed in your closet. We counted about 45 devices that you had created. The absolute obsession that you had with making these things blew my mind. This was at a time when getting you to be self-motivated in your school work was an agonizing task, yet you poured your heart and soul into every creative permutation of bong-building. If you had spent 1/4 that much effort on your school projects or music, you would probably be very accomplished. I did not understand how this obsessive, devious act could be so important to you. For months and months after we found this, you wanted to argue and debate the merits of pot smoking. You were certain that you were getting the "real" information, and that everyone else out there that said pot was bad was full of shit, or perpetuating some conspiracy. You made my life, and everyone else in our households' lives, a living hell with the arguments and acting out. I was trying to keep a relationship going at the time and I had already felt like a guest in Rick's house. I lived in fear that he would want us gone because he couldn't deal with the drama that you were creating. I also feared that you would in some way influence his kids negatively, and that he would want us to leave for that reason. Indeed, I now believe (and have evidence through a text) that you were selling pot to Riley.

Then came many more months of testing, and fights, and throwing bongs away that we caught you with when you thought we were asleep. You have constantly and consistently blamed me and everyone else for things that have not gone well in your life. We have had some seriously difficult times, and instead of trying to help me around the house, and help me by being responsible for yourself, you wanted to challenge and argue every time you did not get your way, or were asked to contribute. Nothing improved, including your school work.

I watched you drift away from the friends that you had since first grade, forget the music that you love, stop participating in sports, refuse to participate in family events and refuse to go on trips. No amount of

41

Confessions of a Heroin Addict's Mother

talking, listening, counseling, or begging would change your behavior. You got involved with kids you would never bring to the house, because you said we "embarrass" you. You always asked me what your friends would possibly want to do in this "hell hole" that we live in.

The climax of all of these events was a couple of months ago, when you had it out with your dad. You insisted that living with me was what you wanted to do, because you could not deal with him or his girlfriend anymore. I agreed to have you live with me full time, instead of splitting it between your dad and I, but I told you that I would not be any more lax on you than your dad was. You have to understand the enormous burden that you staying with me full time presented. It is NOT that I don't love you, or want you around but your behavior often takes me into a very dark place. I am so exhausted from having to deal with the constant drama, suicide threats, acting out, broken doors, broken cabinets, dressers, the fights to get you up, calls to the police, knives being brandished in my face… how can a mother deal with the agony and exhaustion that comes from this behavior? You also understand that my boyfriend, with whom I have a wonderful developing relationship, lives an hour away. When you are with me full time my opportunity to spend any time with him is extremely limited. Of course this is not your fault but it is the reality of the situation. Consequently, I am left alone to deal with all that you dish out. I have had to face the reality that this is more drama than I can ask a new partner to understand. I've had to put all my personal relationships on hold.

Your friends, with whom you do massive quantities of drugs (according to your own account in your letter to your Highland Ridge friend), were fearful for you. When they took you to Primary Children's Hospital, you were threatening suicide. Zoe knew that you had nearly overdosed around the time school had started, and she didn't want to see you harm yourself. You were then transported to Highland Ridge because of statements that you had made on a suicide questionnaire, as well as testing positive for Xanax and pot. This was such a traumatic experience for me! I had no idea that you were abusing Xanax. I knew nothing about near overdoses. It's as though you were leading a completely separate life that I didn't even have a glimpse into. I was so devastated and sad at the thought of losing you to drugs or suicide! My worst nightmare in the world would be for something

Chapter 2: Second Chances

to happen to you. I realized how completely selfish and out of control you were when you knocked me to the floor in the intake room at Highland Ridge trying to get out. You didn't care if you hurt me if it meant you could get out of that door.

In addition to the anguish that your behavior has caused, the financial burden that has come about from all of this is devastating. I was already struggling financially, and it has been incredibly difficult to work while putting out fires left and right with you. It's difficult to even concentrate at times. The last 3 times I have been at my accountants, I have received crisis calls of one kind or another. To have you laughing and making jokes that the ambulance had to take you to Highland Ridge, and the selfies that you have taken with the police when they came to the house, made me wonder if you cared at all. It seems as though you have taken joy in my pain, financial and otherwise.

The final straw happened on Monday (the day you came here). Your dad and I were scheduled to meet with an education consultant in the likely event that we needed to get you more help for the problems that you were having, and to discuss options for you in the event that you could not stay at Eastland. I arrived a half hour early to the appointment. I had just driven you to your final, because you had totaled your car, in the second of two accidents that had happened the same day, the previous Friday. When I opened my computer, the typed messages that you had sent to your friend from Highland Ridge, during your Skype conversation the previous night, all popped up. The things that I read in that letter absolutely crushed me. All of the drug abuse, near overdoses, that you are a dealer, all the girls you've screwed or randomly hooked up with, that you can't stop doing drugs, that you're an addict, that you want to take all of your pills and die, that 20 people had been at my house dropping acid the day before while I was at yoga, that you wished you had friends that like you for more than the drugs you provide…the only thing worse for me, as your mother, would have been to get a message that you had died somehow!

Last week, in our meeting with the school to determine if graduating with your class would even be possible, I mentioned to you that you need to stop dwelling on all of the ways that everyone has harmed you, and come up with concrete ideas for things that might help the situation. I have just stated many incidences where your behavior has had a negative impact on me. I now want to move forward and tell you what I hope for your experience at Second Nature. You are a brilliant, likable, charismatic soul, and I love the energy that you bring to the things that you have a passion for. I feel that in a lot of ways, your opinion of yourself is much lower than the way that you portray yourself to others. I have never seen you show anyone your pain. I have rarely seen you cry, or try things that you don't feel comfortable with. I have seen you give up long before anyone that is trying a new thing could possibly have any degree of mastery at it. I want to see you struggle with something, then succeed at it, through your efforts and persistence. I want to see you proud of yourself for overcoming a challenge. I want you to see that you are likable for being the charismatic, interesting, capable person that you are, and not for the drugs you are providing people. I want you to see that after falling, you can get up and shake it off. I want you to see that you are responsible for your own survival. I want you to see that you don't need drugs to get by in the wilderness, or anywhere else. I want you to see that you are capable of pulling your weight with your team, and that you are responsible and accountable to them for the group's wellbeing. I want you to see that you can trust others to be accountable to you. I want you to embrace the natural world with the reverence that you used to hold for it. I want you to know that you are capable of all of this.

I am so proud of you for being a trendsetter, an incredible musician, a wonderful friend, an amazing artist, and a creative thinker. I love that you feel confident enough in yourself that you lead rather than follow. I just want you to lead in the right direction, and follow no one that doesn't have your best interest in mind!

I have so many wonderful memories of doing things with you, and of the joys that you have brought to me as your mother. I thoroughly enjoyed going through our boxes of photos in preparation for your senior yearbook page. We have had so many joyous, happy, healthy, times. Hiking and biking…that fabulous trip to Costa Rica. So many Christmas, Hanukkah, and Thanksgiving memories with the Watkins family. Camping, and going to Jackson Hole with the Summerhill family. Stargazing and birdwatching. Arches and Tetons. Catching bugs. I am so grateful that I was able to take the first couple of years with you off to dedicate myself to being a stay-at-home mom. I believe that we went somewhere fun nearly every day and I loved every minute of it! We have playgroup friends that we still do stuff with. I loved watching all of your soccer games, cello recitals, orchestra concerts, and recording you as you broke the soccer juggling record. I wouldn't trade these memories for anything.

I love you more than anything in this world. You can do this!

Love Always,
Mom

We fell into a routine of receiving a weekly cluster of emails and photos that I would anticipate and savor, checking to see if he looked warm, happy, and well fed. I marveled at the size of their backpacks, belongings towering over their heads, and sleeping mats sticking out at the sides. I wished that the photos and letters came at a consistent time, or that they would have had an alarm that sounded when they arrived, as I would find myself checking the website link numerous times a day, distracted until I was satisfied. We were also to write a weekly letter, with a little direction from the counselor as to what to include in our letters. I could see what Tyler would write in response to his dad's letters, because all of his letters arrived in one email, but Chris refused to show me what he was writing to him. I just didn't understand what was such a secret that he could not share. It seemed ridiculous not to lay all cards out on the table when we were trying to help. It seemed like a continuation of our years long competition on who was the better parent. Who had a more solid relationship. Who's fault this all was. Who could best say the right words to fix it all.

Letter from Tyler to me, December 1, 2015

Dear Mom,

My first week at Second Nature hasn't been too bad, and now that I'm off of arm's reach, and I don't have to be right beside a counselor at all times, I've been able to integrate even easier with the group. Everybody is pretty cool, and I've got a couple exceptionally good homies here, which always helps. Food is really not too bad if the cooks know what they're doing, but I definitely still prefer your cooking. Sorry I ever took it for granted :(. There are some things concerning me a ton, and causing me some issues. I'm really worried about what Eastland knows at the moment, and I truly hope that you're talking with Carrie consistently while I'm gone. Mr. White, the twelfth grade dean, told me that I was on track to graduate, and it would really cause me some trouble if my time here prevents that. I'm also worried about the college application deadlines that I'm missing. I know I was having school trouble at the end there, due to my depression problems, but I was happy to be done with that term and move on to the next. I really am not happy about missing the next 7+ weeks at school, because I know that missing time at school, from being at Highland Ridge, caused me issues in the end of last term. I really hope to continue at Eastland when I'm back, but if I don't get the chance to graduate this year, then I'll consider switching schools. I also am concerned about the well-being of my foot out in the Utah winters. I'm also sad that I'm missing the Winter's Dance at school, and also my last Christmas and New Years as a child while I'm at Second Nature. These things are very saddening to me. I hope to God that Eastland will let me back in. Please consider that when speaking with them, because I want the best for my future by attending college. I love you a ton Mom.

Love,
Tyler Watkins

My thoughts about Tyler's life story, December 5, 2015

Mom's Thoughts On Your Life Story

Your beginning. Yes you were premature by 2 months, and had slight delays in walking and sitting up, but nothing too concerning to me or your doctors!

- You start out referring to yourself as someone outside "normal" ("learning to walk, learning to speak, and beginning to develop as a normal child would." "I even had a lazy eye!") You did not have a lazy eye. The Dr. may have looked at it and commented that it might be, at one point, but the idea was quickly dismissed. I'm not sure where you even heard that! Your childhood and upbringing were fairly normal

Chapter 2: Second Chances

and typical. I stayed home with you the first 2 years. We had an active social life, and you played well and frequently with other children. Your development was fairly normal; no trauma or upheaval, good and involved extended family, and rich experiences!

- Yes you acted out and had unusual tantrums. Your recollection of one of your tantrums in your story was pretty accurate. Yes you were aggressive when you didn't get your way.

- The 'depression' issue starts coming into your writing described as a "feeling of emptiness." I think that you use that as a crutch. Perhaps the feeling of emptiness was guilt for starting to be dishonest and hiding your lifestyle from us. Perhaps it was disappointment in yourself. You have a tendency to externalize blame for your actions, to avoid taking responsibility.

- Examples:
    - I was premature
    - I was developmentally delayed
    - My parents are too strict
    - I have depression
    - I am not normal
    - My family is not normal
    - My parents are divorced
    - I live in a "high-anxiety" household

- You seem pleased with your secret life; that you were able to get away with it; that your parents "never thought I'd be doing something like that." You are proud of your ability to manipulate. I want you to be proud of your ability to be open and honest instead.

- You are afraid to tell us your "feelings," because you would get in trouble. Yes, you would have gotten in trouble for your actions but I don't believe that you would have gotten into trouble for telling us your "feelings!"

- To think that we didn't know you were lying to us is just wrong. Why did you think that we had lost trust? Why did you think that we looked at your texts and tracked you via GPS? Why did you think that

47

Confessions of a Heroin Addict's Mother

we called you five times a day when you were with friends? Because we trusted you? You are not nearly as good at lying as you seem to think that you are!

- You think that I couldn't tell you were high? Wrong!! I believe also that the 2 accidents (in the same day) were a result of you being high. The second one was not deemed 100% your fault, but I think that your reaction time was slow due to being high. Then, you wanted to blame everyone in the world because you didn't have a car anymore! Talk about spoiled and entitled.

- This next point probably concerns me more than anything else. "The problem I had is not that I was addicted to one drug, but that I knew I could always handle myself, no matter how doped up I was in front of my parents or others." It seems as though you get high on the deception. Do you ever intend to be an honest person?

- To say that your drug use was not affecting your school work or social life is just wrong. You were barely skating by in school and I rarely saw you putting forth the effort necessary for academic success. You dropped all sports, rarely played your cello, and you only hung out with other kids that did drugs…never your old friends.

- When you spoke with me about backing off and letting you be more independent. I knew that you would need this so that you did not fall on your face in college next year. However, you clearly were not ready for the freedom. Things only got worse. I was hoping that you would have to suffer some of the consequences of your bad decisions. Instead, I ended up being the one suffering; 2 car wrecks in the same day! An (expensive) trip to Primary Children's and Highland Ridge because your friends said that you were suicidal, worse behavior and arguing, getting out of the car at stop signs if you didn't like where I was driving you, after giving up half of my work day to haul you around because you totaled your car.

- I am tired of this constant talk of your dad "blackmailing" you. You act as though he got the drugs somewhere else and threatened to plant them in your room. They were YOUR drugs! He just didn't dispose of them when he found them the first time. That is not how blackmail works anyway.

- You blame everything on the "depression" that Highland Ridge caused. You said you're upset that you are missing all of your last year school functions, because of what happened a couple of months ago, and you ending up at Second Nature. What about the Halloween Dance, the 3 senior luncheons that you missed, and the countless other functions that you have not cared about? When I asked you if you were excited for the Winter Formal that you were invited to you said, "Whatever, someone would have asked me anyway." Now you are bummed out that you can't go? You say you are disappointed that you are spending your last Thanksgiving and Christmas of your childhood in the wilderness, but I have to wonder if you would have actually participated as you have missed so many others over the last couple of years.

I didn't mean to write another impact letter. These are just my observations about your life story, and comments that I felt the necessity to make. I really want you to think hard about all of these things, and please try to be honest with yourself, and everyone else, so that you can start to heal. So that we can all start to heal!

Love Always,
Mom

Group Six Weekly Journal Entry to parents, written by one of the other campers, November 30, 2015

Best Week EVAH! Thanksgiving week has been baller. We started off so antsy for Thanksgiving. And not knowing what to expect, we were all very surprised by how much fun we ended up having. The staff team really supported us in providing ample time for games and space for us to process any of our emotions about being away from home. A theme this week, and especially the night before Thanksgiving was gratitude. We did meditations on gratefulness, where staff burnt incense and played music, which created a really beautiful, positive atmosphere.

For our meal, we had two smoked turkeys, cranberry sauce, sweet potatoes, sautéed with onions and brown sugar, and buttered rolls. For dessert we had two huge pumpkin and apple pies. We were all very impressed with how the meal turned out!

More highlights; we're having epic games of MFT (I don't know what this is) and particularly playing Motion, with students and staff. The amount of laughter and humor was over the top. Something from the week that also stood out was that Anthony had his birthday. We celebrated it all day and some of the staff had made an epic birthday meal for him. He had just finished his dessert and he did an unfair trivia question for the dessert pan by asking the group what day his birthday was and the group all yelled out the 29th and the staff all looked at each other, laughed and told him it was the 28th and we all laughed hysterically realizing Anthony had mistaken his birthday and celebrated it on the wrong day. It was hilarious.

We did a group on Sunday and we created a really special space. Staff played music and burnt incense, and we all went around speaking on the subject of what we are proud of in regards to who we have become in life, and then talked about who we want to become, and listened to each other talk about our dreams and ambitions. It was really special to the group, and cool because it was a very untraditional group meeting.

We have all been learning a lot this week about how to take care of ourselves in the cold, winter, snowy conditions. It has been snowing all week and got to probably 0 degrees last night. We have been trying to just focus on the basics of how to be happy with simple things, like a warm meal and a good night's rest.

The sun is finally out today (Monday) and it is so nice to see the blue skies and be warmed by its rays! Anywhoo those are a few of the highlights from the week.

Bye!!!
Group Six :)

This was typical of the weekly letters that we would get, written from a different person from the group every week. I really didn't understand the games or inside jokes, but it was so important for me to hear the

Chapter 2: Second Chances

camaraderie and friendship that was clearly apparent within the group. It was also a little glimpse of what they were actually doing there, as well as the types of activities. This was especially important to me around the holidays, when I felt crushing guilt for sending him there.

Another letter from Tyler to me (he wrote an almost identical letter to Chris), December 2, 2015

Dear Mom,

I was finally able to read my Impact letters from both you and dad. They helped me to actually realize how far I have stepped over the line, and that I have disrespected the family for so long. I'm glad that I was sent here to change my ways before I got caught and received even worse consequences for my illegal actions. Ever since I was a little kid, I have struggled to understand that some of the things I was constantly doing were bad things. I learned, after years of lying and manipulation, to believe my own bullshitting. This lead me to defend my actions, even when there was some part of me that knew they were wrong. I feel so terrible for the actions I took that disrespected our family. Behind all these lies and manipulations, a good side of me realizes the severity of the poor decisions that I have made in the past. My suicidal thoughts were brought on by this good side, due to the realization that I had dug myself so far into a hole. The love and support that I realized I had, is the reason I did not follow through with my bad suicidal thoughts.

I recognized that suicide would be a much much greater loss than to have to change my life. I finally recognized the constant love and support that my family, and especially my mother, have shown me for my entire life. I want to learn how to be an honest and trustworthy young man, instead of believing my own lies. I'm so sorry for the positions I have put you in, and I'll continue to reflect on these feelings for the duration of my stay here at Second Nature. I love you so much Mom.

Love,
Tyler Watkins

Group Six Weekly Journal Entry, received December 7, 2015

At the beginning of the week, therapy day was on Tuesday, like usual, and blue shift came out shortly after the therapists did. The staff that came out were Cory, Reggie, and Ann. Todd also brought his dog, Marley. Early on in the week, Matt found out he was leaving Sunday morning. He forgot his water bottle and butt pad. At the end of last blue shift, two new kids came in (Rob and Tyler), who aren't real new anymore. Both of their impact letters were read at the beginning of the week. The hikes this week were short. We hiked out of Five Mile Canyon and back towards the camp. Saturday night, we got a new kid named Noah. Sunday, we did an Earth phase ceremony for him, and Cayden made Air Phase. This week the therapists came out early.

Letter from me to Tyler, December 7, 2015

Dear Tyler,

I sure miss you! I just read your letter you wrote tonight, and it sounds like you are starting to take some responsibility for your actions. I really want you to take advantage of the solitude and peace in the mountains to achieve some clarity. You are such an incredible person, and I love you so much.

Remember the Alabama Shakes concert at Red Butte? I really enjoyed going to that with you. I miss the good, happy times that we have shared together. There really were so many of them, if you think about it. We have certainly had a rough couple of years, and I realize that a lot of things have been difficult for you. I also understand that you have a difficult time opening up to anyone about your struggles. Do you know that it's ok to tell someone that you are hurting, or that you are disappointed? I'm not sure that I've ever really seen you cry or show anyone your sad side. I really wish that we hadn't had to have moved as much as we did the last 8 years. I know that it was difficult to adjust to all of that change for both of us. I also wish that you had realized how devastating addiction can be on a family when we experienced the aftermath of Rick's relapse, and his lack of commitment to our family, and to staying clean and sober.

Chapter 2: Second Chances

I have always wanted only the best for you. You can overcome this, and find peace with yourself again. Are the mountains beautiful? I want you to camp with me again when you get home. Matt and I are trying to plan another Escalante/Death Hollow Trip next spring with everyone. It is such a magical place and I really want to share it with you! So strange to find fern grottos and cool pools of water in the middle of the harsh, desert, slick rock canyons. So wonderful to be away from devices and distractions. I think that it's good for all of us to unplug and think! I know that all too frequently I turn on distractions like music so that I am not forced to be "inside my brain." A good sincere meditation does a person good. That's one thing I love about hot yoga (and I'm still hoping that I can get you to go someday). It's like a moving meditation. It's physically very strenuous, but once you learn the postures and get into a flow, it's great for the mind. Sometimes I go just to find clarity.

So now some news from the Wasatch Front. Grammy's doctor needs to remove the lump to see if it's breast cancer. She also had a major flood at her house about 3 days ago, so I am going to St. George as soon as the insurance adjustor tells her what they will pay for. She is allowed to hire me as the general contractor on the repairs, but I need to see what the scope of the work is to determine if I can start and quickly finish it for her, particularly so that she doesn't have a torn up house while she mends from surgery.

Grandma and Grandpa Summerhill got a really cute new puppy. I'll try and send some pictures. It only weighs 3 or so pounds, and it just loves to play. It received plenty of attention over Thanksgiving. Matt and I had to keep Moe in his crate so he didn't eat it.

I nearly adopted a cat yesterday from Petco. I came to my senses and didn't, but I sure was tempted! I had not planned on being an "empty-nester" so soon! The house just isn't the same without you and Sparky. I haven't seen Chester for a couple of months. I guess your dad figures that I need a break from everything, and I guess he's right. I have been raising kids and dogs for 30 years! I sure don't miss all of the arguing and worrying though:(

I'm hoping that you do not see Second Nature as a punishment, but rather, a gift. I know that you have been hurting for a while, and I just didn't know what to do to help you. I only knew that you needed a break from your life here, and some time for serious introspection, with the aid of caring people.

You aren't missing any skiing yet. I was going to go yesterday, but I'm a bit under the weather. I've been working my ass off and caught a cold framing a garage last week. I worked with Isaiah Lopez, and he told me I should have just sent you to him, to "straighten" you up! Isaiah is a kid that has definitely made some bad choices, and has faced them, and is making a serious effort to make a good life for himself. I may take him to CA to work on the Smith's project soon. Did I tell you that they want me to do their project? I'm still negotiating with them on the details, but Joan and I are going out next week to get a grasp on the scope of the project. I wish you could go! They are all concerned about you and send their love.

I had breakfast with Sophia and her mom, Lisa, yesterday. She is a great gal! She really wanted to show her support for you, having been to wilderness therapy herself, before coming to Eastland. I really appreciated the talk that we had. She seems as though she is glad that she went, and she feels like it really helped her with her struggles.

Love always,
Mom

Letter from Tyler to his Dad, December 7, 2015

Dear Dad,

I would like to start off by saying that I take full responsibility for any of the instances where I blamed my family for the stupid decisions I made. It was not at all my family's fault that I abused drugs. I have been feeling an extreme amount of guilt since I read my impact letters. It's caused me to have constant thoughts of regret and self loathing during the times where I'm not being distracted by the group. Every night and morning when I lay in my shelter, I find it hard to fall asleep. My poor decisions and the ways I have been disrespectful run through my mind. I wake up well before we need to every day, and after staff tells us to call our numbers and hit the snooze, I have not once been able to fall back asleep, and I'm left to sit and stew in my own mistakes. I woke up

Chapter 2: Second Chances

yesterday morning feeling the worst I had felt since arriving at Second Nature. I worked all day at writing, in an attempt to get my mind out of the hole I put myself in. Steven came after dinner and brought four letters from you, Mom, Grandma and Grandpa. I somewhat expected to get a sliver of positive news, or a happy letter, but instead I received letters that left me with an even deeper feeling of regret and guilt, even more than I had felt after receiving the impact letter. I'm so incredibly sorry that I ever thought that it was at all acceptable for me to disrespect my family when all that you, and everybody else, have given me is support in all aspects including rules to keep me off the dangerous path that I was taking. I would like to let you know that as much as you did not care for my best friend Mason, I was not untruthful about my time spent with him. There was a sense of co-dependency, because he and his family have been a support system for me, in difficult times, when I did not want to go home. I cannot deny that I spent far too much time at his house, and I had smoked weed with him. I did not supply him drugs. Yes, Zoe is a hot girl that uses drugs. I would like to let you know that in the past we had a relationship, but that was during the summer. She is with somebody else, but I had feelings for her for a long while after that. She does not use sex to get drugs from me. I asked her to come and pick me up from the house. I did not think she was going to have 20 or so people with her, but I let them come in for a short amount of time because I knew mom was at yoga. Still not ok, but I would not have let it happen if I knew what was going to happen. Now about dealing. The only reason I was doing that is so I didn't have to waste money on drugs for myself. Not a good move or reason. I mostly sold weed and sometimes acid. I did not sell to people at Eastland, and I did everything to keep that dark world away from my schooling and the people there. I did not accumulate any money anywhere. All I have is about 30 bucks in my wallet. There is no reason to be concerned about safety, because nobody has any reason to be looking for me and I do not owe anybody. A great way to get something like that to happen would be to give you supplier names. I would like you to consider that the things in the message on Skype may have not all been true. That does not help my situation of lying and manipulation, but it's something to keep in mind. To be truthful, I've only had sex with 5 girls, all of whom I trust, and I considered the consequences behind my actions. When I say hooking up, that most likely means making out. I had feelings for every one of those girls. I do not think objectification is ok, and I generally am not one to do such a thing. I had a hard time trusting you, because I was always afraid I would get everything taken away, due to how often it had been threatened. I should have kept in mind all of the wonderful things that you've provided me. I'm so sorry Dad. I love you so much, as well as the rest of our family.

Love,
Tyler Watkins

Letter from Tyler to me, December 7, 2015

Dear Mom,

I've been struggling the last days since I read my Impact letters from you and dad. Each day and night when I'm by myself and away from the distractions of group, I can't get away from these feeling of guilt and regret that I have from my previous actions that got me here. I feel like a terrible person. Last night I got letters from you, Dad, Grandma and Grandpa. These affected my mood greatly and caused me to have awful thoughts about myself. I want to take full accountability for all my previous actions, and the response to my life story intensified that intention but also left me somewhat confused in a few places. I was told by either you or dad that I had a difficult time developing normally, and I have thought that for years now. I am glad to hear that that is not the case but I wonder why I believed that for so long. I'm extremely grateful for the support and fun that we had for the first two years of my life also and all of the wonderful times we had outside of those first two years, up until where we are now. I don't blame my premature birth, believing that I had developmental delays, the fact that you and dad divorced, my depression, or strict parenting for the decisions that I've made. They are just points that I had thought needed to come out in my life story. I wrote it on my first full day of being at Second Nature, in a short period of time. I would like to point out that I am extremely disappointed in myself. The first car crash was my fault, but neither *was caused by me being high, because I was not high. I wasn't getting high on deception, I just knew that if I came home acting fucked up, it wouldn't turn out well, so dishonesty became my habit. My schoolwork did not take a dive until after Highland Ridge, when depression caught me by the reigns. I was not doing drugs until a bit after the car was gone, and other things had happened, like the broken foot and Sparky's death. I also did not drop all sports, I had just lost interest in soccer, due to too much comp practice and the overall intensity and seriousness that needed to be put forth for being on varsity, and the embarrassment I felt being on JV, if I didn't constantly show that effort. I am considering playing this year. Also, cello was always somewhat of a difficult thing to get me to practice long before drugs. Also, please don't assume that it affected my friendships, because I still am great friends with all of those old friends. Don't forget who I was hanging out with before you picked me up to take me to Starbucks. I truly am bummed out about missing Winter Formal. The Halloween dance did not happen, because I didn't have a costume prepared, and I also think I may have been in Highland Ridge when it happened. Senior brunches are also not announced, and I was definitely not the only person to miss them. Also, senior lunch and the Halloween dance are not black tie events that I was asked to. I feel awful about missing Winter Formal regardless of anything I said. I feel deep regret for the many mistakes I've made, and I hope I can someday be forgiven. I love you so much, Mom,*

Tyler

Letter from Tyler for The Insurance Company, December 7, 2015

To Whom It May Concern, regarding insurance on my Toyota Highlander,

Here is my account of the accident that happened as I was turning off of 9400 south. I was traveling east on 9400 S., and I signaled to get into the right lane. I began to slow down well before the right turn was made. I had to have been going around 10 miles an hour before making the right turn that I've made hundreds of times to get to school. I hit a patch of ice about halfway through my turn, and I lost control of my traction, causing me to slide into a woman's car. I could clearly see the woman's reaction, and she did not seem pleased, but there did not seem to be any injuries or complaints about being hurt. The accident did not happen at a high speed, and I can not see it resulting in injury.

Sincerely,
Tyler Watkins

I set about cleaning out Tyler's room, to try to discover more about the life he had been hiding, as I still strived to understand how we got to this point. I had every intention of being the best mother I could be, yet I had fallen so far short of that aim. His room was a disaster. Guilt spread over me again about how small this room was. It was a weird cantilevered expansion on a very old house, sitting on a hill behind the Capitol since before the Capitol was built. His Ikea twin bed barely fit. I had put all of those parts together inside the seven by seven room, for fear that I wouldn't be able to move it in there once it was assembled. I bought him the one that had a drawer under it to save space. Tyler had reminded me so often about how much this situation sucked. I was doing my best, I reminded myself. The decision to move here was a hasty one, and this place was supposed to be temporary. My realtor owned it, and it was available exactly when I needed it. I had to make good on a promise to leave Rick

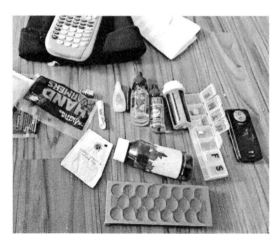

after he relapsed. Fuck drugs and what they have done to people I care most about.

Plates, clothes, mismatched socks, Visine, miscellaneous drug paraphernalia, and homework assignments. I found a crumpled-up piece of paper. It was a history class assignment. I knew Tyler had a great fondness for the teacher of this particular class. He had told me he felt comfortable opening up to her, and indeed, his assignment bore out this fact.

Chapter 2: Second Chances

Writing Assignment - Tyler Watkins

"Wherever I found religion in my life I found strife." Is this true in your life? Why or why not?

Although I agree with this statement, I would not say it is necessarily true. I was lucky enough to be raised by two very liberal parents, who taught me to be the same way from a very early age. They do not agree with religion for various reasons, including religion causing strife within their lives. My mother, raised in a very conservative Mormon family, was touched inappropriately by a Mormon missionary at a very young age. She told her family, but instead of doing the right thing and turning the man in, they told her to keep her mouth shut. I feel strife within a Mormon family as a Non-Mormon. A certain level of strife has been passed on down to me from her side of the family due to our lack of Mormonism within a very Mormon family. This causes less attention to be payed towards my mother, brother and I by my mother's father and step mother. I don't mind though, because I don't enjoy associating with that side, because I'd rather not be constantly preached to. I still love my grandpa, and I know he loves me, and he even offers to pay half of in-state tuition for whatever college I choose. I would not say that is strife. My other experiences with religion remain happy. On my father's side of the family, we celebrate both Christmas and Hanukah at the same time. I have not let other people's religion affect my life in negative ways. Note: On my dad's side, his father is a descendant of the very well known Willard Richards, who was the doctor of the founder of Mormonism, so the religion is truly in my blood.

Note from his teacher: "Tyler - Very honest - Thank you. It is so damn nice having you back!"

Letter from me to Tyler, December 12, 2015

Good Morning Tyler,

It's Saturday morning here in Oakley. I've been spending a lot of time up here because…well I can! The house is awfully quiet in Salt Lake, and I really don't want to be alone down there during the holidays. I have work down there anyway, so I do have to go down for that. Bummer. I saw

Confessions of a Heroin Addict's Mother

Weston yesterday when we had a lunch meeting together. He's working on my branding, and has come up with some wonderful creative logos for the company. I'll try and send them along to see what you think is the best one. He did a great job on it!

Sophia gave me a bracelet to give you but I'm not sure if I can send it up or not. I also have a question in to Second Nature to determine when I can come up and see you. I want to experience what you are experiencing up there, and, you know me, I love that stuff. I actually got a ride in before the snow storm on Thursday. I rode up from the house on my "chicken ride" to the towers above Ensign Peak. Crazy, on Dec.10th, but it was enjoyable and I needed to get my blood pumping.

There are a couple of questions that I'm concerned about that remain unanswered. I have a hard time believing that you kept the "dark side" of your behavior away from your Eastland friends. I have heard rumors that you vaped at school and did Kratom in your car with people at lunch. That would hardly be keeping it away from them. You know that Eastland has a zero tolerance policy. Even one of your teacher's daughters was expelled, and you know what a value that teacher is to the school. You have always been so proud of your "trend-setter" persona, but if you were influencing, or pressuring, or supplying your friends, I am very disappointed in that. You need to come clean about that for a couple of reasons. First, you have been dishonest about so many things that I think you only let us in on what you think we might already know. It's time to be honest with yourself and everyone else about everything. Secondly, Eastland chooses you, you don't choose them. You say that you want to go back, and that you value your friendships and your relationships with the teachers, counselors, and the administration, however, you have not proven that at all by your risky behavior. Your dad and I had a good meeting with Bryson, Brittany, and Carrie the other day and they indicated that it MAY still be possible to graduate, and that they would support you somewhat in doing that. BUT…it will take serious motivation on your part for that to still happen. You have to PROVE that you in fact really want to graduate with your class by your actions, both in the classroom, by attending the scheduled senior activities, and having positive interactions with your peers. We couldn't outright talk about you using drugs during the meeting because of the zero tolerance drug police, but, everyone at Eastland is well aware that you have been doing drugs. They have no indication that you have been doing them at school or you would not be welcomed back, but they definitely spoke in our meetings with an awareness that you have had issues with drugs. Their eyes will be wide open to your behavior if they choose to let you come back. Carrie will send a letter outlining what will be required for you to graduate. I know that working on scheduled projects during spring break will be one of the requirements to make up for what you missed last semester. It would be such a shame not to graduate with your class after 11 years there. But that is up to you!

Another thing that has been weighing on me is your frequent commenting to both me and your dad that, "You have no idea what's going on in my life", or, "Bad things are happening but I can't talk to you about them," but you stop at that. It's like saying you have a secret, but you are not letting us in on it. Why do you say that and then not share? Is someone pregnant? STD's? Overdose? We have no way of knowing what you are talking about, so it only makes us really, really concerned when you say things like that. You talk about us being a "high-anxiety" family, but don't you suppose that statements like that cause us the anxiety? Nothing is more anxiety-provoking than worrying that your kid is in some kind of trouble that they won't find help with, and there is nothing you can do about it, because they won't seek your help or advice. How many times have I wondered if I'm going to get a call that you're dead, or in jail, or the hospital? More than anything my anxiety comes from this. I also feel ashamed around the Eastland parents because I don't know if you have done anything to influence their kids negatively, and I'm embarrassed to tell them we had to get you help. They all know though, news travels fast. Carly even "re-friended" me, probably to get some dirt on what's going on so she can gossip about us. I don't post personal stuff on FB though. Have you considered the legal implications that would most likely happen if someone found out you were supplying their kid? Especially in the influential Eastland group, most of whom have the means to pursue legal action! I wanna kill your drug supplier, so I can definitely understand!

I have a lab that thinks he's a lap-dog that keeps climbing into my lap as I write this, so I better go. Moe misses you too!

Confessions of a Heroin Addict's Mother

It's gorgeous here in Oakley. A soft fog is blanketing the view of the barns and mountains behind Matt's. I'm looking out toward the Uintas, not too far away, thinking about you!

Love Always,
Mom

Letter from Sophia to Tyler, late December, 2015

Dear Tyler,

Hey, It's Sophia. Surprise. Marc told me you were sent to a wilderness camp, and as it turns out, I was sent to one last summer. I know how horrible it is for the first while, and I know that all I wanted was to hear from my friends. So I decided to send a letter your way.

Things at school haven't changed, but more people are wearing bandanas around their ankle. You totally started a thing dude. Also #pray4tyler showed up in the senior lounge again, so for what it's worth, we're all thinking about you.

My wilderness camp was in Arizona, so I didn't have to deal with snow, just cacti (cactuses?). I can't even imagine how cold it would be though. Don't get frost bite, okay?

Honestly, I don't know if it's hell for you, or if this it the best time of your life, but I do have a list of advice for you.

1. Keep a journal. I promise you won't regret it.

2. Learn how to make a fire. It sucks, but if you do it like fifty times in a row it gets easier.

3. Telling people what to do really pisses them off.

4. So does complaining a lot.

5. Embrace the fact that you're in this situation for however many weeks it is. (And don't keep track of the days.)

6. Find a way to pass the time, besides bitching about how shitty everything is, and what you miss from 'real life.'

Chapter 2: Second Chances

7. *Figure out what you want, and just fucking do it. This is a chance to completely start over. You don't have to take advantage of it, but you should at least be aware of it.*

8. *Ration your food.*

I don't want to sound preachy, so I'll leave the list at that.

This is something I wrote when I got out of my camp (Red Rocks). The ground is cold, your body is aching, but you have no choice. You have to keep going. And that's the worst part of this all, isn't it? The fact that you're in hell, and you have no choice but to keep being there. You have to wait it out, hoping you don't lose yourself along the way, thinking maybe you will, but it will be for the best. Sleeping is the only escape now, but it evades you. It knows it's all you have, and as a punishment, it runs. You're left thinking of all that you're missing. School. Friends. Food. Hugs. Parties. You replay the moment you found out about this over and over. You feel alone, even though you know there are warm bodies around you, turning cold as they lay on the ground and absorb the chill of nature. You can't lose control of yourself, you can't scream and say how much you hate it here, and how much you wish you could take back the last six months. You can't run. You can't hide. You are raw out here. And that has the potential to make or break you. So which will it be?

Don't feel pressured to write back, your hands are probably numb anyway. Be safe.
-Sophia

P.S. Hope you like the bracelet

I somehow felt inclined to send the lyrics of the song "Better Days" by Eddie Vedder with the email containing the other letters. I had really listened to the lyrics one day, when I was out on a glorious trail run, with the sunshine just warm enough and the light just perfect. I needed to send this to him. He needed this affirmation of self-acceptance and humility as much as I did the day I heard it.

Letter of Accountability from Tyler to me and Chris, written December 11, 2015, received December 16, 2015

Dear Mom and Dad,

I would like to start off by apologizing for my previous actions that forced you to send me to Second Nature. I'm so sorry especially to my parents, but also to Grandma and Grandpa Rich and Carolyn, Grandpa Arnold, Grammy, Dee, Matt, and my cousins; Haley, Anne, and Mia, and all of the rest of the family...This letter states the things I want to take accountability for, and how I plan to change my behavior. I am motivated to make these changes to show my respect of my family, who has constantly and consistently granted me their unconditional love and support.

My lies and manipulations put far too much stress on my mom and dad's relationships with Dee and Matt, making it hard for me to live in Dee's household, and causing trouble that Matt most definitely did not want to deal with. I recall an instance with my mother where I stated that I would not go to family counseling and that I was proud of being a master manipulator. I am not proud of this anymore, it is a terrible skill that caused me to not only disrespect my family, but also myself.

...My refusal to participate in family events stands out to me. There should have been no argument, considering how much my family does for me. I was always disrespectful when asked to help out around the house with very minimal tasks. I always had excuses. My refusal to go to counseling is a great of example of how disrespectful I was towards my family, because when I finally went to my mom's counselor by myself and with my parents, I realized that both my family and myself could seriously benefit from hearing a sort of middle man, someone impartial. After I was given the opportunity to live at my mom's house full time, I did not show respect for the enormous burden that it would put onto my mom, financially, emotionally and in her relationship. Another example is how I failed to take it seriously when cops came to the house two separate times within the same week. I demonstrated my disrespect for the seriousness of the situation when I took a selfie with cops in the background for my Snapchat. I was disrespectful in having inappropriate sexual relationships. Before that, I was resistant

to sign a contract written by my parents, because it had a list of chores for me to complete, including an agreement that I would not do drugs. I was told that I did not sign this, like I should have anyway, then the consequence would be having cops come to the house, and my dad showing them weed paraphernalia in my closet from a month or so before. I failed to show my dad any respect for all the things he has done for 17 years to support me and help me find a meaningful path in life...I used very strong hateful words during these arguments. I even asked for emancipation at one point. I showed disrespect towards my grandparents by arguing and using vulgar language. As I reflect on that behavior, it really hurts me emotionally to think that I acted that way towards Grandma and Grandpa, who only wanted what was best for me throughout all of my life. I've been stubborn since I learned to speak, and have continued to act the same way all the way up into my teen years. I've struggled with dealing with consequences and had a very hard time being able to change my behaviors due to my stubbornness.

Core Issues Journal - Tyler Watkins, December 15, 2015

What does it mean to be a man?

For me, to be a man means the ability to gain a great relationship with a woman that can eventually turn into a marriage, and end up with a family. To be biologically successful, genetics need to be passed on by having children. A man must be able to have a strong sense of fatherhood at some point in his life, and be able to effectively teach his children the right tools in life. I think my father was successful with this, and I hope to one day be able to follow his example. This is very important to me, and I've believed this to be my path for many years. To be a man, one must have the greatness within themselves to find a great relationship.

Letter from Tyler to Chris, written December 16, 2015, received December 22, 2015

Dear Dad,

I'll start off with what a day at Second Nature consists of for me. It starts off with waking up in my wiggy sleeping bag very early, sometimes even before the sunrise. I look up towards my tarp shelter, put together between two trees with four anchors, then tied together with trucker hitches. I've been consistently waking up from dreams that at first are only nightmares, eventually, turning into dreams of being back at home. This is what causes me to wake up, and I experience some very tough emotions and remorse for the remaining time given to sleep. Each morning, a staff member wakes up, and asks each student to sound off in number order. I am number 5 of 7, now that two people left; and 2 more came in, one of which I was given the opportunity to monitor during my second week. After the sound off, they tell us to hit the snooze, and we are given about an hour longer to sleep. I haven't once been able to sleep during that extra hour. After the staff come up from our camp to our shelters, they give us our boots, and we are given ten minutes at most to have our clothes on and be at the staff shelters with our backpacks. Since I was given a shelter to myself, I've generally been the first one at staff shelters or "staff land." Then, we all go together down to our camp, where we are assigned our jobs for the day, and have breakfast. Breakfast consist of granola and oats which I fiend for constantly, and almost always get seconds. Depending on if we're hiking or not, we either begin to practice minimal impact camping, where we crush and sift our fire pit, bury our shit hole (called the "lat") and pack up the rest of camp, or we go into personal time, where we can work on assignments and letters for about an hour and a half. Some days, we are given time to bust flames. I have now successfully busted two flames. It is an extremely difficult task, and I've only been able to try about four or five times. We then have lunch. If we are staying in camp, we can cook our personal foods on the fire. Throughout the past couple of weeks, I've been struggling with conflicting emotions. I find myself frequently laughing while talking and interacting with the group, but on the other hand, I have strong feelings of depression and guilt in between all those laughs and giggles. This week, I feel very happy. I feel that I have support from my group and positive feedback from staff members. I get a lot from the Jai-hippy-peacemaker-musician staff member Wyatt-Elijah, who brings a significant amount of positive energy to me and the group, through talented guitar strums of ambiance and meaningful hip hop freestyles; along with a great sense of wisdom. Too bad this is his last shift. The last staff shift had some negative vibes that had a tendency to bring me down and it didn't really seem so therapeutic. However, I didn't let these feelings affect my work ethic.

We're given a great amount of group food that goes towards making pretty damn good meals for everyone. Me and my boy Anthony like to throw down some really good campfire cooking. I'm working on dealing with my hard emotions, but it's tough when I miss so much back at home. The stars out here get almost as bright as they are at Bryce National Park, giving a solid view of the Milky Way. To stay warm at night, we have water bottles that we boil and put into a sock to put in our sleeping bags. I've found this to not always be necessary, since our wiggy bags are very warm by themselves, for the most part.

I would like to point out that my friends did not see the self-destructive side of me. I always had positivity, but it left me when I was by myself. I know my friends would stand by me regardless of if I did or didn't do drugs but I want to stop abusing drugs. I know it only brought me more pain. I know how bad drugs are. My blood pressure and heart rate have gotten significantly lower and the last check was 109/80. Much better than before, even when I down half a jar of peanut butter in one sitting. I want to prove myself to be an honest person, and be able to regain at least some level of trust from my family. Thanks Dad.

Love,
Tyler Watkins

Letter from Tyler to me, December 16, 2015

Dear Mom,

I'm really missing all the happy and positive times that we've spent together. Just relaxing at home and watching movies, taking trips to Moab, adventuring, and going to a seriously awesome Alabama Shakes concert. I appreciate the picture of us more than anyone would know. I know I've had some serious struggles with growing up. I wish I had also taken into consideration the devastation that I imagine addiction and drug abuse can bring a family from the experience with Rick. I really appreciate the positivity that your letters bring me, hearing about life at home. It makes me happy but also very homesick. The very chill staff member, Wyatt-Elijah, has been providing me with the experience of meditation through really meaningful guitar chords and burning sage and incense as we meditate. I imagine it's similar to the feeling that you get from hot yoga. I could definitely go for some hot yoga at the moment. :) I love you so much Mom.

Now to answer your questions. For the most part, I have kept the majority of my dark side away from school. I did Kratom at school at the end of last year, and have vaped off -campus a few times with Daniel. I realized that this is far too risky behavior to be doing at Eastland. I don't pressure or influence anybody, and I appreciate people who make their own decisions. I really want Eastland to allow me back in, and if it doesn't happen I'm worried about my emotional state as a result.

The things that I wouldn't mention when I told you and dad that you had no idea what was going on in my life do not consist of people being pregnant or STD's. It was just drug abuse and deep depression that I didn't share with my family. I know you're a lot less superficial than Carly, and don't act like you're in high school like a large portion of other Eastland moms. I wouldn't doubt that Carly wants to find some dirt to spread around to everyone. You're better than them. You're the best Mom.

Love,
Tyler Watkins

Letter from me to Tyler, December 21, 2015

Dear Tyler,

Happy Solstice! I'm sure missing and thinking about you on this longest night of the year. Solstice can help us remember that we are part of a larger order…always changing, always renewing. So many cultures for ages have celebrated Solstice. In Rome, where it is called Dies Natalis Invicti Solis, or the Birthday of the Unconquered Sun, masters even celebrated as equals with their slaves. In Iran, families often kept fires burning all night to assist the battle between light and dark forces. Themes of reversal, rebirth,

Chapter 2: Second Chances

new beginnings, and the reawakening of nature are all part of Solstice traditions. You are in a unique and perfect place to contemplate what Solstice means to you in your own life, with your current, past, and future struggles.

I look forward to seeing your letters with great anticipation every week! I also enjoy the pictures of the group, as well as the weekly journal updates. I wish they did not all come around the same time, as it is a week or so between communications from you. You always have that eternal smile that you (and the rest of the family) are so famous for, while I know you struggle with so many things. Anyway, it looks as though you are making some progress on digging into those hard emotions, and coming to terms with what caused you to be where you are now. While you explore these hard emotions, I really want you to explore the "WHY" element of all of this. I also feel as though you are still only telling us what you think that we already know…you are still not being fully honest with yourself or us on everything. For instance, I have information that you have vaped and done Kratom not on the "outskirts" of campus, but in the senior lounge, as well as the school parking lot. Had I told you that I had this information, you may have used it in your accountability letter, but you still skirted around the truth. It will only harm you, and take you longer to realize the full breadth of your problems, if you hold yourself back from digging deeper and coming clean.

I have been in communication with Mason's mom, Kate quite a bit. Mason is struggling enormously. The Simonsons are in a really tough position, as he is an adult, and they cannot force him to get help. They are aware that he is still using, though almost all of his privileges have been removed. They took away his car, drive him to school, they have taken away his credit card and many other things, but he is fighting and resisting any kind of change. He even used on a family trip to Florida over Thanksgiving. His battles with his dad have heated up tremendously, and his behavior is causing significant strain on the family. Of course, I know very well how stressful that can be. Mason is also refusing to go to family counseling, so nobody knows how they can help him.

The Mason friendship is a really difficult thing for me because I really want you to be able to finish at Eastland, but I don't want you to come back and renew your friendship with Mason, as I don't believe that the two of you are good for each other. If I had my wish, I would move to another state or area to keep you away from a friend that is toxic to you (and you to him). With graduation so soon, I don't think that is the most pragmatic option. You are sooooo close!!! That being said, your mental health is more important than your education, in my opinion, so the jury is still out as to what the best option will be for you. It will be impossible for us to tell you that you cannot have any contact with Mason, but my hope is that you will be better at setting your boundaries with him by that point.

Mason's mother was wondering if you could write a letter to Mason to tell him how you are doing, what you are learning about yourself, and anything else that might help him dig himself out of the hole that both of you have dug for yourselves. Your unique relationship as his best friend, as well as your own experience in the wilderness, might be of some help to him. This would be a good opportunity for you to start establishing some boundaries with him. You can discuss what things will be inappropriate for you when you come back, recognize and name your triggers to him, and tell him the things that you know might be hard for you to see, do, or be around. You have had the gift of being stripped of interference out there, so that you might be introspective about these issues. Kate is beside herself on what to do for Mason. As a mom of a kid that I love that is in the same position, I totally relate and empathize with her. She thought that it would be better if the letter doesn't come through us, though I think that your counselor should see it. If he thinks that it is ok, just send it directly:

Mason Simonson
PO Box 12345
Salt Lake City, UT 84222

Sophia was also hoping to get a short note. She felt really badly when she was in her wilderness program because nobody sent her any letters. She didn't want that to be your experience. Maybe something quick to thank her for her consideration.

I am incredibly moved by Ms. Butter's poetry package that I am bringing up there with your Christmas stuff. She has included a large amount of poetry that was not necessarily assigned, but that she thought might be meaningful to you. I read some of the poetry and I want to read the rest... incredible! She also poured her soul into the letter that she wrote you. You have so many people that love and want the best for you.

How is everything else? The elements? The hiking? I'm happy that you are taking pride in your camp cooking. I trained you well after all! Was all of that peanut butter consumed after a hike? Did you carve your spoon? Are you going to teach me how to bust a fire? You can start the fires when we camp next year if you ever want to again! My guess is that you will look back fondly on this journey that you are on, and, like the rebirth of the Sun this Solstice...shine a little longer every day!

All of my love… Mom

Letter from Tyler to me and Chris, written December 21, 2015, received December 22, 2015

Dear Mom and Dad,

I just wanted to let you guys know where I am now that I've been here for a month, and how thankful I am for all of the things I have taken for granted at home. I'm so sad when thinking of all the awesome things I'm missing out on, especially during the holidays. It's hard to think that the only Christmas music that I heard during this year will be that which was played in the senior lounge months ago as a joke. I miss being able to have conversations with my family, and even being able to personally let you know that I love you, and say goodnight before sleeping in a warm bed in a heated house. I miss lying down at times where I just need to relax a little. Instead, I have to sit on a foam pad, and be at every activity on time, or suffer consequences. It sucks when I always get all of my things done, and most of the rest of the group just sits around. I miss having food whenever I want, enjoying homemade meals with my family, and being able to cook for myself. I miss my friends, and even being able to communicate with friends. I want to be back at school, where I can actually learn, and get things done to prepare me for college. As I sit out here, I get more and more sad about everything I'm missing. I'm so bummed that everyone is on Christmas break living it up in their warm houses while I'm out in the woods

71

reflecting on all these things. I know I very well deserve to be stuck in this shitty position that I put myself in, but I know I want nothing more than to be back home with my family and friends. I can't even take care of myself like normal. I barely have time to comb my hair every few days. I'm getting an extreme amount of chafing in between my legs and my bucket showers aren't doing the job. I'm starting to get extremely uncomfortable and sad. I didn't mean to rant about how shitty this place feels at the moment, but it's been running through my head a ton. I really miss you guys, and Chester. I love you so much, and I hope Christmas at home is everything that it was in the past years that I've had at home. I'm writing this from my sleeping bag.

Love,
Tyler Watkins

Letter from Tyler to me and Chris, received December 22, 2015

Dear Mom and Dad,

I've decided to be totally accountable for all of my past shit, because I'm so tired of being stuck out in wilderness during my senior year.

I'll start off with the "why" element of all of this. The truth is that I thought it was fun, and I was having a good time. When I thought about the consequences, I would justify my actions, or simply disregard them in the first place. This is a great way to really screw yourself over with the law and other things.

Now about Eastland, and my "dark side." I have not vaped on campus, but I did do Kratom in my car last year. Kratom fucking sucks, but I somewhat remember taking a few Kratom pills in the senior lounge. In my mind, Kratom doesn't matter. What does matter, is that I had done acid at school once, and I had smoked dabs, a number of times, before school, and put in eyedrops, so I didn't look fucked up. I did make a decision not to get high at or before school on a frequent basis, but it shouldn't have happened at all, especially acid. Now, about selling things to people at school. I had sold weed to close friends in my grade a couple of times, and I sold acid to a very close friend at school. I truly did not like exposing my friends from Eastland to drugs, but it got tough

Chapter 2: Second Chances

when a good percentage of my grade started doing drugs and other things. I never should have brought such a dark world into my family at Eastland, and I never will again.

Now about Mason. We both had gotten sucked into the world of doing drugs and partying. We had thought that it was just fun and games. We started off by just smoking weed but moved on to hallucinogens, and later to harder drugs like Xanax. Mason had not taken the drugs to the level that I had, but I noticed after Highland Ridge that he had seemed to ramp it up, and it actually worried me for the weeks I was back. He seemed to be almost at the point that had gotten me sent to Highland Ridge, which I have accepted was too far. Now that I've thought about it, and realized the conflicts and troubles that drugs have caused our families, I think the only thing I can do is try to help him realize that it's not doing him any good for himself or his relationship with his family. I want to help Mason get out of this self-destructive cycle. I will do my best to write him a letter before the therapists leave, but it may have to wait until next week. It's sad to hear that they are having similar struggles, and I know the fight or flight position Mason must most likely be feeling right now.

Now, onto the hardest part for me to be accountable for, but it must be done. Dealing drugs isn't just illegal, but it's also dangerous, and it can lead you to doing worse and worse things. I was dealing weed at a larger scale than I had previously said. I sold a half a pound in about a week and a half and that's the most I've ever sold. The money accumulated from this is gone, as it went to drugs and food during this last summer. I was also selling Xanax during the summer, and a little bit during the school year to public schoolers. Here's a list of the drugs that I have done: marijuana, alcohol, acid, mushrooms, salvia, Xanax, Adderall, OxyContin, Hydrocodone, MDMA, Codeine, and I've tried cocaine. I'm so ashamed to tell you guys this, but I think it's the only way to gain your trust back, by being totally honest. I'm so sorry I allowed myself to do this, but I know I won't let myself go this deep into that dark world ever again. The fact that I had access to this kind of thing was dangerous, because I had money and didn't care. I've lied so many times about where I was and what I was doing. It got completely out of hand, and I would come home high, and be high around the family. I'm so ridiculously sorry for doing this to myself, and bringing my unacceptable actions into the lives of my loved ones. I love you so much.

Sincerely,
Tyler Watkins

Letter of Accountability – Tyler Watkins, written December 16, 2015, received December 22, 2015

I've come to realize over my time here, and through my sessions with Steven, that I need to open and be honest about my actions, including the ones that harmed me most. There is one situation that has caused me a significant amount of pain, and I've been unable to accept what happened. I decide that I would open up about it finally, in a therapeutic manner during sessions, but the thought of being honest about it to my parents brought me a great deal of stress, due to it being so difficult for me to process myself.

At the beginning of the school year, during the first week, I had an experience with drugs that I originally considered an overdose. I talked about it with Steven and concluded that it was not an overdose, but a very close call that could have left me in the hospital very easily, but thank God that it didn't.

After saying goodnight to dad and going into my room, I took a dose of OxyContin and multiple bars of Xanax. I was being extremely irresponsible after taking the painkiller, and I didn't think about the risks of taking another depressant until I already had. I immediately regretted what I had done. I began to get extremely high and lay there with barely the ability to move. I tried to send a message to Mason about what was going on but I couldn't even type a message. I blacked out shortly thereafter.

Luckily, I woke up in the morning for school and forgot what had happened. I didn't realize what had happened until later the day after. It took me into an extreme state of depression and suicidal thought. I was so disappointed in myself and that I would even allow myself to do such a thing. I was able to pull myself out of my dark headspace thanks to my realization that I couldn't follow through with my thoughts because of everything that my family has done, Eastland, and the awful thought of how that would affect these people.

Continuation of LOA, written December 17, 2015, received December 22, 2015

...Aggression toward my family should never happen, regardless of the situation. The aggression I'm talking about would arise when conflict happened and both my parents and I would go into fight or flight mode, causing us to escalate the fight and aggravation. After my time at Second Nature, I believe my family will further benefit from the continuation of family treatment. The couple times we had all gone, I had already noticed great improvement with understanding and other things that help me avoid creating conflict, solving them instead.

... I've needed to, and finally have realized that I don't need drugs to be out of my depression. I've realized that here at Second Nature, because when I'm hanging out and spending time with my group buddies, I don't feel that emptiness that I used try to fix with drug use. I can solve that by hanging out with friends when I'm back home, but I will choose not to incorporate drugs into my arsenal of coping skills. If I'm not doing drugs, then I don't have any reason to be dealing drugs. I haven't been having drug cravings while out here. Maybe I'm distracted by the cold, but it's a good feeling, not feeling a need for an artificial mindset. My cravings for drugs have shifted into cravings for food. I will not do drugs for my happiness anymore.

...Something else that will help a lot is if I'm happy about the decisions that I'm making. My poor decisions in the past have most likely put me in the most depressive states I have ever been in. I never want to have those feelings ever again, so if my levels of self-respect increase dramatically, and I'm positive about my decisions, then I will be more happy, which will in turn, aid my motivation for school and many other things.

I'm going to benefit greatly from all of my reflection and realization of the poor choices I've been making, and I believe it will result in positive changes for the betterment of my future.

Sincerely,
Tyler Watkins

Second Nature, December, 2015

For Christmas we were mostly supposed to send letters, more encouraging and void of the pointed remarks about how his behavior had affected the family, much different than the letters that we were asked to send when he was first sent to the wilderness. We could include photos but not too many, as he would have to carry them in his backpack, already impressively large. Going through all of the boxes of years of family photos it was difficult to narrow my photos down to a handful of happy memories, there were so many. As I selected the best, pictures of him and Sparky, pictures of camping trips, first bike rides, all of the typical American family standards, I struggled to find photos from the last few years. Years of a slow retreat into himself. He would sometimes briefly open a window into his world but only to tell me he had secrets I would never know. Enough to drive a mother mad with worry. Did he tell me these things because he really wanted to tell me something? to antagonize me? to taunt - like a school child "I have a secret" - a sick need to be in control of some piece of information?

They didn't want us to give gifts but I received permission to knit him a pair of socks. They were far too fancy for the conditions he was in and I knew they would be. I just held onto some kind of hope that all of those stitches that I put through the needles with my own hands, to form some beautiful socks, an act both tedious and time consuming, would let him know that I really did love him. A representation of my willingness to form yarn into something to give him warmth against the elements – much like the quilt that I had made him while he was in the hospital for the first three weeks of his life. I had started the quilt long before he came two months early, but finishing it became a symbol of my resistance to feeling utterly helpless in the face of the situation. It was the only thing that I could do on his behalf, other than pump milk every two hours to give to the nurses to feed him. The beginning of his life was spent dealing with things that were out of my control in caring for my child, and I found myself in that place once again. Every stitch in the quilt, as well as the socks, was an attempt to keep my baby warm.

I took a road trip and travelled a couple of hours over the mountain southeast of my boyfriend's house. I went the wrong route the first time, unaware that the pass was closed for the winter. Matt's puppy was in the back chewing up something on his first road trip. The packages were to go out in the late afternoon, so I had to get them there before they made the delivery to the remote camp. The campsite was far, and through a maze of high-desert jeep roads, an incredible distance away from the office and supply house, ensuring that the kids wouldn't think of walking or hitching out of there. Most parents lived somewhere much further away. I had missed the shipping deadline and used that as an excuse to get closer, to catch a glimpse of where he was taken. I had my son kidnapped right before the holidays. The least I could do was make sure he had something for Christmas. I made some ginger cookies as well, though that wasn't really allowed. I just put Group Six – not who they were from, to let all of the boys know they were loved by someone.

Christmas 2015

Dear Tyler,

Merry Christmas! I'm missing you here across the mountains to your west. I had not really wrapped my head around what having an "empty nest" might feel like! I will say that it is quiet without you and Sparky around… and I haven't seen Chester for a couple of months. The quiet is not all bad, it's just that change is really hard sometimes. It's hard, but necessary and inevitable. My only consolation is that you are in a good place for self-discovery and self-awareness, and that the change will help facilitate your growth so that you will move toward being self-sufficient, and happy. Sometimes, a mere change of scenery, being out of one's element, will help a person understand themselves better. I found this to be the case when I went to Japan as an exchange student in high school. My intention was to escape what I found to be a painful, tumultuous family situation, but what I found was a deeper understanding of who I was, both as a part of my family, as well as outside of my family. I do believe that the experience that you are having at Second Nature can be much, much more than just a change of scenery. The skills that you learn can become tools for understanding the metaphor of struggling in the wilderness as it compares to your struggles in life. You are learning how to try…fail…try again…and succeed! I'm guessing that busting a flame is a perfect example of this.

I am forever grateful to my dad for sharing his love of extreme outdoor adventure with me. It seems to me that our backpacking trips in the Wind Rivers were my happiest memories. Honestly, the mosquitos were horrendous, the bear threat real, and the extremely long hikes that we endured, sometimes in the rain, were crazy. He pushed us so beyond the point of exhaustion once that I was puking from over-exertion. We were hiking down to a lake only about a mile away but with a serious amount of elevation loss, that required bouldering over massive chunks of granite, the size of cars. Each one required us to lower ourselves down, around, or over them. My brothers ended up getting to the bottom, dropping their packs and heading back to help the girls get their packs down. It's the first time that I'd ever seen my dad look worried. As we lay exhausted on the beach of the lake at the bottom of the gorge (Gorge Lake I believe was the name) that night before we retired to our tents, the most spectacular shooting

Chapter 2: Second Chances

star display graced the sky. We usually went in July, so it was probably the Perseid meteor shower or something like that. I still remember it vividly as one of the highlights of my life. I wonder if we would have even noticed it or appreciated it had we not been lying on the beach exhausted from our hike! When we hiked out of the Gorge the next day, we noticed that someone had scratched out the name Gorge Lake on the sign and replaced it with hell. So I guess we went to hell and have wonderful memories to show for it!

I am sending you a bunch of tiny pictures as I know that you have to carry everything and I wanted you to remember some of the many great times that we have had over the years! Most of those pictures were from the photos that I had in the basement. I had to take photos of the photos and have prints made, because they are not on my computer. I spent a bunch of time reminiscing over more recent photos that are on my computer that I did not have time to print off… more recent stuff…though when I studied it further, I realized that there are no pictures that I have of you, save for the couple of birthday pictures at the concert, and at breakfast, and our pictures of Sparky's last hike, that are more recent than a couple of years ago. You see, you stopped wanting to do stuff with me. I want my old Tyler back again! I know that those old times were good for all of us….not perfect but perfectly imperfect! I want to watch a meteor shower on the beach after a long hike with you.

Enjoy the simple things out there this Christmas. Your peers, the smell of the pinion and juniper forest, the birds. I'm sure that you are identifying a number of good birds out there and I hope that you might share with me what you see. I still think that you should look at ornithology, because I believe that you have a special appreciation of our feathered friends. So what if it won't make you rich, you could do all right as a college professor. Wes and Jennie have done well for themselves, following their bliss. I have included a letter from Jennie with this Christmas package. They are in Florida right now studying mosquito repellent. Perhaps you can go do research with them this summer.

Confessions of a Heroin Addict's Mother

Please remember that our gift to you this year is one of love, mental health, self-acceptance, and responsibility. Only through these things can you find true happiness. Everything else is just "stuff" and doesn't really matter in the broad scheme of things anyway. I know that reading is not your favorite pastime but I'd really like you to read "The Four Agreements" when you get home. It contains four really solid principals that have meant a lot to me since I read it. To summarize them;

1) Be impeccable with your word

Speak with integrity, say only what you mean. Avoid using the word to speak against yourself or to gossip about others. Use the power of your word in the direction of truth and love.

2) Don't take anything personally

Nothing others do is because of you. What others say and do is a projection of their own reality. When you are immune to the opinions and actions of others you won't be the victim of needless suffering.

3) Don't make assumptions

Find the courage to ask questions and express what you really want. Communicate with others as clearly as you can to avoid misunderstandings, sadness, and drama. With this one agreement you can completely transform your life.

4) Always do your best

Your best is going to change from moment to moment; it will be different when you are healthy as opposed to sick. Under any circumstances, simply do your best and you will avoid self-judgement, self-abuse and regret.

I usually dislike self help books, which is strange with a degree in psychology, but all of this just makes sense to me. I think that the 4th agreement is especially valuable to me. What freedom from my own self-judgement has come from knowing that there was simply no more that I could have given something, after looking back and knowing that I did my best!

Merry Christmas to you and warm hugs! I'll love you always,
Mom

Chapter 2: Second Chances

Letter from me to Tyler, December 28, 2015

Dear Tyler,

I just love this picture of you and your cello and had to share it with you! I can't wait to hear you play again...It's been so long. How was your Christmas? I've had such a tough week with you gone, hoping that you are getting some perspective and mental clarity, but missing you terribly during the holidays. I know the weather has been particularly harsh this week and I am confident that you are learning to care for yourself as you realize that you can survive this extreme climate, and that you can survive the challenges that you will surely face at home when you are finally here!

The last letters from you were very difficult for me to read, as I am sure they were difficult to write. It's hard to be honest and confess when you know how we would feel about the things that you were doing. I appreciate your honesty in saying what you surely needed to tell us. I have played over and over in my head the scenes of the life that you were leading, as you were trying to present to the world a happy, well-adjusted, private school, cello-playing, sweet kid. I just can't fathom the energy that it took you to live the lies that you were living. I now have a better (or worse) picture of WHAT you were doing, but I do not think that you have yet come to terms with the WHY part of the picture. I don't feel that you can remain clean and move toward some productive college years until you understand why you felt the need to take the drugs, sell the drugs, provide drugs to your friends, and treat your parents, your family, and yourself in such a disrespectful way. I'm happy to hear that you think that counseling is something that you now see value in to help you explore these deep-seeded issues. While you are in the wilderness receiving counseling, and having the time to contemplate these things...you need to come to some understanding of the WHY part of the picture. Did you think it would make you more popular? more likable? You did mention that it was "fun," but what made you start in the first place?

You didn't know it was "fun" until you tried it but you had to know how disappointed we would be! Is that what you were trying to do? Disappoint us?

Your life has not been bad. Though we know from research a person's experience of his or her life struggles is subjective, or personal. Look at all of the pictures of the fun times that we have had through the years in the little snapshot sheet I sent at Christmas. Were they not "fun" times? Moving into your college years you are supposed to be creating in yourself a person that can work within the norms of society (like them or not), educate yourself to be able to take care of a family, and become a contributing member of the human race…not a destructive force! You have always said that you want a family, and even recently, while in Second Nature, you mentioned that you wanted to be a father and spouse in your "Becoming a Man" writing. Do you think that the lifestyle that you have been leading can get you even close to being the man and father that you want to be? What would have become of you if I had been a dealer and drug abuser as I tried to raise you? If I had influenced and sold drugs to my friends and lied to my family about it? You say now that you see that this was wrong but did you have any guilt regarding your actions at the time that you were doing them? I'm worried that you are "finding God in a foxhole" by telling us these things to get you out of the wilderness, but that you have no intention of maintaining your "clean-living" behaviors once you are home.

You are going to be 18 in August. I am almost past the point of being able to influence you, your life, and future at this point. This is the last-ditch effort that we are making to try to get you on a path to becoming a person that I, and YOU, can be proud of! Are you going to make the right choices for yourself? I can only be there to verbally support you, listen to you, and make suggestions, if you chose to hear them. Your choices are going to be on you! My job as your Mom is to have you take over my part and look after yourself. That is not saying that I won't always care what happens to you, but my influence will be greatly diminished. My hope is that from this day forward you will care for yourself the way I care about you! LOVE ALWAYS!!!!

We will get to talk to you on Wednesday I believe for our first family counseling session. I can't wait to hear your voice. I came up to Duchesne to drop off your socks and Christmas stuff. I was trying to imagine you out there. I took Moe with me for his first road trip and hiked him for a little while outside town. It is beautiful up there. I'm looking forward to coming up to spend the night in a couple of weeks when Steven says it's time for that. I'm going to LA to work for the Smiths on their Uncle Bob's house clean-out. I went to check it out a week or so ago. What a mess:) Uncle Bob was a hoarder so it should make for an interesting project! I'm taking Isaiah with me to work. I'm trying to coordinate the timing of that with a visit up to you. We should know more this week. Still trying to get the go-ahead from the Smiths on timing. I really need the work though so I hope that it turns out.

Matt says Hi! We missed having you here with his girls on Christmas morning. I can't wait to hear the updates from your group journal. I really do savor getting any information about what you guys are doing. I wish that everything didn't come at one time...letters, journal, and photo updates but I guess that's just how the cycle works.

Talk Wednesday! I love you so much...
Mom

Letter from Tyler, Core Issue Journal, written December 24, 2015, received December 30, 2015

There's a large amount of things for which I'm thankful, but I have the tendency to take a number of things for granted. Being here at Christmas has helped me realize many things.

I'm extremely thankful for being able to go to my school, Eastland. Without Eastland, I'm certain that I wouldn't be even close to as smart as I am today. I also do not doubt that I would have gotten into more trouble at an earlier age, and I believe I would have had a much closer chance at getting fucked over by the law or with other situations. I'm so glad that I was able to learn to play the cello at a young age, because I know that without Eastland that most likely would not have happened. I love my school and how it has prepared me for college.

Confessions of a Heroin Addict's Mother

I'm so thankful for food, music, being able to have had a car, being able to try new things, and being accepted by my family. I'm thankful for being given the chance to change my ways instead of being shunned.

Letter from Tyler, written December 25, 2015, received December 30, 2015

Merry Christmas Mom and Dad!

I wanna say that this is a really meaningful day for me out here in the Uintah Basin, and the staff has really made it as good as it can be. I'm so thankful for the things sent out. I have the pictures and the pearl bracelet. I'm feeling significantly better now than I have been in the last while, and it's so great to hear from everyone and have support from so many awesome people. The Christmas package sent meant more to me than you can imagine. I can't wait until I can get back to the real world and start back up at Eastland with my teachers and counselors that give so much love and support. That really isn't something you can find anywhere else but at Eastland, and I can't begin to imagine what it would be like without such caring teachers. I also want to say that the socks mom knit are amazing and I'm not going to destroy them by wearing them out here. The staff is treating me with respect and recognizing my efforts. It makes it seem like this place really isn't too bad when it seems as though they see something different in me than the others in the group. I can't wait to get back home and be with my family and leading a normal life. I love you so much! Merry Christmas and Happy New Year.

Love,
Tyler Watkins

Letter from Tyler to Chris, written December 29, 2015, received December 30, 2015

Dear Dad,

I'm doing alright in the crazy cold weather at the moment. It's really not too bad other than the morning, when we wake up and it's negative 10 degrees. This Christmas was awesome, for being in a wilderness

*program, and I was really able to be thankful for the little things in life,
although the days leading up to Christmas had me struggling. I got
everything that was sent up but the cinnamon bears. It was all freaking
awesome and it made the day great, along with the staff being super
cool, especially with me. They seem to get along with me exceptionally
well. On Christmas Eve, we had a fairly normal day, and on Christmas,
staff made us pancakes with sausage, then for dinner we had some
seriously good ham and sweet potatoes. I'm happy for any food at this
point. We stayed in the tent for 3 days which was a godsend. And yes,
we've had snow on the ground the entire time I've been here.*

*It's never been difficult for me to get along with any of the staff or
students, and the staff really seems to have taken a big liking to me. I've
been hinted to that I'm moving to Water Phase soon. It seems to take
longer than my 5 weeks here for other people in the program.*

*I realized how stupid the path I was taking truly was shortly after I
wrote my impact letter, and for the past few weeks, I've been accepting
it more and more. I'm unsure if there is more to be added to the list
of stupid things I've done, but I was honest about all of the worst
things I've done and I won't hesitate to let you know if other things
not mentioned come to mind. I understand that it must be hard for
you to understand that I did such a ridiculous amount of drugs for fun.
Something I'd like for you to consider would be the fact that drugs
make you feel a certain way and it seems like it's just fun, at first. Then
one starts to get to a certain point where drugs are on their mind a
lot, and they begin to look for that sense of euphoria in any way they
can. That would be better know as addiction, and while I don't think of
myself as being addicted to one thing, I did feel addicted to a different
state of mind, and that may even be worse than addiction to one thing.
The drugs and lying most definitely led to more guilt and depression.
Something I've been talking about with the seemingly oldest staff
member, Todd, is that we both think that a good part of my depression
is brought on by guilt. I definitely created a depression cycle.*

*I can see myself going back to Eastland after Second Nature and
finishing out the year strong as hell. I see myself living with both you
and mom. I know my friend who I have done drugs with in the past*

*won't try to bring me back into that world. It's completely within my
control to not get into those things again, and I'm confident with myself
that I will not let it happen. It's hard to shut out all of my friends who
were in the drug and party world, because that happens more than
you can imagine with Eastland kids, too. But, I have enough respect for
myself and enough self control to say no. I know I can go to Eastland
once again and I'll be able to make the right decisions. I know I'll
participate in the family and have empathetic feelings for the family.
I've always had the motivation to succeed in life. After Second Nature,
there won't be any drugs to get in the way of this motivation. I care!*

*I'm not trying to manipulate anyone anymore, and I've realized how
fucking stupid the things I did were. I never got off on being deceptive.
It was just a way for me to get away with doing the absurd things I
was doing. I totally understand why it cost me just about everything.
I'm so sorry that I cost you guys a ridiculous amount of money. I know
the ridiculous cost of Second Nature, and I'm so sorry that it ended up
coming down to this. That money will not have been wasted. I should
never have done anything that could jeopardize my academics, and I
know I can redeem myself during the rest of this year. I never meant to
push away my family. Even I am struggling to believe that I had done
this to myself and my family.*

*I am definitely ready to hear from both you and mom and I'm
advocating for a phone call that should be within the next couple of
days. I'm not used to not hearing from my family for such a long time,
so I'm really anxious to get to speak with you after being out here for
more than a month.*

*When I get back, I plan on seeing Star Wars with you, going skiing on
my rad new skis, getting coffee, watching movies at home in blankets
on the couch, playing with Chester and Cosmo, making food, looking
at nebulas with the telescope, going on hikes, playing music, playing
games, getting coffee and donuts, getting Indian food and catching up
on all the time that we've missed together. I'm going to be on Water
Phase very soon, once I bust a few more flames. You don't need to be
on Water Phase to get a phone call. I feel like I'm doing an awesome job
in the program. I haven't had too much time to read the poems from*

Mrs. Butter, but the letter she wrote meant so much to me and the few poems I read seem to relate to my situation more than I ever could have imagined. I miss you a ton, Dad. I know I'll get to see you soon!

Love,
Tyler Watkins

Letter from Tyler to me, written December 30, 2015, received December 30, 2015

Dear Mom,

It's been an extremely long time since I've seen you and heard your voice. I can't wait to get back and work on playing the cello song Julio, so I can play it at family dinners. I haven't really been having too much trouble caring for myself during this stay at Second Nature, and I realize that caring for myself was something that I've always been able to do fairly well. I think that contributed to getting away with the ridiculous things that I was doing because it made it easier to hide things. I'm confident when I get back that I will be able to take even better care of myself than before.

Writing that letter last week, days before Christmas, was extremely difficult for me to write, and it ended up putting me in a pretty bad place afterwards for a little bit. I had a feeling that it would be just as tough or tougher for my parents to read what I had written as it was for me to write it, and realize that the situation was even worse than you had originally thought. I'm so sorry, Mom.

Since Christmas, I've had the most positive attitude, and my actions and self improvement have helped me in becoming a leader in our group. In fact, half way through this letter, I learned that it earned me a phone call. I had an awesome session with Jason, and I'm in a really good spot at the moment. The last staff shift was really recognizing my efforts, and once I bust a few more flames, I'm going to be able to move on to Water Phase. This is awesome, because I don't know of anybody making it to Water Phase in the amount of time that I've been here. The two students already in Water Phase at the moment, got on Water Phase after 10 and 15 weeks.

Confessions of a Heroin Addict's Mother

I never wanted to disappoint you and Dad. I honestly thought that I would get away with all of my poor decisions, but I'm happy to have been able to come clean about the stuff that was deep in my thoughts. I know my life has not been bad at all. It's actually been awesome. I love the snapshots you sent me of my childhood and they stay in my pocket at all times. I was checking them out this morning and thinking back to all those rad times.

I know that being a clean person is necessary for becoming a good father and raising a child properly. I'm happy to say that I know that can happen.

I had covered up my guilt by doing more and more drugs and making bad choices. This only made me more guilty. I don't want to give myself reason to be guilty anymore.

I'd be so happy if you would drive up and spend a night up here as soon as possible. That would be so rad. I'm sure my efforts in the program will allow you to do that pretty soon. We'll have fun. I'm so happy to get to talk with you on the phone. I love you so much, Mom, and I'm happy that I'm in a good spot emotionally.

Love,
Tyler Watkins

Life Report on Man's Search for Meaning - Tyler Watkins, written January 5, 2016, received January 13, 2016

Reading a Man's Search for Meaning really puts the hardships that I face in my life into perspective. It made me realize that I have truly been given so much in my life, and the tough times and problems I've had are nothing compared to that which was faced in Nazi death camps during the second World War by those with Jewish blood. Upon having this realization, I also came to notice that Viktor E. Frankl has a very different perspective, and the things he learned from his survival of the time spent within concentration camps are very important ideas and words to keep in mind during my life.

Some of the feelings that I noted Frankl having and writing about within

Chapter 2: Second Chances

these camps, are a much more intense version of some of the emotions I have had while at Second Nature. For example, the emotions that come up when I am missing the things I used to have, and being away from all that I love. Those within the concentration camps felt a longing for simple things. They would often, as written by Frankl, find a sense of "wish fulfillment" within their dreams while they slept in extremely close quarters on their sides. I have found myself having this sense of wish fulfillment in my dreams nearly every night, where I dream of being back at home with the simple pleasures I took for granted while I was out of treatment. The perception of time noted by Frankl stood out to me, as I've had a similar feeling during the time I've spent here. Frankl states that weeks seem to go by quicker than days. This was likely due to the immense suffering and torture that the Jewish people endured. I am not having a tortuous time out in the wilderness and the days go by very quickly. This makes weeks fly by at a very significant rate.

Frankl observed that during the struggles constantly faced within the camps, men found inner strength by pointing out a future good to look forward to. Frankl says that it is a peculiarity of man that he can only live by looking into the future. I agree with Frankl's statement, and believe that inner strength during difficult times can be achieved by looking forward towards a positive life goal. Looking into the past at mistakes is not beneficial, but focusing on the present in order to follow through with imminent tasks at hand is important, while keeping future goals in mind to boost inner strength. One must "turn life into an inner triumph." A quote that I would like to keep in mind is, "life is like being at the dentist. You always think the worst is still to come and yet it is over already." This is important to me, because I realize that I will have hard times in the future undoubtedly, but I believe that hard abuse of drugs is a part of my life that is in the past, and stopping the use will be extremely beneficial towards keeping my life ahead of me on a good path.

I have a tendency to have a sense of vagueness and ambiguity in the way that I reflect on my emotions and actions. Something important I read was, "life does not mean something vague but something real and concrete. Just as life's tasks are very real and concrete." This pertains to me, because I want to be much more open with my feelings to those around me and stop putting on a guise for how I truly feel. I want to be real with myself. I know this is an important step to maturing.

Frankl talks about thoughts of suicide and other difficult thoughts felt by those suffering in the concentration camps. Many realized that life was still expecting something from them. This is very brave, considering the daily beatings and mistreatment that they went through. I myself have struggled with thoughts of suicide in the past, but I have been able to bring myself out of these hard feelings by realizing the potential I have, and thinking of the time and support put in by my loved ones. Killing myself would affect my family far too much. I have a responsibility to finish unfinished work, and that work would be growing up and getting my life on track! I cannot get myself into that position again and I can't throw away my life! I have loved ones waiting for me! These things were on the mind of those in the Nazi camps and it kept their heads in the best spots possible for their situation.

"The crowning experience of all, for the homecoming man, is the wonderful feeling that, after all he has suffered there is nothing he need fear any more except God" (93).

Letter from Tyler to me and Chris, written January 3, 2016, received January 13, 2016

Dear Mom and Dad,

I decided to write this letter due to some things on my mind that have been bringing me some serious concern. I'm extremely worried about what happens after my time here at Second Nature. I've noticed that everybody here is getting sent to aftercare after their time here. My worry is that it always seems to happen, and I won't be able to do anything to change that, even though I'm working hard here. I really have been thinking a lot about going back to Eastland after Second Nature, and I think it's the best option for my future as well as my emotional well being. All I hear about schooling at aftercare is that it's extremely easy and doesn't require a serious amount of work. I don't think that will benefit me at all, and I really want to end my senior year at Eastland strong. I'm just so worried that the option of going back will be thrown out the door for some reason, and I want to be able to graduate with Eastland. Otherwise, I feel like the last 12 years would be a complete waste of time and effort. I know my teachers care so much, and that level of effort from a teacher is impossible to find anywhere else.

This has been on my mind an extreme amount the past days since our phone call, and I really don't like the thought of not being able to go back. I know it would hurt me a lot and I hate to imagine how it would affect my family, who has invested a huge amount of time, money, and effort to have me attend Eastland.

Love,
Tyler Watkins

The New Macho
By Boysen Hodgson

He cleans up after himself. He cleans up our planet. He is a role model for young men. He is rigorously honest and fiercely optimistic.

He knows what he feels. He knows how to cry and he lets it go. He knows how to rage without hurting others. He knows how to fear and keep moving. He knows joy, and shares gratitude. He seeks self-mastery.

He has let go of childish shame. He feels guilty when he's done something wrong. He is kind to men, kind to women, kind to children. He teaches others how to be kind. He says he's sorry.

He stopped blaming women or his parents or men for his pain. He stopped letting his defenses ruin his relationships. He stopped letting his libido run his life. He has enough self-respect to tell the truth. He creates intimacy and trust with his actions. He has men who he trusts and turns to for support. He knows how to make it happen. He knows how to roll with it. He is disciplined when he needs to be. He is flexible when he needs to be. He knows how to listen from the core of his being.

He confronts his limitations. He's not afraid to get dirty. He has high expectations for himself and those he connects with. When he makes mistakes, as all men do, he holds himself accountable. When he falls, he gets back up. He practices compassion, for himself and others.

He knows he is an individual. He knows we are all one. He knows he is an animal and part of nature. He knows his spirit and a connection to something greater. He looks for ways to serve others.

He knows future generations are watching his actions. He builds communities where all people are respected and valued. He takes responsibility for himself and is willing to be his brother's keeper.

He knows his higher purpose. He loves with fierceness. He laughs with abandon, because he gets the joke.

Core Issue Journal, *The New Macho* - Tyler Watkins written January 4, 2016, received January 13, 2016

The New Macho poem has many ideas and feelings that every man can strive to achieve within his life. There are some things in which I am proud to say I have practiced within my life, but there are many things I need to add into my life and actions.

My focus will be on the things which I need work on. A big problem for me is honesty vs. deception, and this was brought up in The New Macho. I like to think of the good part of me as a role model for others, but the dark side of me is the exact opposite. I want to only have the good side. I want to know that I can be rigorously honest and be optimistic not only on the outside, but also on the inside, instead of merely appearing like I'm happy. I want to know that I'll have enough self respect to tell the truth. I've learned how I can respect myself. I need to learn how to listen from the core of my being. I want my actions to create intimacy and trust, rather than doing the opposite, like they have been. My previous actions are not something I want future generations watching.

Things that I have done that reflect the ideas in The New Macho *bring me hope about my future self. I clean up after myself and after the planet. I've really shown my ability to hold myself accountable. I seek to master myself. I'm a kind person to men, women and children. I'm disciplined when I need to be along with being flexible when needed. I have high expectations for myself and my friends. I look for ways to serve others. I know I'm an individual but we are all one. I am an animal within nature.*

The New Macho *explains the attributes of being a man, not just any old version or skewed idea of one, but a right and honest one.*

Letter from me to Tyler, January 4, 2016

Dear Tyler

We are finally through the holidays! Yeah!! It just was not the same without you around. It's really hard to think about you out there in the elements when we are at home. I absolutely feel that this was necessary though. I also feel that you are learning the fine art of enjoying the little things in life. Having a simple Christmas without lots of gifts and things really does let a person know what is truly important. We have had enough "lean" years that this is not your first "simple Christmas," though being in the elements and away from family is a first.

I can't wait until we can visit you! I want to experience the adventure that you are on first hand so that I may better relate to you…but mostly I just want to give you a big hug! It was so great to hear your voice last week when we were finally allowed to talk. You had more maturity and wisdom than I had ever heard, and I want you to keep striving for honesty and openness as you continue to explore the actions that have taken you to the Uintah Basin.

You have come clean with your "stuff," now I must come clean with mine!

I have not demanded enough of you. I have allowed you to get away with not participating in family events because I was too weak or tired to fight the battle with you. You should have gone to Moab with us in the summer, as well as the many other outings, trips, and events that you opted out of.

I have not demanded that you help more around the house with chores and other obligations. You do your own laundry, but in retrospect, I realize it's probably because you didn't want me going through your pockets! You should have been helping with the household chores as well. When you get home I will need your help fixing the items that you damaged in your fits of rage, (broken door, broken dresser, broken cabinet, etc.).

While you have always been angry that you felt you couldn't "divide and conquer" your dad and I over the many years that we have been divorced, I actually have, many times, allowed you to manipulate the situation between us. It has been extremely difficult to parent you because of our incredibly different parenting styles. So many times I have felt caught between the two of you when I disagreed with either you, or him, or both. I feel that I have always been the scapegoat for the family problems, and I have been caught between the two manipulators. You guys manipulate, I placate, everyone suffers!

I had significant relationship struggles in the last 5 years or so with Rick, and it distracted me from seeing what a terrible situation that you had slipped into. I was too self-absorbed to see it.

I allowed my work to fill most of my time, because I understand how to work even if I don't understand everything else that is happening around me. Work is so much less complicated!

I should have demanded that you get a job. You had too much time on your hands.

I should have demanded that you get more involved in things like volunteer work through your school, or other opportunities. You need to see how so many others live in order to really live yourself, and appreciate what we have been blessed with. Think about my Nepali refugee students when I was teaching building construction, like Puspa and Kumari. They lived in huts in refugee camps their entire lives before coming here. The first time they saw running water was in India on the way here. I'm sure that you can empathize with that now.

Even though we have taken a ton of hard knocks financially in the last 8 or so years, with the recession and other major life upheaval events, we

Chapter 2: Second Chances

still have a place to live that is warm at night, and we still have food to eat, even if I do grow most of it. I have allowed you to make me feel bad about feeding you "too many homegrown vegetables" (as if that's a bad thing!). You have to understand how painful it is that you should be critical of that when; 1) I love gardening and 2) I do it for our own "food security." I have allowed you to make me feel bad about our tiny house that we rent. This would not be the time for me to buy a house with so much uncertainty. You know all of the reasons behind our need to move into something cheap, flexible, and month to month. I was not happy with having to move out of our beautiful Emigration Canyon house but you must understand that I had told Rick that I would not tolerate a relapse, and was forced to stick to my guns and leave. The state was threatening to take away his medical license and forced him into a 3 month rehab for doctors, it had gotten so bad. I know that was hard for you…the whole situation. We were comfortable, you loved the kids, it felt like a "family." You could not possibly have known the extent of his drug problem and how it affected all of our futures together. It is so hurtful for you to constantly throw out there what a "shitty" place we live in now. I'm doing the best that I can for now, and I will not allow you to make me feel bad about it.

You know what they say…"Hindsight is 20/20." We can look at the things in the past with the present knowledge of what the outcomes of our actions and decisions were. It is much easier to pass judgement on what we have already done than to anticipate what will be the right decisions moving forward. We can only use the knowledge of what "didn't" work to come up with some solutions to what might work in the future. When you get home, I'm sure we will have some sort of contract that we ALL must live by, for EVERYONE'S happiness and mental health. We will all do our best to abide by whatever the established rules are. I'm sure that we will have help in drafting this contract from your counselor. I'm sure that the contract will include things like the continuation of counseling, family as well as personal. It will probably include you attend meetings like NA (Narcotics Anonymous), or some other more intensive aftercare type situation, or both. It will probably include you getting a job. It will probably include the option of a more intensive "inpatient" hospital for a long time if you cannot stay clean and sober or abide by the contract. You will likely have a contract with Eastland as well. Remember that graduating

95

Confessions of a Heroin Addict's Mother

with your class is not a given. Your school will know fairly quickly if that is something that you are motivated enough to make happen. Your dad and I are discussing your living situation. You are going to have to agree to go live with him at least as often as you are with me. I had allowed you to live here full time prior to your stay at Second Nature and I really suffered through that horrible time. I won't hesitate to say that it dragged me into a terrible, dark place. There is a possibility that your grandparents will let you stay with them, possibly with your dad there, at least at first. This would make getting to school with no car much easier. You have lots of friends in that area that you might be able to carpool with. Living with your grandparents might ease you into a home situation a little more easily. They won't put up with crap, though. We obviously will not be able to buy you another car after you wrecked the first one. I will be in debt for a long, long time from all of this.

On a lighter note…everyone is doing fairly well here right now. I'm happy that the holidays are over. We kept it pretty simple and tried to just enjoy some good hikes, walks with Moe, and gatherings with friends. I've been looking for 6 months or so for good hikes in the East Oakley area that I was sure must exist somewhere. They are starting a new trails foundation for that area to help develop, mark, and explore the trails for hiking, horses, and mountain biking. I have been wanting to GPS track anything we find to add to their collection of trails. We found a well-marked one last week that was just awesome. We hiked Moe the snow dog forever, mostly trail busting, except for maybe one other person that had gone before since the last snowfall. The snow was really deep so it was kind of tough. I think that next time I'll put skins on my skis and skin up, or take snowshoes.

Matt gave me a cooking class with him and we did it last night. Fun!!! We learned how to make home made pizza. I didn't have the heart to tell him that I could have taught the class. It didn't matter though. It was a good thing to do together and I got a few more recipes. I'm a little closer to convincing him that I need to build a pizza oven in the backyard.

Alex Sorenson's grandpa passed away last week. Just so you know so that you may offer condolences when you get home. He has always been such a good friend. I hope that you guys can remain friends when you get home. Sophia just moved to a duplex with her mom and siblings last weekend (divorce??). I don't know them well enough to ask, but would really like to get to know them better. They have been very supportive through all of this. Let's all get together when you get back.

I was supposed to be leaving today for CA to work on the job for the Smiths. They are still trying to get project financing in line before I can go…bummer! I really need this job. I've been filling my schedule with crazy little odd jobs and framing jobs until I hear for sure when I'm going out. I lost another big job too so that sucks. The life of the contractor I guess!

By the way…have you seen my REI backpack? I can't find it. Seems like you had it for something. Did you leave it somewhere? I had called Sorensons and Kate after you went to Second Nature to see if you had anything at their houses and they both said no.

I can't wait to see you…are you still wearing your bracelets? I sure enjoyed seeing the Christmas pictures and all of the cute fun things the staff planned for you guys on the holiday!

I'm sure that you are having experiences up there that you will never forget!

Love Always,
Mom

A New Year
CHAPTER 3

January 5, 2016

The wretched holidays are out of the way. On to a new year, a fresh start. We had waited with great anticipation of this day to finally see Tyler in his element, in this place where the transformation was to take place. Hope, worry, guilt, fear; all difficult to pare out. I had wanted to stay overnight at the camp as some parents did, but for one reason or another, this was not suggested. Perhaps that was more for the parents who were coming from across the country, their kids kidnapped like Tyler to get them there, only taken on a plane, instead of driven over the mountains. Their captors, mercenaries of war against the Troubled Youth of America.

Chris and I were in the odd position of having a kid that was nearly an adult, yet still needed both of us to be in agreement with each other; be co-parents and co-conspirators in our child's life. As much as I hated the fact that after being divorced for ten years, we still had to speak daily, the strangest part of it all was our indescribable bond with each other as we recognized that we were the only people that understood this situation, this child, and had an empathy for each other as we shared our common pain. Nobody else could know. I certainly had not and could not share with Matt all that went on with Tyler out of fear of scaring him away from an otherwise wonderful, budding relationship.

Chris and I would take separate cars and stay in separate hotel rooms at the only place that was not a dingy fifties motel in Duchesne, Utah. A letter had been sent out to parents in anticipation of their arrival that included a section on local lodging. This place had been suggested for convenience, as it was directly across the parking lot from the office/warehouse/home station for Second Nature. The other suggestions had included Stein Erickson in Park City and other high-brow locations. Clearly we were not the typical clientele, as a stay at Stein Erickson was

Chapter 3: A New Year

reserved for once in a lifetime events, such as anniversaries and honeymoons, to people like us. I couldn't imagine staying at such a luxurious place while my kid was freezing in the elements, and to me, the two-hour drive between Park City and Duchesne was impractical.

Duchesne is stark and barren yet beautiful and awe inspiring. A cold, high desert landscape dotted with sagebrush just west of the convergence of the Duchesne and Strawberry Rivers. The Dominguez-Escalante Expedition had come through. French-Canadian trappers had come through. Oil companies had come through. Kids from dysfunctional families had come through. The searchers of converts, fur, oil, and therapy had seen something in this place.

Long ago, the land had been leased from the Ute tribe for sheep to graze. Then, in the early nineteen hundreds, President Roosevelt had declared the area opened for settlement after purchasing the land from the Utes under the Allotment Act of 1891, and for a time, it was called Theodore. Lotteries were held. Tickets were given with a number, and numbers 1-111 were allowed to make their claim. A large circus tent served as a trading post and post office. The first winter was harsh with many still living in tents and the spring brought flooding and hardship. Many gave up their claims after the first winter. One man was reported to have said he must "give up his claim or his wife, because she wouldn't live here."

We had a parent meeting the night before going to the camp, with all of the parents from around the country congregated in the cozy, nicely decorated meeting room at the Second Nature headquarters. We passed through their operations as we headed back to our meeting place. I imagined Tyler being processed and outfitted after being kidnapped and taken there, guilt and hope wrestling each other for the upper hand. Anxious parents sat sheepishly looking at each other in the room, around a coffee table of cheese, crackers, and water bottles; strangers with a common pain.

Say your name and tell where you are from. East Coast, West Coast and not much in between. No others within driving distance like us. People with the means to spend forty to fifty grand out-of-pocket to try and save their kids, or finance it for years and years, like me. No promises. Ambiguous success measures. Just hope.

99

We learned some communication methods that our kids were being taught at the camp, and the parents quickly connected to each other with our stories. Openness and bonding come easily when you are in a room of parents humbled by the task at hand. We were all out of our circles of judgmental friends and colleagues who didn't understand what went wrong with our families that seemed to have everything. "Checking in" with our feelings, as our children were being taught in the wild, we cried together. One couple was reluctant to go out, having been told that they did not want to be seen by their child. Most of these parents were not experienced outdoor enthusiasts and some time was taken to outfit them with proper gear. Layers of clothing covering layers of guilt. For some reason, the parents from California whose son told them not to come would be camping overnight, though we were not invited to do the same. Perhaps it was part of their treatment plan, to force them together when they didn't want to be. We could only guess and trust that there was some method to all of this.

The next morning, we met early at the designated spot across from the hotel in the parking lot with those going to camp six. It was me and Chris and a mother whose husband was on a business trip, so she was handling this alone, being driven by a kind man who was training to be a counselor and who assisted in our son's therapy. We drove forever through the raggedy, blue collar town of Duchesne on the highway, then to smaller roads outside of town, to an even smaller maze of never-ending jeep roads way outside of town. I'm fairly good with directions but I lost track of turns on the jeep roads as we chatted with the other mom, trying to pass the time more quickly until we got to see our sons. I thought about how far away the camp was from everything. Tyler had told me that one of the kids had eaten some mushrooms that he found in an attempt to get high and had become violently ill and sent back to the headquarters for medical attention. I wondered if sticking kids in a remote camp would do anything at all if they went to those lengths to get high anyway.

Our arrival was a surprise to Tyler, but he seemed really pleased and excited to see us. He looked great. His hair, long and messy and falling on his shoulders, looked beautiful to me. He had gained twenty pounds so they sure weren't starving him. He looked happy, content, and at peace.

Chapter 3: A New Year

No complaints of the cold or elements were heard. My relief was palpable. If my child was fine, then I was fine.

We sat in a large wall tent, taking turns talking with just the three of us, then with the counselor going between the two families in group six that were visiting today. Tyler was adeptly making himself a snack with his ration of tortillas and peanut butter from his stash. One of his camp mates was given the task of seeing to our comfort. He awkwardly poked his head inside the tent flap, probably worried that he would interrupt the war that he had been made privy to through the reading of Tyler's life story and our Impact Letters. He offered us bags of snacks which consisted of Cheerios and raisins, without any salt or sugar, as was the rule at the camp. We were in the tent with the warming stove, sitting on ground chairs that were held in a sitting position with a plastic buckle, a luxury our kids must earn by working through the stages. When the temperature got to be near zero, not freezing but zero, the kids got to sleep in the wall tent with heat. Otherwise, sleeping was under a tarp stretched between trees. The last few weeks had been tent nights.

Marley, the counselor's dog, sat next to me, sensing that I was a dog person, but not trusting me enough to let me pat his head without emitting a surly growl. I was used to those who sought comfort through proximity while rejecting me at the same time.

Steven, the main counselor, and founder of Second Nature, had migrated back and forth between Chris, Tyler and I in one tent, and another tent containing the mother who was visiting her son without her husband. I felt a little sorry for her. This was a lot to bear without support and I was thankful that Chris and I could at least attend together, despite the space of years since our divorce.

Shifting gears between family dramas and different circumstances seemed easy for Steven, who's confident yet caring demeanor was perfect for his position, and I was grateful he was Tyler's main counselor. He was large in stature and bald enough to look intimidating. Oddly enough, his son was a cellist and took lessons from the same teacher as Tyler in Salt Lake. He remembered Tyler from past cello recitals and I had recalled seeing their last name on the countless printed programs that we had read as we sat waiting for our child's performance, counting the number of times we would have to listen to "Twinkle, Twinkle, Little Star," before

101

Confessions of a Heroin Addict's Mother

Tyler was to play, the more advanced students placed toward the later part of the recital.

Tyler was referred to as "The Senator" at camp. He had tried his hand at manipulating Steven, not in regards to his physical situation at camp, which he had adapted to easily, but by twisting his stories, how accountable he thought he should be, and what he would agree to in an attempt to change his circumstance. Steven had repeatedly asked him if he ever intended to be an honest person. Steven thought that he was a particularly tough case because he was so smart, and at first he had doubted his methods with someone like Tyler. The discussion was productive, though heated at times. I wished it could have all been a happy reunion and the tough questions could come later, on a different day. I wanted to savor the time with Tyler, having missed the holidays together. For some ridiculous reason Chris made a really big deal about how much "his" family had been affected by all of this, and kept bringing up the fact that he and Dee had been together for eight years. He made some glib comment about my relationship with Matt being new, recent and somehow not as legitimate or important as his. I was furious. I'm not sure why this set me off so badly but I think we were both looking for someone to blame as we jockeyed for the "best parent" position. Who better to look good in front of than the counselor trying to figure out why your kid is messed up? We ended the session with some optimism about his future as he opened up and told us what his feelings were, which was a truly rare moment.

I had to go to the bathroom so badly after sitting for hours in the tent. They sent me up to the latrine area, which was close enough to the camp to be seen, so nobody could use a bathroom break as an escape opportunity. I had to take off my coat and then my Carhartt overalls and got a real taste of how biting the wind was. When the kids went, they had to yell out their name every ten seconds or so in order to be located. I couldn't imagine anyone trying to trek out of here. We were miles and miles from civilization.

We then joined the rest of the group, sitting around the glowing fire and having a surprisingly good time. I was intensely interested in the other kids there. I was doing my own compare, contrast, and analyze exercise to see how similar or different they were from my son. The kids went around the circle, talking about each other using the "easy critique," which was usually something positive that person was particularly good at, then the "hard critique," which was something difficult to say but offered some constructive criticism that the individual needed to work on. I could see that some of the kids had a difficult time coming up with something good to say about a few of the kids, especially the one whose mother was there to visit. This made me feel even worse for her. When it came to talking about Tyler, I could tell he was popular with his peers and they exuded over-the-top praise on him for being a leader and an all-around cool guy. Then the hard part came. Tyler had a way of smiling constantly even when he was telling a painful story. They said his happy demeanor just didn't match his words and they felt like he was hiding some real pain and not being honest with himself or anyone else. I was sincerely shocked at the openness and astute observations that were coming from these kids, and I was impressed that a group of teenage boys could feel so comfortable talking about their feelings. I felt so good. If nothing else, Tyler could possibly learn to express himself and "check in" when he needed to talk about something difficult. I felt so close to him at the moment and felt like all of this pain would be worth it for everyone in the end, when he was finally home.

Letter from me to Tyler, January 11, 2016

Dear Tyler,

I can't tell you how pleased I was to see you last week! The time just flew by when we were out there. I have played over and over in my head a movie of what I think your day must be like so it was nice to compare it with your reality! The area has such a stark and Zen-like beauty that I'm sure must add to the opportunity for meditation and self-reflection. I was even thinking that at a later date maybe we could go out there and spread Sparky's ashes and have a little ceremony for him. Damn I miss that dog.

You had a more mature air about you. I was pleased with your openness and your progress as you have become more accountable to yourself, and to us. I was really impressed with the maturity and insight that you and your peers displayed as you communicated the strengths and weaknesses that you see in each other. I hope that you can carry away from Second Nature the communication skills that you have learned, especially the check-in. We learned a lot about the communication model that you guys use in the field at our parent meeting on Tuesday night, before the visit on Wednesday.

We are working on some things as we try and figure out how to help you navigate your way into adulthood. The webinars from Second Nature are informative and helpful. We are working on a home contract in the event that home is determined by all to be the best place for you to be. We are all still trying to figure that out. We will need your input on the contract, particularly which kids you think will be good and bad influences on you and what kind of back-up plan, and back-up to the back-up plan you will employ when things get rough. You know that the temptations and pressures will not change, but you can change how much of it you allow yourself to be exposed to, and how you react when triggers present themselves. I am not confident that you have good plans in place, and one of your peers expressed the same concern that we have about your problematic relationship with Mason and what you're going to do about it. I'm guessing that you have expressed concern about this matter to the group as well. Mason's parents will not allow you to see him either, so we are all on the same page about the unhealthiness of yours and Masons' friendship. But, he is not the only issue or friend with which you have had a problematic relationship. You will really need to be honest with yourself and us about who you think will be healthy to keep in your life…only you know for sure. I'm hoping that you will be able to see the bigger picture as you work toward getting into college and becoming a productive and healthy adult.

If you can come home, you will also need to find some good NA meetings and a sponsor that will be able to help you through the 12 steps. Would you want someone like Zach Dempsey to be your sponsor? He's really a good guy, doing well, and committed to his "program" of sobriety. He sponsors a number of guys but is not Rick's sponsor anymore so there is no conflict there.

I've been busting my butt trying to fill in the work that I lost or that has been postponed. The Smiths are still trying to figure out when I'll be going to CA to work on their Uncle Bob's place. I sure wish I knew cause it's hard to schedule other work and stuff. I'm doing a tiny remodel for someone near Sugarhouse right now.

I don't know if I told you that Grandma and Grandpa are going on another mission. Funny one though, as they are going on a local mission. They still need to go to the Missionary Training Center and everything during the day and then they come home at night. They are doing their week at the MTC right now. I think they will be working with local missionaries in the Utah County area.

I'm sitting here with your dad at Crown Burger having a meeting on everything. Sorry that we got into a fight in front of you…It was inappropriate timing. We really are, for the most part, on the same page when it comes to your care and future. Funny, the cop that came to the house the first time is sitting a few tables away.

I can't wait to see you again! Matt and I are trying to plan another Escalante trip this summer…hoping that you will want to participate.

Love Always, Mom

Letter from Tyler to me, written January 13, 2016, received January 13, 2016

Dear Mom,

I'm so happy I got to see you last week. That meant a ridiculous amount to me, especially since it was pretty much a surprise. The session with Steven that we had was a very good one, and I feel like we all got a lot from it. It really showed the progress that I've been making here. I'm glad you and Dad were able to hear a lot more about what goes on here at Second Nature.

I have started working on a home contract but I really want to think it through. What I put in my letters will be a rough draft for sure, but I think a home contract is a necessary measure for my return home, if it is to happen.

I know I will not be able to hang out with Mason any more. The other friends I think I probably should not hang with are Zoe, and the people

I did drugs with or partied with. It's mostly just Mason and Zoe along with the public school kids I met through them. It's going to be hard to say goodbye to them but its going to have to happen.

If I get the chance to come home I plan on finding NA meetings along with a sponsor. I don't know who I could have sponsor me other than Zach Dempsey so we should talk about that. I really have a lot of investment into the program and I'm going to be on Water Phase soon after I get 10 more flames busted. I will make Air Phase in order to get myself to come home.

I've been really missing out on things like music that I had at home. Music is a huge coping mechanism for me, and I miss it a ridiculous amount. I'm working hard to give me the chance to come home.

Love,
Tyler Watkins

Letter from Tyler to Chris, written January 13, 2016, received January 13, 2016

Dear Dad,

Before I answer your questions, I just wanted to let you know where I am in the group, and where I am emotionally, since I've seen you guys. I am in a really good place with the group. I've been taking a huge leadership role, even more so lately than before, and we are all functioning at a whole new level. Last night I was having a pretty tough time emotionally after Noah and I talked about music we like, like Mac Demarco, and it brought up a ton of memories and feelings. I checked in about it, but I still was having a tough time the rest of the night. Listening to music and playing music is something I've used as a positive coping mechanism for such a long time, even when I was very young. I'm really missing all of the things that I had back at home and I can't wait to get back home and experience all that I've been missing so much.

I'm so glad we got to talk for so long last week. That was so meaningful for me. Everyone observed the good relationship that I have with my parents and they all thought that was amazing. The session we had

Chapter 3: A New Year

with Steven was really helpful, and it was probably the best session I've had so far. Steven and Jason have really done a good job helping me realize my situation, and they give me motivation to do the right thing.

I understand your reasoning behind me making Air Phase in order to come home. I've always planned on making it to Air Phase since getting to Second Nature. It's not an option in my opinion to not make Air Phase. It seems as though I either make air phase and come home or I go to treatment at Provo Canyon which is not an option in my mind. I'm extremely close to Water Phase, but I'm being held back by only having busted 5 flames when I need 15 to get into Water Phase. It takes a lot of patience to start a fire using friction with sticks. I guess they want us to learn persistence, and to keep trying without getting frustrated.

Upon my return, if I get the chance to go back to Eastland, I understand that a contract will be strictly enforced and I'm prepared to follow that. I want to be challenged the remainder of the school year because I need to prove to everyone that I'm capable and have huge amounts of potential.

I plan on putting a lot of effort into school, cello and finishing off my Senior year strong all around. I want to list more things, but I don't have too much time before Jason leaves with letters. I also want to do some form of martial art to help me get my angst and anger out.

I still need to write to Grandma and Grandpa, but I've been totally overwhelmed with trying to get everything I can done. I want to keep a great relationship with Grandma and Grandpa while redeeming myself over time for my past poor interactions with them. Also, I need to take full accountability to Dee for everything. It makes me sick that her custody situation with Jess could be in jeopardy because of my behavior. I feel so bad. I'm sorry that I have had a negative effect on your relationship with her.

Love,
Tyler Watkins

Core Issue Journal - My Potential – Tyler Watkins, written January 11, 2016, received January 13, 2016

...While at Second Nature, I've recognized the potential I have. There is so much I can accomplish with my group, myself and my family. Since the beginning of my stay, I've been able to be a big voice in the group, and I've been motivating the others to do their work. I've recognized the potential I have to work in a group setting and be a leader. I have also learned skills that brought me the realization of my faults in the past, and will help me change my actions and reactions in the future. I have done a great deal of becoming more accountable for my faults and poor decisions. My potential for the future has increased dramatically due to my new-found ability to realize when I make mistakes, and how to handle them...

Ideas on a Home Contract - Tyler Watkins, written January 12, 2016, received January 13, 2016

I am writing this contract for if I earn the chance to go home after my time spent at Second Nature, in order to keep me on the right path, so I don't fall back into my old patterns.

- *No use of drugs of any type*
- *No selling drugs or affiliating with drug culture*
- *Solve conflicts appropriately without raising voice, using vulgar language and acting physical*
- *No arguing if asked to do a chore or participate in a family activity.*
- *No hanging out with bad influences and people I used to party with. This would be Mason and Zoe and those associated with them*
- *Use healthy coping skills and mechanisms instead of abusing drugs. This would be listening to and playing music, working out, yoga, meditation, some form of martial art or way to get out my feelings, focusing on school, reading, spending time with family, skiing, having physical activities, spending*

time with friends who are positive influences, seeing movies, forming solid and healthy relationships and doing the right thing

- *Drug testing*
- *Going to some form of NA meeting and finding a sponsor*
- *Opening up to the family with how I feel*
- *Going to family and personal counseling*
- *Continue with all my positive activities*
- *Graduate from Eastland with better grades than ever before*
- *Go to all school activities*
- *Follow a positive path and lead much healthier lifestyle*
- *Be sober!*
- *I have more to add but limited time. This Home Contract is very important to me and my want to come home and lead a good life.*

Tyler Watkins

Letter from me to Tyler, sent January 18, 2016, received January 20, 2016

Dear Tyler,

It was great to talk with you again last week! I can't wait until we can do that any time we want. I miss being able to chat whenever, though you had become fairly disconnected for quite some time. It broke my heart when you said that you didn't feel close to either dad or me before you went to Second Nature. I hope that through your experience that you have come to realize how much we truly care about you and your wellbeing.

I'm sorry that I've been somewhat self-absorbed in the last couple of years with all of my own relationship and living arrangement issues that we have had to endure. The number of times that we have moved has been most unfortunate and inconvenient for both of us, as well as losing the "family" that Rick and I had melded together. I know that was difficult for you.

I was hoping at least that we could maintain a friendship with Riley and Lilly, but I was mistaken in thinking that. Oddly enough, I did run into Riley at Einsteins when your dad and I were meeting James to discuss options for you. Right before meeting with James, I opened my computer to find your letter that disturbed me so much. 20 minutes later we had our meeting with James and the need to take quick action for your health and safety was starkly apparent. Riley came into Einsteins while we were in the middle of discussing what to do with you and I was an emotional mess! He was home from Cal Poly for Thanksgiving…so weird to see him at that moment! I have lost all contact with Lilly. :(I guess "step-parents" and siblings have no visitation rights. So sad. I really do feel like that loss had a big impact on you, as it did me. I have such fond memories of the good times that we all had together when things were going well.

I've had a few conversations with Mason's mom this week. She's really upset that there has been no letter to Mason, as she is beyond knowing what to do with him. He has completely withdrawn from the family. I'm glad to hear that you realize that you cannot see him or Zoe, but I do not believe that a big scheduled "good-bye" will happen. Mason's parents will not let him see you or any other friends for that matter. They are not giving him any money and are currently driving him to school. The little bit of money that he got for Christmas he spent on drugs so Kate took the rest away. You need to write him a letter before you come home to say goodbye and maybe offer him some help and advice as his friend. I already told Zoe months ago that you were not going to be coming home, though I'm sure that she will hear that you are. You will need to set a distinct boundary with her, and those associated with her, that is unwavering.

Kate told me that the kid named Jonathan that we think you were buying drugs from…the older one…got arrested. It's been big news in your social circle and I guess that Mason found out via text messages. He got pulled over on a traffic stop, the cop smelled pot and searched the car and arrested him for other drugs. Not sure if he's in jail or not. I guess I don't need to tell you that you were teetering on the edge of serious trouble and really were lucky that you didn't get caught. You are never, ever to have any contact with him. We do have the extra phone that your dealer (Jonathan?) probably gave you, so we can certainly charge it up and get

Chapter 3: A New Year

your contact and history off of that if we need to. I am hoping that you will be motivated enough yourself to want to stay out of trouble but that will certainly not prevent me from being vigilant about who you are communicating with.

We will talk more on Thursday about the contract and what it needs to look like, so that we might be able to come up with a final draft between us that is manageable and acceptable. If you come back to Eastland and expect to graduate with your class, attend NA meetings, have some kind of physical outlet, and do scheduled school activities, you will be certainly too busy to get into any kind of trouble. There will be no other way to graduate if you are not immediately on top of it. Eastland has made that abundantly clear. The thought of graduating next year from West or somewhere else doesn't sound all that great, so it will be up to you to show us the motivation that it appears that you have found in Second Nature.

I really am encouraged by the great distance that you have come emotionally, as well as with your accountability. I am proud that you have become a leader within your group. You have so much potential to be a positive influence on others and I have great hopes for your continued progress on that account. Perhaps you may become a sort of mentor (not preacher) for people that are struggling. I noticed that someone in your group was reading Dharma Punks. Have you read it? I read a review of it and it sounded really interesting. It's about someone who was completely on the wrong track and made a total turn-around. I'm not quite sure how Buddhism relates to Punk rock but apparently the author has some ideas about their relationship. I'll have to read it. I also want to read Man's Search for Meaning. It sounds great. I appreciated your thoughts on it and how it relates to your own experience.

I better wrap up. I have a big bid to do for finishing up Jeff's house so that he can get it on the market. I am also marching in a Martin Luther King celebration from East High, up to the U, with Matt and Moe later this afternoon. Everyone is doing well here. I've been a little under the weather but on the upswing now.

LOVE YOU!
Mom

Letter from Tyler to Chris, written January 19, 2016, received January 19, 2016

Dear Dad,

It's been so great to hear from you in a positive tone and see that there is recognition of the progress I've been making here at Second Nature! I miss you a ton! I'm so happy to hear about all the awesome things going on at home and in your job. Tell Jess I say congrats on her 3.9. That's amazing! Also tell Dee that I'm super happy that she got a raise and a bonus. That's so rad. The family seems to be in an awesome spot. I can't wait to try the mini vitamin blender :) I can't wait to go skiing with you!

I've busted 8 flames and a ton of embers. I'm getting really good at it lately. I'm still sick, but everyone with cold injuries have come back from base and are doing a lot better. The group is doing fantastic at the moment. It's really awesome to have a huge sense of motivation back, so I can prove to everyone how awesome I can be if I try. It seems as though I now have even more support than ever, and I can do anything. You're the best.

I'm so excited to be able to come home soon. I'm working hard at my personal therapy now that I really know that I have so much potential in a group setting. That's why I decided to let you guys know in my last letter that I was having some negative emotions.

After writing to mom, I'll start writing to Grandma and Grandpa, and Dee. I'll be sending a letter to Mason ASAP even though it's hard for me. Can't wait to talk with you!

Love,
Tyler Watkins

Letter from Tyler to me, written January 19, 2016, received January 19, 2016

Dear Mom,

Talking with you last week was awesome! It'll be so nice when we can

Chapter 3: A New Year

actually have real conversations whenever we want. I'm feeling a loss of connection since I've been gone for so long. I recognize how much you and dad truly care about me.

Thank you for being accountable for the moving that happened so many times the last few years. It's hard to hear that you saw Riley during a really emotional time. That must have been extremely difficult. Riley, Lilly, you, Rick and I had so many awesome times camping and hanging around the house.

I'm sorry for not sending a letter to Mason yet. I've been working on finishing all of my yellows and expects from this week. It also is going to be a very tough letter for me to write. I will try to get to it before the therapists leave today, but we just had a random snow storm fly in and the letters to Grandma and Grandpa are more important at the moment. It really sucks to hear that Mason is in such a shitty spot right now with the family. It's also hard to hear that you told Zoe that I was not going to be coming home.

Jonathan was one person who I got illicit things from but most definitely not the only one. It's crazy to hear that he got arrested but it was surely coming considering the path he was leading. I could easily have been in a similar boat. The extra phone was something I got at the thrift store for like 50 cents. I didn't even think it would work. Drug dealers don't just give phones to people. I am definitely motivated to stay away from trouble at this point.

I would like to talk more on Thursday about the contract ideas so that we can get a final draft that we all agree with. I'm going to be a really busy dude the rest of this year. I plan on being immediately on top of all my shit when I get back to school. It would totally blow to have to go to public school, or to graduate next year, instead of this year.

It's so nice to hear that you and dad are really recognizing the progress that I've been making over my stay here at Second Nature. I plan on being a mentor for those struggling when I get home. I'm going to be on Water Phase soon, then I will be able to read Dharma Punx. I'm super excited about it.

113

Great to hear that everybody at home is doing well!

Love,
Tyler Watkins

Letter from Tyler to Rich and Carolyn, written January 19, 2016, received ??

Dear Grandma and Grandpa,

I'm sorry it has taken me so long to write to you guys. I've been so busy working with the group and getting all of my assignments finished. I've been working extremely hard here at Second Nature to become accountable for my previous actions, and to be a much more functional person within society and with my family when I get back home. I'm so excited that my efforts here have given me the ability to come back home and go back to Eastland to finish off my senior year stronger and better than ever, instead of going to an aftercare for the remainder of my childhood.

I would like to apologize for the enormous amount of mistakes that I made over the last few years, starting with smoking pot, and eventually moving on to harder drugs. I began to show distance and immense disrespect towards my family. I had dug myself into such a deep hole of addiction and manipulation that I was not able to recognize the terrible path of self destruction I was on. At some point, it became inevitable that I would get caught up in the law, or die. I'm extremely lucky to have been given the chance by my family to come to Second Nature and change my ways for good. It helped me truly recognize that I was riding dangerously close to the edge and could have fallen off at any moment. I now have a whole new level of motivation, and feel positive about gaining back the trust of my family, school, and friends. I want to prove to the people in my life that I have all this potential that I now see in myself. Having a second chance means so much to me, and it's so nice to hear and read from my mom and dad that my improvements are not going unnoticed.

I'm so sorry for the conflict that happened at your house when I had Mason's mom come and pick me up from the house, and it pains me greatly to think back to that night. I remember telling Grandma, "I love you and I'll see you in a few days." Those few days turned into a few months, but I'm looking forward to it so much when I get back.

I plan on spending a lot of time with you guys when I return, and I would really appreciate being able to stay at your house sometimes and be closer to school. I can't wait to help Grandma with shopping at Trader Joe's, and get togethers at Tsunami. I want to go antiquing at different antique stores with Grandma. I deeply miss those times we had. I want to play guitar with Grandpa and talk about music and animals. We can work on projects together like tying flies and doing leather work. I've been thinking and it would be super cool to make moccasins and a belt. It would be awesome to go camping and enjoy the outdoors. I can't wait to see Gita and Sadie. I miss my family so much and I really am having so much homesickness and worry about how the family is going to look at me upon my return. But I'm confident that I can show everyone that I have made big changes.

Soon I will be making Water Phase, and soon after that I will make Air Phase so that I can come back home and continue my life in a positive light.

I can't wait to spend time with you guys! I miss you so much! Have a wonderful birthday next week Grandma!

Love,
Tyler Watkins

Core Issue: Gratefulness - Tyler Watkins, written January, 19, 2016

I have so much in my life to be grateful for, but in the past I've overlooked so many of these things that I've now come to realize are so amazing. There are so many things I'm grateful for in the past, present, and future.

I'm so grateful for my family, and their love and support for so many years, even when I've been disrespectful. My family has provided me with the best education possible. I'm so happy to say that I've gone

115

to Eastland for 11 years, and will hopefully be able to finish off my senior year. I'm so grateful for the ability to play music, and I love so many different types of music, thanks to playing cello since the second grade. I'm grateful I grew up in a household where my parents are very musically involved. I'm so happy my parents introduced me to music at an early age. When I would lay in bed, sleepless during my toddler years, the only way to get to sleep was intense music. This has helped me become musically oriented and benefit from its healing effects.

I'm so grateful for my mom's cooking, and for her helping me learn to be a "foodie," and have a love for great food. At this point in my life at Second Nature, I am simply grateful to have food at all and not go hungry. I have also learned skills to be able to cook food that I enjoy.

I'm thankful for my dad's knowledge of biology, art, music, and film. It has given me a great love for the outdoors and a curiosity for the world around us. He's helped me learn guitar and allowed me to teach myself how to play instruments and experiment with different musical genres. He's also taught me to love movies and films with directors like Wes Anderson and Quentin Tarantino. He nurtured my curiosity about what it takes to make a film that can catch the eye and attention of the viewer.

I am so thankful for my life.

Letter from Tyler to me and Chris, written January 19, 2016, received January 19, 2016

Dear Mom and Dad,

I just wanted to let you guys know where I've been with things the last few days.

While I'm very happy that I know I am close to being able to come home after making Air Phase, I also am having some troublesome feelings coming up that I decided not to ignore.

I really want to prove to Eastland that I am now seriously motivated to do my work, and I recognize that being in uniform 100% is an important way to demonstrate that. I'm just really worried about it, because I

Chapter 3: A New Year

am kind of having a loss of identity for how to look and dress. I know you say I need to get a haircut and you guys don't like the look I was portraying before Second Nature, but I would like to say that the way I dressed and looked was not because I was trying to look as though I was some badass drug dealer. It was just how I looked.

Yes, my hair is long, but that is not because of drug culture. I just like having long hair. I dress more like a hipster than anything else and it's not related to drugs. I plan on following the dress code when coming back to school, but I don't want to completely change the way I look by cutting my hair (although I think a trim and a few inches off is necessary). I want to be able to be myself.

Something else that has been on my mind is my friend situation. I recognize the fact that I need to part ways with Mason and Zoe, but it's really been weighing on me. Mason was my best friend before the drugs came into play. We've been best friends for the past three or four years, and it will be tough for me to just straight up say goodbye to him through a letter. It's also tough for me to think about shutting Zoe out completely, because our relationship also did not just consist of drugs. And, I have a lot of friends associated with her that also don't have ties to drug culture. It's just very tough for me to shut out the friends I spent the most time with this last year, and go back to my friends at Eastland whom I never did much with out of school. I also had some feelings of betrayal towards my Eastland friend group, because it sounds as though Alex, or somebody, brought attention to my vaping and Kratom. But I was not the only one associated with those things.

Also something I've been thinking about a lot was the serious amount of stress I felt from having to move back and forth between houses and never truly having a choice. At this point, I really want to live with both Mom and Dad, but there's some things that worry me. So much stress was put on me to always have to round up all of my shit and pack up like I'm moving every week. I never felt as though I had any say in the matter. Another thing that worries me is that if I go back to my dad's house, there will be a ton of trust issues with Dee. I totally understand why, but there were already problems between Dee and I beforehand, where I felt like she wouldn't ever have a positive attitude in my presence. I want to change this, and I also want to take accountability to her personally. I'm just worried about what's going to happen when I come back, and what my living situation is going to look like.

These things were pretty overwhelming for me to think about the last few days and it even caused me to be depressed for the past bit and curl up into fetal position and lay there when everyone else was playing hacky-sack. Just letting you know how I've been feeling instead of ignoring it.

Love,
Tyler Watkins

The manipulation was to begin again. This letter infuriated me for some reason. I felt like all of the progress made had been lost and his politician side was taking over. Once he got a little hope that he might be able to come home, instead of going to a boarding school or an aftercare program, the arguments began. A hundred pages of understanding that he couldn't hang out with certain friends, dress a certain way, affiliate with "drug culture," and drive a wedge between his parents to be able to manipulate his situation, was wasted. It was all bullshit. Senator Tyler, after being voted back in, renegotiates his campaign promises. Tyler was famous for pushing the limits on everything, including the school dress code. He was put into after school detention so many times for dress code violations but he continued to try to find new ways to push the limits. It almost always felt like he was seeing how much he could get away with. Perhaps I should be more understanding when he expresses his feelings. I've just seen how this negotiation works so many times.

Letter from Tyler to me and Chris, January 20, 2016

Dear Mom and Dad,

I just wanted to let you know my thoughts on my self-image after having a session with Steven and Jason. In my other letter to you both, I stated my feelings toward my style and how I make myself look. I wanted to touch on how this sense of style and attention toward the way I appear is a very superficial thing that I do and have learned to do. I want to say that this is a small fraction of the things that I care about in my personality and how I treat others. I care greatly about my respect towards other people. I want to be able to show kindness, compassion and empathy towards other people and those who need attention or help when they're in need. I care about my future greatly and I want to see myself succeed and I want to gain the trust back from my family.

Love,
Tyler Watkins

Tyler Watkins' Home Agreement:

Family Statement

It is our hope that our family can be close emotionally, and that we all will help each other live happy, fulfilling, honest and meaningful lives. We are strong, ethical people that believe in being good to ourselves and to others. We know how amazing Tyler is and we all support his positive journey forward into adulthood. We're a family of moderation and good decision making. We take pride in our strong work ethic. Now that Tyler has completed his journey at Second Nature, we expect him to use the skills and the tools he has learned to stay healthy and to live a happy life. The entire family has learned new skills, as well. We will all implement these skills into our family life. Most of all, we are a family that recognizes how fortunate we are to be together, and we are all appreciative of everything our family, friends and community provide us. We expect Tyler, and all of us, to understand this statement and live an honest, meaningful, and charitable life.

Communication

You have gained some amazing communication skills. We have all been introduced to these skills. We will all practice active and reflective communication to match your already strong skills. "Checking in" is a powerful tool for all of us to practice. We want these skills to become second nature to us. We will use these healthy communication skills daily, especially when tense moments arise. We know that we can solve most issues with strong, healthy communication. We will all work hard to communicate with respectful language. We will all use cursing at a minimum. We will not use curse words in anger. Again, respectful communication will be practiced in our homes.

Guidelines

The rules explained here are based on our values and the spirit of your two families. You will have the same basic guidelines at both households with a few small differences. We expect you to follow the guidelines at both homes, and your mom and dad will support each other's specific home guidelines, while expecting you to uphold the basic guidelines which are laid out in this agreement. We are in agreement on the things that are contained in this contract. The choice is yours, every day, to live within these parameters, or not. There will be privileges and freedoms gained for doing so, and consequences for not.

Sobriety

Obviously, maintaining a healthy mind and body requires that you do not use/abuse or possess any mind-altering substances. This includes all illicit drugs, alcohol, and tobacco. There will be absolutely no arguing the merits of using any illicit drugs, such as marijuana, or any others. Any drug paraphernalia will not be allowed in our homes, in a car, at school, or on your person. This includes all illicit drug paraphernalia, vape devices, and tobacco/nicotine devices. This also includes (but is not limited to) Visine, hand warmers, cigarettes, vape oils, rolling papers, glass pipes, pill cutters, pill boxes, cough syrup, packaging material like small baggies, rolled up papers for snorting, and, of course, pills or other drugs. Homemade devices are also not allowed. If we find any of these things, we will assume that you are using, even if your drug test is clean. You will also remove yourself from any situation where drugs and/or paraphernalia are present. For dealing with your addiction, you will be seeing your therapist at least once a week, and random drug screens will be required. These will be the most advanced drug screens possible. We expect you to follow your Relapse Prevention Plan.

The backup plan, if you start to struggle with either sobriety, heavy depression, or aggressive/manipulative behavior, is that we will do whatever it takes to keep you safe and healthy. We will follow through with professional support such as ER visits, inpatient care, outpatient care, or residential treatment, until you are stable and functional. For example, your parents will determine when to send you back to Second Nature or Provo Canyon Hospital. As this agreement applies to you being in our homes, even after you are 18, if you refuse treatment, we will ask you to leave our homes until you are willing to receive help.

As drug dealing and drug abuse are not tolerated in this family, the consequences will be very clear. Any illegal substances/paraphernalia brought into this home, into your grandparents' home, or into any family members home, whether yours or another person's illegal items, will void ALL privileges. We will call the police without question. We will consider professional support, but we will defer to the leadership of the judicial system.

Manipulation and Lying

There will be no lying and manipulation. You will continue to work with your therapist on skills and techniques to prevent lying and manipulation. We will all use our communication skills in a positive way to help you get away from manipulative behavior. Your mental health depends on honesty and integrity. We expect you to be honest. As discussed in the sobriety paragraph, we will turn to treatment to support you if you become lost in manipulations and lies as that will be a sure sign that you are heading down a negative path. After you are 18, you will be asked to leave our homes if you do not agree to treatment.

Education

This entire family believes in you finishing high school. It's expected that you have gained a new respect for your education. You should now have the ability to organize, prioritize, and complete your school work. You are almost 18, and we expect you to be self-reliant and finish your school work on time. If you return to Eastland, we will require that you follow their School Agreement without argument. You will thank them for this final opportunity and work very hard to complete their requirements. No matter what school you attend, you will consistently arrive to school on time, go to each class on time, not leave campus during school hours, and you will leave school only after the day is completed. You will use all study halls for studying only. You will attend all tutoring sessions that are recommended by Eastland. We expect you to join the Chamber Orchestra, and participate in all music practices during and outside of school. As you are a gifted

Confessions of a Heroin Addict's Mother

cellist, we expect you to continue lessons with Evan. We will financially support you in all of your cello endeavors. As empathy is so important, the school and our family will require you to join volunteer programs/projects during your last months at Eastland. These projects will be determined by the Eastland administration. If you return to Eastland, it will be required that you consistently follow the dress code and respect the administration that has given you a second chance when they really didn't have to. It will be your job to respect and honor their amazing support of you, and our family.

We also believe in college education. We all know how intelligent you are and we know that you will go so far, if you stay clean and sober, stick to your goals, be honest, and work hard. At this time, your dad does not have funding for college, as he used up his funds on Eastland, your health care issues, and Second Nature. You should continue to work with your mom and Grandpa Arnold, to earn any scholarship funding they can provide. As of today, you will follow guidance from counselors, family, and your own research about college applications, financial aid, loans, and scholarships. Most individuals in this world have to strike out on their own for college. You will need to do the same. We believe you have the determination to move forward with your education. It makes us proud to know that you care and understand how important a college education is to your future. We will support you as much as possible with your educational goals. If you fail to strictly follow the Education Agreement and the possible Eastland Agreement, the consequences will be expulsion from Eastland. We will have a dialogue and work toward a solution to fulfilling your requirement to graduate from high school at that time.

Health

To succeed in life, we all need to stay physically and mentally healthy. Our whole family will move forward with a strong plan for physical activity. If you return to Eastland, you will play on the soccer team if the coach will allow it. We believe that team sports provide an unequaled opportunity for many aspects of both physical and mental health. Another option would be to get involved in a martial art, in which you have already expressed interest. If you do this, a regular attendance schedule will be arranged with your parents around whatever job you are able to get. If you are on the soccer team, you will follow the coach's rules and suggestions for being a positive member of the soccer team. You will attend all practices, all scrimmages and all games, whether you play j.v. or varsity. During the soccer season and after, you will have a physical exercise plan and you will employ it.

We realize that you are an individual and that you have your own identity. That being said, we expect you to respect yourself, family, school, workplace and friends. You will be expected to consistently keep up your hygiene, including cutting your hair to a reasonable length.

We expect you to be a loving and caring partner in any relationship. We also expect you to always practice safe sex. We are always available for discussion about relationships and sex, and hope that you will approach us with questions and concerns. You need to consider the physical, social, and emotional impact that random "hook-ups" have on your partners and yourself. If you do not follow the Health Agreement, we will have a dialogue to discuss the situation and the consequences.

Work, Money and Chores
This family has a strong work ethic. We expect you to have the same. You will apply for a part-time, mainstream job upon your return home. This will be a job that has regular paychecks, managers that are always present, and multiple employees. We would like to see you gain an understanding of what it means to work within a structured environment, including scheduling, organization, healthy communication, and hard work. You will need to make enough money to pay for car insurance, a car, gas, dates, etc. You will have conflicts with your school, social, music, family life, etc. You will need to prioritize and organize your daily, weekly and monthly schedules to maximize the most meaningful calendar not only for yourself, but also for others. We will fully support your work life. We will help you get here and there when we can. We will also support you with building the skills to organize a busy and meaningful life.

There will be chores for you to do at our homes. We will have a weekly structured list of chores for everyone. You will have an allowance. We will negotiate the dollar amount upon your return. It will be fair and reasonable. We understand that we live in an expensive world. You will respect our financial allowance decision and you will respect our chore list. Chores will be done without nagging and you will work hard to complete each chore correctly, without complaints. We will assist you in opening a personal checking and savings account immediately upon your return. You will be required to place at least 10% of your weekly job and allowance pay into your savings account. We will have full access to observing your bank accounts until you are 18. We hope that you will continue to follow a strong financial path of budgeting and saving throughout your life. We will always support you by helping you understand and build the skills necessary to navigate the financial world. If you do not follow the Work, Money and Chores Agreement, we will dialogue until figuring out a solution.

Friends

As we have discussed, the friends you choose should support your sobriety and mental health. You have identified certain friends who are not to be trusted any more. Namely, Mason and Zoe and the public school kids that you met through them. There are certainly other friends that should be included in this list that you have not mentioned. You have committed to not bringing dysfunctional friends into your life. You will agree to not associate with the friends that you are to name from this point onward. If we see any issues here, we will have a dialogue. We will discuss and figure out what is happening and how we can resolve the matter. Privilege loss will be considered. You will bring home any and all friends, so that we can meet them. There will be no excuses. For every time you go to a friends' house, you will need to bring them to one of our homes. If you do not consistently follow the Friends Agreement, we will discuss the consequences and loss of privileges.

Family

Family is always a priority. We are proud to be available for each other. We support each other and will always help each other. The love of family is undeniable and strong. You will live by this belief when under our roof and hopefully throughout your life. You will attend family functions such as family dinners, celebrations, holiday gatherings, and vacations. We all realize that sometimes your life will require a discussion about you not attending family event, but this will be rare, perhaps 1% of the

Chapter 3: A New Year

time. Again, family is a priority. Along with events, you will consistently engage in everyday family activities and chores, such as making dinner, joining us at the dinner table, cleaning up after dinner, and cleaning up after all messes. You will keep your room at both homes consistently clean, as well as all living spaces in our homes. We feel it is important that you understand self-motivation and empathy. You should be able to keep up with family responsibilities without being asked all the time. Self-starting and correctly finishing a task is important in our family. All of this applies to any house you are staying at or visiting. Your grandparents can always use your help. You should voluntarily visit them and help them with whatever they need, such as yard work, snow removal, heavy lifting, playing games, or just hanging out. They have all given so much to all of us. We will all respect and help them on a consistent basis. If you do not consistently follow the Family Agreement, we will discuss the consequences and decide which privileges will be rescinded.

Technology

The smart phone, computers, and television all play an important role in modern life. All of us understand how amazing these technologies can be, but we also understand the dangers of these distractions. While you are 17, your phone will be monitored by both your mother and father. We expect you to pay for the monthly cost and repairs to the phone. There will be no inappropriate usage of the phone, computer, iPad, or television, such as pornography, drug dealing, etc. If we determine there has been inappropriate usage of technology, we will indefinitely rescind the privilege to use it. Social media is also a wonderful tool, but poses a large distraction You will "friend" us on all social media outlets. If you do not consistently follow the Technology Agreement, we will have a discussion to figure out possible consequences.

Car and Transportation

Transportation was a lot easier a few months ago, before you lost your given car which was your designated mode of transportation. This has created a new transportation dynamic within this family. You are required to arrive to school, jobs, lessons, activities, and family functions on time. We will assist you with transportation to these events, with your understanding that we have jobs and other priorities that will require all of us to be creative with your transportation methods. Some of these methods may require rides from approved friends, other family members, public transportation, and bicycle. You will be able to use a family car only when it is approved by your dad or mom. You will be required to pay for your own insurance. Insurance is the law, therefore you must have current auto insurance in order to drive any car. You will take the designated defensive driver course that is required after 2 accidents in the same day. Your mother got an extension from the judge to accommodate your Second Nature stay. The only available day to take it is on February 8th. Insurance will be outrageously expensive for you if you don't take the course. With a good part-time job, you can handle liability insurance. The car is a huge responsibility. You will be held 100% accountable, by law, for all infractions. Even if you have earned enough money to buy a car, while you are 17, we will take away and sell your car, if you drive under the influence of ANY illegal substance, drive recklessly, or hurt anyone with the car. There will be no discussion of consequences if you drive under the influence, or possess any illegal substances/paraphernalia, whether yours or another person's. We will immediately take possession of your car, sell it, and turn you into the police, without question or dialogue.

Parent Commitment

The past months have shed light on issues within our entire family. Our commitment is to be the best parents and role models we can be for you. We will remain firm and follow through. We will continue to support your positive path forward. We are committed to family therapy. If we see red flags, we will hold a family meeting and figure out what measures to take in order to support you. Your parents will attend support group meetings with you, when you or we feel it is necessary. With all our love, we will always be there to support you. We will always talk through issues, fears, and successes. We will celebrate successes. We will respect you as an individual and we understand that perfection is not possible, although we will not let that statement be used as a copout. We have gained back some trust, but it will take acting in accord with this agreement to build a new level of strong trust that is lasting and meaningful.

Conditions Specific to your Mom's House

You will in no way influence Matt's girls in a negative manner regarding drugs or anything else. You will help out when we are at Matts and you will attend planned social and family events and vacations when your school and work schedules allow. There will be scheduled chores. You will need to help your mom fix the items in the house that you were responsible for breaking. This includes replacing a door, fixing a cabinet door, and fixing 2 drawers.

If things don't work out
If you are not succeeding at home, it will most likely be a result of struggles with sobriety. We will help you get the help you need. After you are 18, if you refuse to receive family approved professional help and support, we will ask you to leave our homes. If any illegal activity occurs, as discussed in this agreement, we will immediately report it to the police and we will not pay for an attorney. This is our back up plan, but we sincerely hope that things will work out, and we will not have to employ it.

Steven had laughed and said our contract was more complete than some he had seen written by lawyer parents...especially the verbiage used when listing drug paraphernalia (including but not limited to). Chris and I had written individual contracts and had merged them, both too stubborn to let each other edit out anything, attempting to outdo each other with our individual expectations. I haven't even included the summary spreadsheet here because it was so over the top and redundant. We were stupidly thinking that we could reverse any parental disappointment that we had over seventeen- and three-quarter years in three months' time.

Reading back a couple years later over this list I realize that we were asking for absolute perfection. No slip-ups. Nothing. We scrutinized every defect and frailty that he had ever embodied. Was perfection too much to ask? If we didn't include it in the contract, would he think it wasn't important to us? In listing everything that we expected we had asked him to be Superhuman. Would we be disappointed in anything that was not complete adherence to the contract? Would we be able to fulfill our end of the contract? Would it be a military state in our homes to enforce this? We must have overwhelmed him because so much of it quickly became a waste of ink. What choice did he have but to agree with all of this to leave that God forsaken place? How many young men have found Jesus in a foxhole?

Homeward Bound
CHAPTER 4

The contract was agreed to and a pick up date was set for us to drive to Duchesne. My son was coming home! Tyler had a shorter stay than most at Second Nature and I'm still not sure if it was based on the fact that we were out of money and they knew it, or if it was a result of his progress. He had moved through the stages quickly and was proud to be a formative leader in his group. For some reason, his work ethic was a point of pride for the first time in his life, though he had sometimes lamented that he did not make his group mates responsible for themselves when he did their chores for them. Why did he see the signs of codependency in himself before I had noticed them in myself?

He had already been at the base camp office for a couple nights as a result of getting frostbite on his toes and the back of his heel prior to coming home. As he told me a wave of guilt swept over me...who sends their kid into these elements? They brought kids there with cold injuries to heal, but it was time for him to leave anyway. I was ecstatic to see him again. My child was finally coming home! It was a surprising and anticlimactic drive back to Salt Lake. Chris slept as he had been away working and hadn't slept much the night before. I drove all of us back in my truck, stopping at Arby's as I was sure Tyler wanted food that hadn't been cooked over a fire. Nobody really ate, anxious for what was to come.

For some reason, the decision had been made for him to go and live at Chris's house when he got home. Chris had been all protective and self-righteous, thinking that if he could just impose himself a little more, he could straighten things out. I tried not to be resentful. The plan was for him to stay with Chris for a couple weeks, then go live with his grandparents until he graduated. They were very close to his school, and he also had a number of friends in the vicinity that could help carpool him to school for the last couple months.

Chapter 4: Homeward Bound

We received a call from Second Nature. Tyler had been such a stellar example of success in their program, and he was so well spoken, that they wanted him to be a guest speaker at the parent meeting for those whose children had just been sent to the program. They were meeting at a hotel in Salt Lake for an orientation, and to learn what they could expect while they and their child moved through this frightening experience. Tyler and I went together and both shared our different experiences and observations of the ordeal we had just been through. I sobbed tears of joy as he eloquently expressed his appreciation for the program and what it had done for him. He was a picture of perfection! Handsome, together, and honest. The relief in the parents' faces was obvious as they asked question after question and listened to the horror we were experiencing prior to the decision to send him there. Their child too could be saved! One of the parents asked Tyler what his plans for the future were. When he said he wanted to go into sales the room just roared with laughter. He was a natural!

What we did not know that night is that he had already relapsed within about a week and a half of being home. He had found some wine and proceeded to drink a bottle and a half of it at a sitting. He had searched it out, looking for something to provide him with an altered state. None of the relapse plans and back up plans were summoned. Chris sent him back to me.

He never really even tried at school when he got back. The school administration carefully tailored a plan that was very forgiving and if he put some effort into it, he could still graduate. He had said when he was in the wilderness that he was very concerned about the opportunity to graduate with his class, after spending the last twelve years with them We were baffled as to why he wasn't trying harder to comply with the plan presented to him. My intuitions had been correct about his carefully chosen manipulative words to get himself out of the wilderness. At Eastland, they were watching him very closely. His teachers said he was not putting himself into the work. He was warned. He was given a stern lecture from Bryson, the dean, who told him the instructors said he wasn't trying. He was given one last chance to turn in an important assignment, in order to pass a class required for graduation. Instead of doing the assignment, he didn't come home that night. Chris and I met him at school in the

129

morning to meet with Bryson. We weren't even sure that he would show up, as we waited anxiously in the parking lot for him. He was already at school. After contacting him on his cell, we met him outside the building that housed Bryson's office. He stumbled towards us, a shoe untied, and looking disheveled. The kid had one last chance to save himself and this is how he shows up? What had he missed in all of the communication? Had he been given too many chances by all of us, and he figured he'd get another one? Visibly irritated when we arrived in the office, Bryson told Tyler he was going with him to speak with the teacher for whom the assignment was due. They marched off together, Bryson looking angry and determined, and Tyler with one shoe still untied. We went through his backpack while he was with Bryson and found a cigar, a bottle of Corona, and no books or work. He was also definitely high. Obvious to everyone, I was sure. He was expelled.

I felt like I had been sucker-punched. All of the work and sacrifice. The shame and disappointment were overwhelming. It was as though he had sabotaged his own success. Could he not see what this would do to him? To us? What was so important that he just couldn't put in the effort to finish? A couple hundred thousand dollars down the drain with only weeks 'till graduation. I had to ask the parent in charge of graduation and senior activities to take my name off the parent email list. It was too hard to get the emails, telling of the exciting events ahead. She was a good friend, so I felt bad having to say anything. She didn't need to be the one feeling guilty.

"I'm so sorry, that wasn't very sensitive of me," was her response, which made me feel bad for even mentioning it. I should have just deleted the emails. I found out many months later that his classmates had carried his picture at graduation. Their lost comrade. I didn't know, because I hid from the world for a long while.

Without the hope of a diploma, a GED or other equivalent would be necessary. I had to go out of town to California to work on my friend's house, and had no choice but to leave Tyler alone. I had left Tyler a list of phone numbers, so that he could try and arrange a meeting at our nearest high school with the counselor to see about attending the last bit of the last semester, and possibly graduating with their school. Eastland was highly stringent academically, and from a college preparatory standpoint, he

Chapter 4: Homeward Bound

had way more total credits than he needed to graduate, but he didn't have what the public school required. Financial literacy and health. There was no possibility besides getting a GED, or a regular graduation (if he did computer classes) for a diploma at Horizonte Learning Center. He would be going from one of the best, most expensive schools in the area to a school that primarily served dropouts, refugees, and English learners.

We met with the counselor when I got back from California. She worked tirelessly to find him options. She called me the day after our meeting with her, and told me her story. She was a mother who had been there too. Her son had nearly died of an overdose. As she sat in the ER, she told me she had thought to herself, "What if he dies?"

Then her thoughts turned to, "What if he lives?" The hell of enduring the pain was more than she could continue to deal with. A mother knows what she can handle. I recalled the day when the school psychologist got mad at me for telling her that if I had my kids in the opposite order, I would have stopped at one. It was not that I didn't love Tyler with the vastness and enormity that cannot be understood until you are a mother. But a mother doesn't want to feel helpless or see her child suffer.

When I was in college studying Cognitive Psychology, I learned that a hamster mother will cull her litter when she gets stressed, or when she can't provide enough for her offspring. If you have ever seen the ferocity with which an animal mother will usually defend her young, you might understand how far she would need to be pushed to actually kill them. I am not in any way suggesting that I ever did or would consider this, only that I fully understand that desperate feeling of helplessness.

New Beginnings
CHAPTER 5

June, 2016

Tyler did get his GED and then moved to his first apartment. I got married and moved to Oakley. At the risk of sounding anticlimactic about it, the beautiful event was overshadowed by other events. I had waited until Tyler was out of the house, in order to not bring his problems into my new marriage. It had been nearly ten years since Chris and I were divorced. Tyler was not eighteen yet. He had about six weeks to go, but he had found an apartment in the Avenues, with a couple guys looking to fill their third bedroom, and was willing to make the move. It looked like a great situation. He'd be living with young, driven, college guys, in a great location near the University of Utah. Maybe something would rub off on him. I gave Tyler and his housemates the furniture I did not need, as I combined my life with Matt's. That lasted about six weeks before he was threatened with eviction for partying too much and disturbing the neighbors. I lost all of the housewares and furniture I had contributed to Tyler and his roommates because they thought they should be able to keep it for the inconvenience of taking a chance on him. Then I ended up helping him with a hasty move, as they wanted him out as soon as possible.

In all honesty, about half of this book I wrote as it happened, starting about a year ago. In going back to fill in the rest of the story, our lives had become so chaotic and overwhelming that I find I don't remember why certain decisions were made. Way too many decisions had to be made. I believe that I have a sort of PTSD from the grief and pain of all of this. Or perhaps it is similar to the pain of childbirth, that is long forgotten in order for us to go on, and possibly procreate again. That being said, for some reason, it was determined that Tyler would go live with his grandparents for a couple months. I don't remember why. Chris took him out to gather job applications in the Sandy area, where his grandparents,

132

Carolyn and Rich lived. Chris and Tyler had a good, and successful day, and Tyler was in the upstairs office getting ready to fill out online applications for the jobs that he had found that day. As Chris said goodbye to his parents downstairs, they heard a thud on the floor from above.

Huffing

Letter from me to April Runyan, to be forwarded to friends, for an email-intervention, June 12, 2016

April,

I would be totally comfortable with people having my email. You may forward this information also, so that everyone knows what happened.

Most of Tyler's friends know about his struggles with addiction, and the complications that it has added to his life in the last couple of years, so this should not be totally unexpected information. Tyler had just detoxed himself from painkillers, which I understand is a very difficult thing to do. On Friday June 3rd, I got married, and we had a lovely ceremony with just my kids and my husband's kids at our home. Tyler attended, and seemed to have fun. The next day we left on a 4 day, 30 mile, backpacking trip through Escalante with the kids for a "family honeymoon." We all had a really good time, and Tyler said a couple of times that he was glad that he came. We got home on Tuesday night, and the deal was that Tyler was going to go live with his grandparents for a couple of months. He was going to work and save money for an apartment, which he would get once he turned 18, on Aug. 1. His last apartment that he had moved into had been a disaster, as his lifestyle and partying got him thrown out. He seemed excited about working at a few of the places that he had picked up applications for with his dad on Thursday, and he went upstairs to work on his resume and fill out online applications. His dad was downstairs saying goodbye to Tyler's grandparents, when they heard a thud, as Tyler hit the floor. By the time his dad got upstairs, Tyler had no pulse. Chris did chest compressions until he came around and started breathing again. He was taken to the E.R. He had huffed "Dust-Off," and was the one in a million who's heart stops when huffing. He said he didn't know why he did it, other than poor impulse control. He was sent to a behavioral hospital by

133

the E.R. docs, which is where he is right now. It is uncertain where he will go after this.

I am hoping that this clears up any rumors. Please email me if you have questions. I am asking for those who know and love Tyler to offer support for his clean and sober lifestyle, which he certainly needs or he will die. Not everyone gets a second chance. If you would like to email him, you may send me an email, and I will get it to him. I'm certain that Tyler will be unhappy with me contacting his friends, but I really don't care. I only want him to be healthy and happy, and know how many people love and care about him.

Eva Summerhill

Letter from Kyle to Tyler, June 14, 2016

Dear Tyler,

I love you, man. You've always been a great friend to me throughout high school. Please get better soon. Stay strong.

Love,
Kyle

Letter from Alex Sorenson to Tyler, June 14, 2016

Yoooooo Tyler!

I'm sorry about everything, man. I love you, bro! We need to hang out as soon as you get out. But more importantly, you need to stop doing all of the things you're doing, bro. I know that this is your life, and that I have no right to tell you what you should or shouldn't be doing, but I care about you, man. And from my point of view, I'm seeing you go down a dark path, and not living your life to its fullest potential. The things you're doing are very dangerous, and aren't worth it, man. There's so much more in life for you to experience than just having your life revolve around drugs, bro. It really hurt me when I heard about this, and I know it hurt many other people. I want to see you succeed, especially because I know for a fact that you can do it. You're one of my best friends, and I miss hanging out with you. I miss how it was when we were younger, like in middle school, and we would hang out all the time, and do tons of crazy shit. I miss you, man, so get better soon!

Alex

Letter from Taylor to Tyler, June 14, 2016

Hi Eva, This is Taylor from Eastland. Thank you so much for allowing us to write Tyler, Here's a little note from me:

Tyler,

I never got the chance to write in your yearbook when it was being passed around at school, so I am glad I have this opportunity to write you! I hope you are hanging in there. I know we were never very close, but having said that, I am so grateful that you were part of my Eastland experience. You are such a great kid, and you always made me smile. I can't even imagine what you are going through, but I hope you know that you have your entire senior family rooting for you! There are 71 people who love and care deeply about you, and hopefully that provides some comfort. You will be in my thoughts and prayers, Tyler!

Taylor

Letter from April Runyon to Tyler, June 16, 2016

Tyler,

I want to hear from you at Thanksgiving. I want to see you at Christmas and New Years. I want to see you next summer. I want to be able to text you and call you to swap stories. I do not want to be sitting, surrounded by everyone else that loves you as much, and more than I do, at your funeral. I do not want to have to see your parents cry anymore. I do not want to have to comfort our classmates as they worry endlessly about how you are doing. But that is what I will be doing if you don't get better. I want you to know how worthy you are. How loved you are, and how valuable you are. I want you to understand how much we all want you to be healthy and happy. I can't make you stop using. I can't make you see your worth. You have to do that on your own. However, in anyway I can, I will help you. I love you. I love you. I love you. You are

Confessions of a Heroin Addict's Mother

worthy. You are worthy. You are worthy. You are valued. You are valued. You are valued. You are enough. You are enough. You are enough. Please take this to heart. I know you have probably been hearing things like this a lot but please try and HEAR them. UNDERSTAND them. Keep them inside you. It's up to you and you alone to get better, but you are surrounded by people that want nothing more than to help you and see you succeed. Please Tyler, do it for me, for your mom, for your dad, all your friends, all your family, for anyone really, do it for us until you learn to do it for yourself, and then never stop.

I love you more than you know.

April Runyon

Letter from Alyssa to Tyler, June 18, 2016

Hello, My name is Alyssa. I was Tyler's classmate and we were close friends since 7th grade. Is he still in the hospital? If he is, how is he feeling? April said we could send him a letter through you, so here is mine:

Dear Tyler,

I'm so heartbroken that this happened. I know you have been going through difficult times for many years, but this year especially. I want you to know that I care about you, and you mean a lot to me. We've been really close friends since 7th grade, and since then we've gone through many things together. Our friend groups changed, we'd fight, then once again we'd become best friends, and to this day we continue to be friends.

Even though things might not have gone in the best direction for you, please do not give up. You're a smart and charismatic person, and can keep moving forward in life. Everything will be good, at some point in the future.

Just know that you have my support, and the support of our whole class. I love you, and I hope you feel better.

Love,
Alyssa

If you could please get this note to Tyler, I would be very grateful.

Alyssa

Letter from David, June 16, 2016

Dear Tyler,

Hey buddy, I am so sorry to hear about what happened. I am really grateful that you were brought back to life, and I think that you have been given another chance at life. You are an amazing kid, funny, talented, smart, and just nice to everyone. You have so much ahead of you, but you can't let drugs pull you back. Friends who only want to party with you are not really friends. I know that God has a plan for you, and that He loves you, and knows you. I would encourage you to kneel down, and sincerely ask for His advice and love. He is only waiting for you to ask. I promise that you are His son, and that He cares for you more than any of us can understand. I hope that you can figure this stuff out. I love you, man.

Sincerely,
David

He had been sent to Provo Canyon Hospital, a behavioral health hospital. We had nothing to do with it this time. There was no choice. He was what they call "blue-sheeted," which means that the doctors requested that he go, and going was mandatory. At this point, we did not think it would do much to help him, but it was not our decision. I printed out his friend's letters and took them to him, a paper intervention of sorts.

I was already scheduled to work on round two or three of clearing out my friend's Uncle's house in Glendale, California. I desperately needed the income, and I had been waiting on this for a while. We were in limbo again as to how long Tyler would be in treatment. After a week or so, I had asked if I could pick him up at the hospital on the way out of town toward California, where he could help me and I could look after him. However, this was against medical advice, and if I took him, the insurance would not cover his stay. So instead, Chris had to send him on a plane a few days after I got to California. I felt bad, but I couldn't tell the Smiths that I was taking him. They wouldn't be happy with him being at the house because of all of his problems, but I had no choice. I had to work, and I had to keep an eye on him, and quite frankly, he worked his ass off helping me and it was really good for both of us. I had also hired a couple of young gals that were just out of college, who had helped me on a previous trip. They were fun to work with, and I think that Tyler felt great about the amount of help he was able to provide. We all had a good time taking a break at an Armenian restaurant, while trying something that looked like a football or boat-shaped pizza with two eggs for eyes, called khachapuri. It was great to see him engaging in smart, fun conversation with girls close to his age.

Upon arriving home, we stayed at an Extended Stay America, while he found a room to rent in the classifieds. I thought he found a good living situation. He'd be renting one of three rental rooms in a house that the owner also occupied. What could go wrong? It was close to the community college if he wanted to take classes, and there were tons of places he could work within a short bike ride. He did get a job as a bag-boy at a grocery store. The job lasted two weeks.

I got a job doing the staging of a house that needed a number of landscaping and fix-it projects, in preparation to be listed for sale. I had Tyler and two other kids work with me on that house. The three of them had worked well with me on remodel projects on numerous occasions. I went to pick him up at his house and had to wait a half hour. When I finally got him in the car, he was so nauseated he could hardly talk. I could tell he was high, but I had a commitment to finish this project so I took him anyway. He lay on the grass with my clients asking who he was as they walked around him. I just pretended like I didn't hear them. What could I do?

Chapter 5: New Beginnings

Jackson

Jackson Hole. Raw magic. It's a place that I've always considered home. I've only actually lived there for one full year, and on and off for another summer, but vacationed there most of my life. I was fortunate to have had my dad purchase a house on the outskirts of town through a foreclosure auction many years prior. Solo trips. Family reunions (or, "ruin-ya's, as my grandad called them). Trips with my kids and their friends. There had been a trip with my friend Shonna, her son, and Tyler, where we had walked with the kids in a Burley stroller on the bike path in front of the majestic Tetons. There had been trips with people I dated, though they had to sleep in a tent outside, because it was my dad's house rule. Trips as a contractor to remodel and remake the house with Tyler in tow; spending his time with friends he had so easily met at the skate park on the outskirts of town.

A memory of a long-ago Jackson trip drifted into my head. It must have been January or February, 1999. It was some kind of school break for Weston, thirteen years Tyler's senior, with the caution and wisdom of an old man. We had traveled in a storm along the Hoback River toward Jackson, knuckles white and nowhere to pull over. The snow, covering every inch of the road's shoulder, quietly stole my ability to stop the car and nurse. Tyler, a hungry infant, five, maybe six months old, screamed inconsolably for food, and I was engorged with milk but unable to do anything. Not the first, nor the last time I would be full yet helpless. Full of milk, wisdom, knowledge, love, that for whatever reason; circumstance, pride or stubbornness, he couldn't or wouldn't take, or I couldn't or wouldn't give. The album by Vangelis, "1492," was the remedy for the moment. Intense music calmed him from birth; became a necessity for sleep. The more intense, the more it soothed. He was always somehow calmed by intensity.

He doesn't want to go this time. Afraid we will see the track marks when we float the Snake River, or go to Granite Hot Springs. His way of letting us in on the secret he has kept for three weeks. Such a short time, yet way too long, when you consider how much damage a needle can do. Neil Young has a song about it. I guess Tyler thought that us hearing it would be easier than seeing it.

I was planning to go anyway with Matt when Chris called in a panic, and told me to call around and see what hospitals had a detox bed open. He said that Tyler was so violently ill he could hardly move, and was vomiting profusely. He was in tears as he described Tyler's room when he picked him up in Taylorsville to meet me at the Heber Valley Hospital E.R. Needles...he has needles now. But we knew that already. Chris didn't want me to see it, just to meet him at the hospital. Test after test was run. This was more than just detoxing from heroin, and it was more than they could handle at this hospital. They sent him back down to LDS Hospital in Salt Lake where he was admitted to the infectious disease department. They let us drive him this time, to save the ambulance cost. In a hospital gown with I.V.'s still in his arm, he lay in the back seat of my truck as we drove him an hour to better help. Endocarditis? Hepatitis? HIV? Sepsis? Back at the hospital where he had come into this world, they were determining if he had a disease that would take him away from it. I thought again of how helpless he looked as a four lb., four oz. preemie, I.V.s sticking out of the top of his head, and as orange as a carrot from jaundice. And now, how helpless he also looked, as a six-foot, three-inch 180-pound young man, vomiting his guts out in a bag and doubled over with pain, crying and screaming shamelessly, as though he were that newborn again, unaware of anything but his own pain.

In the Beginning

At what point can I separate myself?
In the beginning everything came from me.

Nuzzling at my breast,
So tiny, so helpless.

My milk would let down at the slightest whimper,
Soiling my shirt if I did not attend to him quickly.

Now I have to ignore my impulses,
My motherhood.
Eva Summerhill

It took three days to figure out that he had sepsis, which is a very serious blood infection that can kill you if not treated quickly. Thank God everything else was ruled out, but he still had to get over the infection. How could this have happened with a few weeks of injecting? Nurses, infectious disease doctors, an addiction doctor, a crisis counselor, and people trying to sell their recovery programs bopped in and out of his room.

My hope was that this would be his rock bottom, that from here on I should not have to remind him of how dangerous his behavior was. He voiced his fear of what damage he may have done to his body. Perhaps this horrible darkness had held a lesson for him. A recovery program was chosen from those presented to him as he rested on the infectious disease floor of the hospital for five days, recovering from the infection and detoxing from heroin.

Dayspring, Late September, 2016

Supposedly, co-dependents forget to take care of themselves. I certainly did not stop my exercise routines. My sanity. My meditation. I rode Round Valley on this day with my friend Kathy, trading the leading position to push each other, each needing the therapy of a hard ride for our different reasons. She kept looking back, either to make sure that I was back there, or to make sure that she was beating me. I don't mind competition from her, though. It's the competition from myself that I struggle with. Always striving for better, faster, more likable. Never quite good enough. My tires rolled over the rocks with a lot less fear and effort than they had a few years prior, as I rode with a new confidence of what my body and bike were capable of. All of the images of cheesy inspirational quotes on posters about accomplishment and perseverance washed through my head, as I climbed in the autumn afternoon. You know, posters that usually show someone on top of a mountain they had climbed, or doing some other physical challenge. Riding was nothing. I could do this. It was the rest that I struggled with. I needed to get back, so that I could attend the family therapy meeting at Dayspring, the intensive outpatient program that Tyler was sent to after he was discharged. Now that is a challenge that nobody prepares you for. No posters hanging on anybody's walls show a struggling family trying to support their addict child.

My first meeting with Tyler's group and their families started with an assessment of what we were feeling at the moment. I would learn that this would be how his counselor would start every family meeting. It needed to be an emotional description. Simple enough. Tired. The words came out quickly enough that I knew that my true emotions had been tapped. Doug, the counselor, would have preferred an emotion and not a physical state, but that's how I felt. Tired. I then realized that I was sobbing. I tried to keep it in control, but I lost it. In the front seat, in front of everyone. My body shaking as I tried to choke back the tears. "Welcome to Dayspring," Doug said, and kindly looked at me.

Tyler and I are linked in a way that I can't explain. When he drugs himself, he drugs me. When he threatens suicide, he kills a little of me. I saw myself suffer when it was him writhing in pain in the hospital. We would laugh at something in unison, that, why it was so funny, neither he nor I, would be able to explain. But we both somehow knew it was hilarious. For fun, we would sometimes go to the massive Asian market near his school, and stroll the isles, clueless as to what most of the products were.

"What do you suppose this tastes like?"

"I don't know, let's get it and see." Or we would buy something based on the funny English translation on the package. The melon candies... "that would make you smile with beautiful voluptuousness," or some other nonsense.

This was one of the good days. We were looking for his third apartment, where he would live while attending Dayspring's Outpatient program. I had seen the "for rent" sign while driving home from visiting Tyler at the hospital, and realized it was within walking distance to Dayspring. We arranged to have the property manager showed us the room. He was a stern, but seemingly reasonable, guy from Bulgaria. He spoke with a predictably strong, thick, and songlike accent, but each time that he knocked on one of the three shared units that he showed us, he broke into a strange, high, nasally sound; a complete departure from his regular speech. Each time it happened, Tyler and I could hardly contain our laughter. I turned toward him as I was trying to keep it in, and realized that he was trying to hold back his laughter as well, which made it

Chapter 5: New Beginnings

all much worse. "Mainnnntennnennnce" was our word for the rest of the day.

Chris and I tried to let him do his thing, muddle through living on his own, and the lessons one learns from just doing it. He liked his two roommates, though he didn't pick them. He was assigned to them by the landlord. He became fast friends with one of them, who was outgoing and handsome like Tyler and also like Tyler, seemed a little aimless. He was in school at the time, so I thought maybe that would motivate Tyler to see that you can have fun, but still get stuff done. There were three separate studios with one shared kitchen and bathroom. The building would have been beautiful with its stately arts-and-crafts architecture, and the location was stellar, in the Avenues area of Salt Lake, but years of slumlord style maintenance had rendered the place a dump.

Running late yet again. A lifetime of running circles around a kid who could never quite do it on his own. I was baffled that as a child he needed a prompt to open a door, or to turn a page after coming to the end of reading it beautifully, according to his therapist when he was seven. ADD. His teachers said that they could teach him, if he weren't playing under his desk, or doing backflips in the back of the room. I remember mornings where I had to go sit in the car while he got ready for school, the maddening anxiety overtaking my ability to control my fury. Unable to understand his lack of initiative, his lack of empathy, and his apathy towards the fact that we were going to be late, and miss the bus for the third or fourth time that week. That his behavior would cost me an hour and a half of my morning to drive him when he missed it and I would return home frazzled, angry and behind schedule. I felt like he was antagonizing me. Pushing my buttons, and forcing his sick sense of control over my day, my time, and my sanity. Some mornings would be so rough that the neurotic dog would hide under the deck, forcing me to crawl under and get him before heading to chase the bus. Even the poor dog was afraid to face the palpable tension in the air. Tyler called it a "high-anxiety" family, yet he antagonized everyone, and caused most of the anxiety. He was a master button-pusher and manipulator. Our first family counselor had said that we should let him feel like he controls something. That he felt helpless in his life, and was seeking to control something about his existence. The way I saw it is that he created a tornado that we would all get sucked

143

into, pulling everything in his path into its vortex where chaos and turmoil were his master plan; his creation.

This morning I'm late taking him to the doctor to follow up on his four-day hospital stay, two weeks prior. Three times I call him, to make sure he is ready, as I drive down Parley's Canyon from Oakley. In the first call, I tell him that the weather is horrible, with the first of the season rain-snow mix. The second call is to make sure that he will be ready when I pull up so we won't be late. The third, to say that I'm there. He says hold on, he's not quite ready. Five minutes I wait. Late yet again.

Soon after moving in to the Avenues apartment, someone's mother had messaged Chris on Facebook. Who knows how she had linked Chris and Tyler? Her son had recently been with Tyler, and had overdosed. Tyler had called 911 and "saved him." But he was the one who had bought him the drugs. His friend had thanked him for getting them. Savior or killer? Tyler said Savior. His friend had asked him to get the heroin for him. He had thanked him. It was his choice to ask, pay for, and take the drugs. Tyler was unable to see that he would not have OD'd if he hadn't helped him get high in the first place. Probably in some strange sort of denial, he only believed that he had done him a favor by getting him his fix, and had done him a second favor by calling 911 when he was unresponsive.

I needed to run hard and long. I needed to change my Pandora from the mellow Indie Folk Radio station I most frequently listened to and blast Rage Against the Machine. It suited my mood. I understood teen angst music, as a forty-nine-year-old mother, possibly better than when I had been a teen. Being both cathartic and chaotic, it set my pace for the speed that I wanted to run, fast, hard, and away from these feelings. Music was my drug of choice. The only thing that I can listen to when I have too much on my mind is music, but not just any music. Pop won't cut it. Too hoppy, bouncy, and joyful than anyone has a right to be. I can't even listen to comedy when I feel like this, though, on good days I love *Wait, Wait, Don't Tell Me* on NPR and the joyful variety of *Prairie Home Companion* when I am not weighed down by grief. When I'm overwhelmed, I can't even listen to the news. Today it will be music.

Chapter 5: New Beginnings

Drowning, Mid-October, 2016

I have always thought that I would somehow die by drowning. I was a competitive swimmer from seven or eight years old through high school. We were on the swim team at the YMCA as kids, then on the country club team, when we weren't swimming for the high school. I was good enough to set school records, be the captain, and make it to state. I know how to swim, though my fear of drowning persists.

Perhaps it was the amount of time spent in the water that made me fear drowning. Or that feeling of panic when an ocean wave catches you off guard, and fills your nose unexpectedly. Or the memory of my alcoholic coach at the YMCA, who would throw hard rubber toys at us to make us swim faster. Or perhaps it was the time when I was a teaching assistant in a swim class for handicapped kids, and a Down's Syndrome boy twice my weight panicked in the deep end and jumped from the kick board, holding me underwater and leaving me to fight to get him off me, and swim us both to safety. To me, these days, motherhood was drowning me. It seemed that just when I was able to get to the surface and gasp for air, I would get pulled underwater again.

He called me. A rare and welcomed moment. This time it wasn't to ask for anything. No groceries, gas or rent. It wasn't a crisis moment. He wasn't detoxing, or telling me that he had to move. Just asking how I was doing. One of the things that I have struggled with in all of this has been his inability to show empathy. Any understanding of the financial and emotional impact of his behavior was lost in a cauldron of anger and blame. What I did not know, yet, was that he had been suspended from the outpatient program. I would be blindsided yet again. In retrospect, I think that he had called to soften the blow I was about to experience.

I had also received an angry call from Chris before I arrived at the family group therapy session. He was still unaware of Tyler's suspension from the program when he called me, as was I. Chris was spewing hate and blame at everyone. He had told me he wouldn't be coming tonight to the family night at the outpatient clinic. The place that was dealing with the very issues that we were facing in this family. He had missed all but one of the three and a half hour meetings on codependence, and the family cycle of addiction. Chris said he wasn't responsible for any of it, and wouldn't be blamed for Tyler's problem. We exemplified everything that

145

I had learned, through participation in the meetings, that explained how this was a family problem. We were swirling around in the crazy cycle of addiction. Addict uses, family gets angry. This causes addict to use again, which causes the family to get angry again. Get me off of this merry-go-round! Tyler would later tell me, as I called him to find out his part of the story of the suspension, and to ask why he hadn't told me, that he had used right after a fight with his dad on the weekend. Blame everywhere. Nobody was taking personal responsibility for their part. Tyler had surely planned on getting high by not taking his Suboxone, which reduced cravings, but also keeps you from feeling the high when you take the heroin, then he blamed his using on his dad because of the fight. I decided I would not tell Chris about the suspension. I was tired of being the mediator between the two. Tired of being manipulated by both of them, blamed at various times by Chris, by Tyler, by myself. Just tired. It was Tyler's responsibility to tell him. I hadn't made the choice to use.

Donna was in the hall when I got there, as I ran in a few minutes late.

"You're Tyler's counselor, aren't you?" I had recognized her from the hospital when she came into his room to explain the details of what their program had to offer, and to make recommendations for him. She was not what I might have expected from a substance abuse counselor, and I had met a few. This is a field frequently populated by addicts in recovery themselves, or boisterous self-confident types. I had to strain to hear her very soft voice, asking for clarification, or for her to repeat information frequently. Tyler spoke very highly of her though; she had made a connection with him. Upon talking with her, I found her to be direct and firm, underneath her very soft-spoken persona. She was no pushover.

She said she was his counselor and pulled me into her office, through the room of clients and their families, where Chris, Tyler and I should have been. None of us were represented.

"Where is he?" I asked. She couldn't say much, because he was now an adult. My child, who was unable to make good adult decisions, pay his own bills, and be independent of my help, was too adult for me to be told why he had been suspended. It was obvious that he had relapsed, as clean drug tests were a requirement of the program. She had to dance and skirt around telling me, while simultaneously laying it all out there. I felt like

Chapter 5: New Beginnings

her empathy toward a struggling mother allowed her to carefully choose words that would help me comprehend. I know that lingo by now.

"You have to take care of yourself, that's what your focus should be," she said, as though saying my son had died, there was nothing that could be done. "You understand that recovery for someone his age is very difficult, don't you?" This was not the first time that I had heard it. With an already dismal rate of people who relapse when on heroin, I was hearing again that his age made it even more difficult?

"Are you going to Al-Anon?"... "Let God and let go," as though someone, something could ease this pain, if I just give in to them. I don't trust many people. How can an entity or program I don't understand take this pain from me? This is what drowning must feel like. But instead of dying in four or so minutes I felt as though I remained in a constant state of drowning. I'll gasp enough air to keep me going for a bit, get pulled back underwater, then spit it out again long enough to take another breath, only to be pulled down again.

Dharma Punx

Tyler was supposed to be going to a meeting every night while he was suspended from the outpatient program. He had read the book called *Dharma Punx,* while in the wilderness. I had seen the book on one of the kid's mats as they huddled around the fire, and I had inquired about it. They were allowed to read different books as they moved through the stages. Earth, Fire, Water, Air. *Dharma Punx* was reserved for the highest level. When he had reached that level, he read it, and told me that it was about a guy who had lived a punk-rock, violent, and drug-filled lifestyle, and that he had turned to Buddhism for his recovery. Not only had he become a counselor and written books, but he had also started recovery meetings similar to AA, but based on Buddhist principals. I found out about the meetings many months before we actually went, because of some research that I had done on one of many restless, insomniac nights I had while Tyler was in the wilderness. I would spend all night searching for anything and everything that I thought might spark something in Tyler.

His car wouldn't start, so I used the opportunity to come down to Salt Lake and jump the car, and suggest that we go to a Refuge Recovery meeting together sometime. Overcoming addiction needs to be something an

147

addict does for themselves, but I had rationalized that perhaps I needed to lead him to something that he might connect with, let him know that I supported him, help him realize that he wasn't alone, and he could find others out there like him looking for a community. He agreed to go, and was completely open to it. Because it was at the University, I hoped, and I'm sure he did too, that there would be other young people there. Others who had gotten off-track really early. Others who had a long life ahead of them.

In the car, on the way there, he kept lamenting over the idea that he was just entering college age, but could not enjoy the college party life that his friends could enjoy. He had no friends that didn't use drugs except a couple, and he struggled to find activities to do with them. I don't know when he got the idea that all of college is a party, or where he quit having an interest in things that used to give him pleasure; music, soccer, making things, bird watching, astronomy. I kept bringing those things up in our conversations, hoping to spark something deep inside of him. But

they were things made minuscule by the euphoria that drugs had brought him, coursing through his veins, and making everything else mundane in comparison.

I had sent him pictures of birds that I saw out on my hikes and bike rides, and asked him to identify them for me. The kid who used to have a sincere interest in ornithology, a gift for identifying birds, down to the minutia of rings around the eyes, or other characteristics that I had difficulty discerning.

Such joy I recalled from going birding in Northern Utah at Willard Bay with Tyler and five of his classmates on a school biology project. A glorious day filled with sincere interest in the subject, as well as lots of the typical shenanigans reserved for teenagers. The kids were teasing the friend who seemed like he was just along for the ride, and though the birds were right there, was reluctant to pull out his camera to snap photos. I pulled over frequently, because someone wanted to run through the field to get a shot of a group of egrets or herons, or to look for that owl we

Chapter 5: New Beginnings

were told roosts in a certain tree behind the storage garage. I had French fries all over my car from the drive-thru and from packing seven of us in my Toyota Highlander, the six-foot, five-inch daughter of a basketball player in front to fit her long legs. I miss those days. The chaotic parental bliss of experiencing noisy teenagers when they are joyful, fun, and not angst-filled.

On our drive to the meeting, I remembered that I had taken a photo for Tyler last week while on a bike ride. I had pulled over to let an uphill biker pass, and scared a little owl out of his sleep and across the Mid-Mountain Trail. It was a rare glimpse of a shy, nocturnal creature. I was able to snap a picture on my phone as he turned his head backward to stare at me, his eyes seeing through me to my pain, connecting to me in a way that felt like a higher power. The owl seemed to tell me,

"Send the picture of me, he will know who I am, you will see who he is yet again."

I have never been superstitious, but the occurrence of owls in my life over the past few years has been uncanny. I could count five or six occasions where an owl sighting was followed by some disastrous event or argument. Perhaps it was my mind's way of making sense of the world. To turn a coincidence into an act of good or evil. There is so much ambiguity in our world that our minds need to make some sense out of it. I hoped that this owl would bring a different story. Tyler identified it as a Screech Owl when I showed him the picture. That's all he had said, though. No excitement or further inquiry. We just kept driving in silence to the meeting.

We searched for the meeting but to no avail. I had emailed the organizer in the morning to make sure that it was happening and received information that it was. We inquired at the information desk in the Student Union building, and they sent us to a lady that was walking

Confessions of a Heroin Addict's Mother

toward us down the hall. She knew nothing, but a man sitting in the lobby nearby must have seen our searching, disappointed look, because he called out to us,

"Are you looking for the Refuge Recovery meeting?" We sat down with him. He seemed so calm. At peace with himself. He exuded a reassurance that I embraced for the moment. We used the opportunity to ask him about Refuge. Perhaps our inquiry was too pointed for someone that we had just met, but he unflinchingly shared a little of his story, and what differences he saw between AA and Refuge Recovery. He had an unstuffy hipness that I could see Tyler might feel comfortable with, though he was much closer to my age than Tyler's. He said that he had been uncomfortable with AA "politics," and the warnings that he had received about controlling his language. Without making it a point, he dropped language that did not make me uncomfortable, and knowing Tyler, probably made the guy seem more "real" to him. Not self-righteous or judgmental. The meditation had helped him, he said. In AA there were steps to build upon, and here there were not. He felt like "spokes on a wheel," that could all be discussed and practiced at any time, worked better than moving through steps for him. He told us some stories about his early life and how tumultuous it was living as a musician in Laguna Beach, very close to where I lived in college. I knew of some of the places he would hang out, and had some understanding of the reputed craziness of that area up the canyon, as I lived near there in college. It was where Timothy Leary had lived, and it was reputed to be the LSD capitol of the universe. He listened intently as Tyler opened up to him about some of his experiences. We had our own meeting, there in the lobby of the Student Union Building. It felt comfortable and natural and I was filled with gratitude to Ray for sharing a moment with us.

Refuge Recovery is a search for freedom from suffering. It is non-theistic. Everyone always asks how they can become "happy" in life.

"Hell," he said, "I'm just looking for peace." I wanted to know more. Hell, I just wanted some peace too. Tyler would go to a few meetings off and on over the next few months. I wished he would go more, but I had done what I could, increasingly gaining the understanding that he had to do this for himself.

150

Chapter 5: New Beginnings

Me Time, Late October, 2016

I realize that I am ultra-driven and move at a pace that most people don't understand. Maybe I learned it at school, as I walked the large University of California, Irvine campus in the ten minutes between classes. My motto has always been "walk with purpose." I get impatient waiting for electronic doors to open at the market when they require that I slow my pace. I get impatient with people that seem unaware that they are blocking the entire grocery isle, with their five kids, wrestling around a sideways-parked shopping cart. I don't know if I'm that annoyed because I'm in that much of a hurry, or if it bothers me that some people don't consider others. I go out of my way to think about others, sometimes enduring personal harm or sacrifice. I would learn later that this is a hallmark of co-dependent types. Character traits that frequently are considered a good thing in society would mark me as complicit in my sons' addiction. Being thoughtful, helpful, empathetic, and always putting others first.

"Now it's time for me," I try to convince my reluctant self.

I hung pictures today. Finally inserting myself into the home that I have lived in for four months. After being single for nearly ten years, I got married to Matt and I moved to Oakley. I have decided to allow myself to feel like I belong here. I'm trying to find respite in the most bucolic of settings, with a thoughtful and caring man. We built our garden together with its planter boxes and arbors. We planted vegetables and had a cut flower garden from which I would share bouquets with the neighbors. I tried to make myself feel comfortable residing in his world, as I sought to find a touch of peace and serenity amidst a sea of turmoil. It's not like Matt does not make me feel welcome and comfortable. The restless feeling is something I probably impose upon myself; anxiety as a result of the interruptions, the worry, and the fear of getting unsettling phone calls. Just when I think I can relax, something turns me inside out and disrupts the quiet peacefulness that I had found or created. I don't want to get too comfortable anywhere. The solace I attempt to bring to my life, by doing things that are healthy for my psyche, competes with feelings of guilt for not paying attention to what is actually going on. In the past when I let my guard down, indulging in an hour and a half yoga class, the result was a party at my house, behind my back, with twenty people dropping acid in my kitchen. On numerous occasions, I was interrupted

151

as I worked with my accountant, my phone ringing with various different crisis calls, forcing me to leave, unable to continue concentrating on tasks that required more focus than I could possibly give them, under the circumstances. These meetings were followed by a quick apology and reschedule with my accountant, fully aware that she heard the whole conversation. I am trying to learn to accept that things may not ever change with Tyler. Giving up on your own child seems counterintuitive to my maternal instincts. That my child's sink or swim moment may just result in drowning. But he could drown, or we could drown together, with him pulling me under the water with him, unable to detach the tether that holds us together.

Mother's Day

My tears held the weight and acidity
of every parent who had suffered helplessly.

They burned and created little canyons down my tired skin…
worn thin with worry and susceptible to erosion.

An addict's mother…the sedimentary rock
in the geology of humans.

Eva Summerhill

Sparky's dog collar. A picture of Tyler as a baby, sitting naked on a furry blanket. A picture of Tyler being held tightly by Weston. A hap-

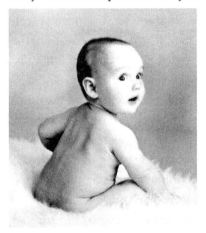

py fourth grader at school in music class with that silly, goofy smile that I remember so well. A black and white photo of a four-year-old with the cutest face. It had been an outtake of the photo shoot, but was my favorite, because it captured his impish grin and disheveled quirkiness. I realized that the reasons that I had been taking my work upstairs, into the kitchen, and the reasons that I had not settled

Chapter 5: New Beginnings

into my office, were all wrapped up in those photographs and dog collar. I hid them all away. Back in a box in the closet where I didn't have to face them. I could work in my office now.

I had gone to the doctor a month or so before. I found her through Matt, as I worked to settle myself into my new town. She and her husband were his close friends and she knew much more about me than most family doctors would know, though she was careful to keep her medical advice within her office walls. I needed help with insomnia. This was a lifelong problem for me, but the last two years had become intolerable. My helplessness in the situation with Tyler seemed magnified as I lay trapped in my bed, trapped in my head, tossing and turning in a desperate attempt to sleep and not wake Matt up. She told me that she could prescribe sleeping pills, though they shouldn't be taken long term, and this was not going to be a short-term problem.

She sent me to a sleep doctor. As I filled out the questionnaire, the questions hit me hard.
- How many days do you feel like you have let your family down, you would be better off dead?
- Do you have problems falling, or staying asleep?
- Are you in counseling?
- On antidepressants?
- Do you have trouble concentrating?
- Do you have trouble enjoying the things you used to enjoy?

Yes, Yes, Yes, and Yes to all of those things. My setting was different, and though I had been trying to pretend that I could find some normalcy, I knew there was none.

In Hiding

I'm always traveling to another location in my mind
Looking at real estate on the sleepless nights, which are many
At properties way beyond my reach

I dream of living in beautiful hamlets in Europe
With my painted shutters and flower boxes
And maybe a cat
Never with anyone else for some reason

I bought a book once just for the title, *She Drove Without Stopping*
Can I really get away from myself?
Changing my location wouldn't change my situation, or me
The pain resides within

Eva Summerhill

Let God and Let Go
CHAPTER 6

Late September, 2016

The chapel was grand but not ornamental, starkly different from the Catholic chapels that I couldn't resist peeking into on my honeymoon in France, Switzerland, and Italy, four months earlier. It sat perfectly positioned, with its prow pointed toward the mountains of Park City, a sincere attempt at bridging the void toward God. The day before, I was climbing up those same mountains on my mountain bike, fall's glory blessing me with a peace and connection I could not find inside these walls. The congregation held lovely people, old friends and acquaintances of my husband from twenty years in this small mountain town, as well as those who did not know us, warmly reaching out in the spirit of Christianity. I still preferred the mountains. The ceremony, hymns, traditions, and rituals were all foreign to me. I would go to support our connection to a community. My husband's, far reaching, and mine, tenuous and new.

Seven of the twelve steps in a program that we were told might help us recover, make direct reference to God or a Higher Power. I've gone through the motions to find religion and made a couple of attempts to seek my truth, though perhaps more of an attempt was made earlier in my life, long before I thought that some sort of faith would help Tyler and me as we teetered on the edge of disaster, wishing we could just "let God and let go," if only we knew what that looked like.

Though I was a reluctant believer, symbols of devotion have always had an unbelievable draw for me. Retablos in Mexican folk art, creches, crosses, sacred choral music, Byzantine icons, Buddhist alters, and Shinto shrines. Artistic expressions of devotion and passion. I yearned to have as much commitment to my beliefs as those that hold these things dear.

My fiftieth birthday celebration was a trip to Bryce Canyon, my cathedral, with its red rock spires and shapes an architect could never imagine. The sun was hitting the rocks and glowing in the late-afternoon autumn. No words could describe the beauty, no photograph could capture the feeling. No scripture could describe the wonder of that place, that moment, as I sensed what my Higher Power might look like.

In college, I hung out with a friend who was Bahá'i. I explored this faith because I liked their basic principles. To the Bahá'i, all of the major religions held the same truth that was presented by a different prophet, depending on the needs of the people of their particular dispensation. There were a lot of couples with different religious and ethnic backgrounds that embraced the faith because it did not negate anyone's religious beliefs. Weston and I even marched in the Martin Luther King Day parade through South Central Los Angeles with the Bahá'is. Weston, my towhead blonde toddler on my shoulders, marching through Compton.

With Weston in tow, I frequented the Hare Krishna temple in Laguna Beach where we lived. I enjoyed the chanting more as entertainment or a cultural experience than anything, and the greatest benefit to a poor college student such as myself was the free Indian food after you had

Chapter 6: Let God and Let Go

listened for an hour and a half or so. After I moved to Utah, I was sometimes drawn to Huntsville, Utah where the Trappist Monks chanted, and you could buy honey in the store to help support them. The music moved me, but I had to close my eyes to appreciate it, as the chapel was more like a Quonset hut than a church. I had pieced together what worked for me, I suppose.

I was raised Mormon in the Church of Jesus Christ of Latter-day Saints, and my family moved from Utah to Catholic country, South Bend, Indiana, at the age of five. There was Notre Dame, fish on Fridays, ashen foreheads on Ash Wednesday. Faith was the precursor to betrayal. Betrayal that became the foundation for my lack of trust. Eight years old. Baptized November 6, 1974; the age of reason and free agency. Capable of telling right from wrong, able to make a choice. Shortly after my baptism, an event would cause me to question everything about my religion. Was it me that chose to be touched by him, that way? Me that chose to touch him...the disgusting hardness under his missionary suit? The missionaries were idolized in our home, in our culture. The Primary song, "I hope they call me on a mission, when I have grown a foot or two." The piggy banks filled, so that one day we could pay to serve God, to sacrifice a couple of years in our prime to spread His word. He couldn't possibly be at fault. Missionaries don't do bad things. They are called by God, examples of His goodness. I would hold my secret for a year, too ashamed to tell anyone. Though he made me, I touched him too. I had free agency. I was old enough to make a choice, old enough to be baptized, after all.

I was to learn that I was less important than him. Less important than the fuss it might cause. Less important than the Church and what it meant to my family. Stewardship order would be maintained. God. Church, Family. I was third. "Just don't tell anyone," was the only thing that I heard. The Catholics were the only ones who did those sorts of things. We don't talk about that.

In late October, I attended my nephew's farewell for his mission in a Mormon chapel an hour and fifteen minutes away. Familiar but foreign all at once. The chapel was so plain and unadorned. I've never understood why the Mormons have such beautiful temples yet their chapels were devoid of ornament and style. Did the humble surroundings reflect a pragmatic, modest people? Was it a juxtaposition to their temples, which

157

were exceptionally beautiful with unmatched craftsmanship? It was hard to concentrate and be reverent when the hymns, sacrament, and prayers seemed rote and mundane, as though procedure had eclipsed ceremony and symbolism.

The service was in honor of my nephew and a young lady, who would both be leaving on missions soon. They both gave talks to the congregation, which included the regular ward members, as well as invited family and friends who were there to support their missionary. The first talk was on prayer, and was given by the young lady missionary. It read a bit like a book report, but included some anecdotal stories of how, on two occasions, her prayers had been answered. The first instance was when her grandmother had fallen and broken her hip and had to have surgery. Her prayer had been answered for a speedy recovery. The second was a prayer to help her decide if she should go on a mission. Her answer had come a month later in the form of a "warm feeling" that had come over her. This brought up all of my old confusion. Certainly there were many instances where fervent prayers remained unanswered. Was this girl more worthy than some? Was worthiness even a factor? Where did God's will come into play? What about fatalism, when something is part of a plan? Was an unanswered prayer a sign of unworthiness?

My head was filled with stories told over the years by Mormon friends, or heard during many, many talks in church. My friend told me that one month they did not have enough money for her family to pay both tithing and the car insurance, and a choice had to be made as to which was more important. Tithing was more important; insurance to God. Miraculously, a check for the very amount that they were short came in the mail in the form of a refund for something or another, thus enabling them to pay the insurance. There was a house fire story, where someone's sacred undergarments saved them from burning, but only where the garments had covered their body. Truth? Ward-house legend?

It would be nice to believe. I liked the people that told the stories, and church legends were as fun as any legends. I just didn't, for some reason. I guess that I believed that the story happened, but not the miracle as an act of God. There have been too many innocent people that have had horrible things happen to them, that I can't possibly believe that a cry for help, or an act of devotion, or a prayer, could make a difference.

Chapter 6: Let God and Let Go

I turned away from a formal religious search. My religion became stubbornness and self-reliance. I was, and always would be, an island. I believed that I had an internal locus of control. Nobody outside myself controlled me, particularly not God. I wasn't that weak. Nobody made decisions for me. Nobody made me do anything I didn't want to do. I didn't want help. I didn't need help, and damn it, I could do this myself. I could fix anything. If I relied on someone, I would become beholden to them. Never allow yourself to be beholden to anyone, or anything, for that matter. Then they, or it, can control you. Trust nobody. Question everyone and everything. Be skeptical of everything. If you do it yourself, you can't be disappointed in anyone else. This did not serve me well.

My dear friend in college, Sanjay, told me a story that I have held onto as one of the only stories that I believe, in relation to miraculous events. I don't know why I believed him more than anyone else, but he was so very intelligent, and I had always respected him as a mentor. He had come from India to get his undergraduate degree at Purdue, then his PhD at the University of California, Irvine in Social Ecology, where we met. His father had come from India to join him on a road trip across the Desert Southwest on Sanjay's journey to Southern California to attend graduate school. They had taken a Greyhound, the two sitting always together in the front seat. They were to take their time marveling at the grandeur of the National Parks and attractions as they spent some rare time together. Sanjay's dad was an engineer. Predictable. Rational. Cool. He had never in his life told Sanjay that he loved him, that was not his way. As they travelled through the rock formations of New Mexico, Sanjay's dad told him that he loved him, and that he wanted him to move to another seat. Confused but obedient, Sanjay moved. A massive boulder rolled off the mountain in a rockslide, hitting the bus and killing his father and four others. Sanjay had also been injured, as he was thrown from the bus and down a ravine, and would forever after walk with a limp. I believed the story. Sanjay was the smartest person that I had met, and is now a professor of Health Policy in Toronto. He was not, and is not, a whacked out religious freak. Why had his father had this premonition? This story would be, for some reason, the only believable story that I could hold onto when I had an internal debate about the existence of a higher power.

There is nothing my skeptical mind could possibly refute in this situation. He did not make the story up.

I needed something. I needed to believe in something. Over time, I started feeling that my religion was found in connectedness. Not just from human to human, but from human to other animals. The idea of God residing in all things suited my concept of what God might look like more than any other construct of what God was. Connecting to something or someone connects one to the God that resides within it or them. It's the feeling you get when someone is sincere in their question,

"How are you?" Or when someone makes eye contact and you feel that they truly see you. It's the owl on Mid-Mountain Trail. The friend that isn't embarrassed to ask how you are doing, though they are aware it might be hard to hear the truth, instead of, "I'm fine." It is the message that you hear in an Al-Anon meeting that you feel is directed at you as an act of comfort or reassurance, though cross-talk is frowned upon. It's the hug that is comfortable, and given openly without restraint or embarrassment. It's the way my Sparky dog put his head on my lap when he knew I was down. It's the way I connect with Tyler when he apologizes and tells me he really wants to be clean, and that he is tired of disappointing me. I have to believe it. There is something. I feel it. I have come to know it. But not yet. This realization did not come until much, much later. I had more to learn still.

Merry f*$king Christmas, Christmas Day, 2016

Christmas Eve, which Tyler usually spent with his dad's family, was relatively smooth, as far as family drama goes. Other than Tyler arriving two and a half hours late to his grandparent's house for their traditional Christmas Eve party. His dad had told me he had looked good, clean, and had helped his Grandmother Carolyn clean up the kitchen. We had all been worried, because Thanksgiving had been disastrous. Not only had he shown up late then, but he had also been high, and had sat in a chair the whole time withdrawn from the others, even his twin cousins, with whom he had previously been close, and who were back from college for the holidays. Everyone was furious, but were willing to give him another chance on Christmas Eve.

Chapter 6: Let God and Let Go

Are you staying at our house
tomorrow after your grandparent's
party at 8? If you can drive to REI
parking lot, I can pick you up. If I
know time. I'm worried about snow.

> I can do that, or make it easier for you and just
> go back to my place that night, then hang out
> with you guys Christmas Day by meeting up with
> you to go down to Grandpa's together, and then I
> could spend the night of Christmas at your guys'
> place. It would be easier for you and I like it.

I don't want you to be alone. We are not
picking up girls 'till 11:30 on Christmas
and heading down to Grandpa's.

> I'll make sure I spend it with people not alone

Ok. If you are alright with it.
Who is not with family though?

> It should be fine. Alex moved
> out and I get his room now

That's good I guess. You ok with it?
You're not planning party are you?

> Good idea

161

Don't be like that. I'm trying to help

Mom I'm always joking

You don't need to get kicked out again

I wouldn't

Christmas Eve at the Watkins' household was always a good, yet stressful, time. Tyler's Grandma Carolyn's cooking skills were often the main focus, and everyone looked forward to the gourmet meal and lovely presentation that was always sure to come. There would be little tags near the plates where the guests were expected to sit, and gorgeous seasonal place settings with niceties such as antique Ironstone Transferware dishes. Every detail of the meal was considered days in advance, to the point that the hostess would get so worked up in creating perfection that it was almost difficult to be there. This was not an event where one could arrive late without great offense to the hostess. Tyler had been working all day on a dirty, difficult job for a friend of mine, then had experienced some car trouble, so being late was somewhat unavoidable, but two and a half hours really couldn't be excused by any stretch of my codependent mind. He drove himself home after the gathering at his grandparents', and was to spend the night at his apartment alone, because his roommates had gone home for the holidays and there was a snowstorm that night, making it difficult for him to drive up Parley's Canyon to Oakley, or for us to drive down and get him. It had all been discussed after Winter storm warnings had been heard on the news and holiday plans were being scheduled. On Christmas Day Matt and I would pick up the girls from their mom's in Jeremy Ranch, at eleven thirty, on our way down the canyon to Salt Lake. Then, we would pick up Tyler, and proceed down to my dad's in Alpine for brunch and festivities. Chris and I had spoken a few times via text on Christmas Eve, but it was not until long after the party was over that he texted that it went fairly well, saying that he felt that Tyler was in good spirits. About the same time, Tyler responded to my sixth text, saying he was fine.

I was feeling badly that we did not have Tyler come up somehow and wake up with us on Christmas morning. I was missing the nostalgia of early morning presents under the tree and the all night, restless anticipation of kids waiting for daylight. Our house was too quiet with just me, Matt, and the dogs. We were taking care of Chester for Chris and Dee, as their dog had just had surgery, and a hyper Jack Russell Terrier was too much for him to handle. I thought it would be good to have Tyler and his dog together when he came up at Christmas.

Christmas Day, 9:34 am (from me to Tyler):

Merry Christmas! we will pick you up around noon

Can you meet us at REI parking lot at 12? We will fill your tank

You alive?

Hello?????

Answer the damn phone! so inconsiderate

Christmas Day, 9:37 am (between Chris and me):

> You have Tyler figured out for the day?

I can't get in touch. He's not answering.
Have u spoken? We want to meet at
REI parking lot

> me either

> Super worried. Probably no roommates there either

He won't answer

> What time are you guys heading into the valley?

Planning on picking Tyler up at 12, but I have
received very little communication in 2 days.
We were thinking of stopping at St. Marks to
see Phil on way to my dad's. He has broken
ribs and punctured lung from his accident.

> That sucks. I have tried Tyler for last hour. He was
> in good spirits last night. Just don't know where
> his head is. He agreed that it would be good to be
> with your family today.

Chapter 6: Let God and Let Go

**Christmas Day, 11:30 am, multiple phone calls are made to Tyler.
Text messages between me and Chris:**

> You may have to go to his place and knock on door.

That's what I'm afraid of

You in town at all?

> No. Maybe a police welfare check is needed?

I think you are right…please let me know what they tell you

> You have his address. I need it.

Let me try and find it.

Here it is: 312 I Street #2

> I'm going there

K

What's going on?

Confessions of a Heroin Addict's Mother

Chris calls. Too much to say in a text. Tyler's door was unlocked so Chris had barged into the little studio. His roommates were gone. Tyler lay in bed with a heavily tattooed and pierced girl. An octopus tattooed across her exposed breasts. Someone's daughter, away from her family on Christmas as well. Her parents, probably looking for her. Heroin, used needles, and clothing were strewn about the room. Chris still wanted to have the police come and do a wellness check.

"Call and don't tell them that I went in, so they go in and see the drugs. It's the only way he can get help, get clean."

We are going to pick up my step-daughter, Jamie, despite the chaos, right on schedule, as I comply with Chris and call 911. As I explain the situation to dispatch, I pretend that I don't know that Chris already knows Tyler's alive. The officer calls to ask the details of the situation. Why we were concerned. I crammed a couple of years of worry into a thirty-second call. He was a heroin addict. He was depressed and threatening to kill himself, had nearly died a couple times, and he wasn't answering, though he knew the holiday plans. The officer said he would call me when he got there.

Tyler came to the door for the police. The officer hadn't felt like Tyler was impaired enough to warrant a search of the apartment. I couldn't tell him I knew there were drugs all over the place, because it was a wellness check. He was only there to see if he was alive. No help from the police, yet again. If my son were black, he'd have been arrested long ago.

I was beyond angry. Tyler called me, furious that we had called the police. He said his dad had just seen a little box of drugs or something, that he shouldn't have overreacted. Yeah, there was a girl in his bed. He had just overslept. We should cut him some slack. His phone is glitchy, and sometimes doesn't work. He was sleeping in, like a normal person would on Christmas. All the excuses I had heard, and heard, and heard again. I called my dad to tell him we were still coming, determined not to let Tyler ruin another holiday. I had warned my dad earlier that we had another drama-fest on our hands today, and that we might not make it, before I had even known whether or not Tyler was alive.

166

Chapter 6: Let God and Let Go

Text messages between me and Tyler, 12:39 pm:

Merry fucking Christmas. I'm out

I won't be responsible for your
drug use. I'm not the reason

You're not the reason, but stress is caused by your constant
speculation. I had a girl over. Dad saw a box. That's it. There
weren't drugs everywhere. I'll send you a picture if you like,
but I know you don't care. It was really important to me to
spend this Christmas with my family, since last year that wasn't
the case. You know I have problems with drugs. Is it really
necessary to make me feel even worse about being addicted
to this? It's awful. I don't want to keep doing it, but I don't know
what to do anymore. Now with no support from anyone in my
family, I can't go to outpatient, I can't pay this next month's
rent, and I'm going to be in a terrible position. You and Dad
cause so much tension in my life when I really am trying to
figure things out. A week ago I was really considering being
done with my life, considering all of the things that have been
screwed up the past years. I don't know what I'm going to
do now. I'm in a terrible position. If you're worried about me
being dead, then why would you now put me in a position
where I would rather be dead? Just consider your reactions
to things. I don't have any family to talk to. Tell me why I
shouldn't kill myself now. I have zero reason to be around
anymore. Nothing. I doubt I'll even get an answer to this text.
But when I don't answer the phone because I'm asleep, and
or my phone's dead, you guys have a conniption fit and call
the cops. But I can't even get you to not hang up on me on the
phone. It's actually comical that you don't even listen to me on
the phone and always hang up when you get called out. It's
crazy how you and Dad believe that you can do no wrong, and
are some of the most hypocritical people I know. I don't know
what you want me to do honestly. Give me one reason why I
shouldn't kill myself

Confessions of a Heroin Addict's Mother

If you were serious about seeing your family on Christmas you might have been more concerned when arrangements were being made and actually answered your phone. Instead, you caused me to worry and didn't respond. Another Christmas ruined for me too.

My phone turns off by itself randomly. Not my fault. I slept in like a normal person and didn't realize it wasn't working. No need to call the cops. I thought my phone was on, I'm sorry about that.

I went on with my Christmas plans like a normal person

I tried to enjoy my family, but after that it really was impossible. I had my husband and step-daughter to consider, as well as what all of this drama was doing to our little family. I was going through the motions. Looking for ways to help in the kitchen to distract me. So tired of the status quo. I had really been hoping Tyler would be here. He hadn't been to my dad's for over a year and my dad, without a prompt, had called Tyler last week to let him know that he would be welcome and without judgement. I appreciated the gesture and I had believed that Tyler did too.

A couple hours went by and he quit responding to my texts after he sent the texts about there being no reason he shouldn't kill himself. Again, I had heard it hundreds of times. It was his way to manipulate me, and it always worked.

You There?

Chapter 6: Let God and Let Go

You alive?

????

When I didn't hear from him, I copied and forwarded all of his last texts to Chris. Our conversation:

Text messages between me and Chris:

Tyler called me a couple hours ago screaming at me for 20 minutes about how he's going to kill himself and how we've ruined his life

I hung up on him. I simply can't take any more of it. We then texted back and forth until he said he had no reason to live, and quit responding.

If he continues to threaten suicide, call the police. They have to respond. We'll both call and harass the police until they actually find a way to enter his apartment. He needs to be arrested. We can't have him selling drugs and living this nightmare. It has to stop. If you don't hear anything from him and you are in fear, call the police again. They can write a parking ticket or maybe help a dying kid.

He hasn't written anything for hours

Confessions of a Heroin Addict's Mother

> Call the police. Tell them he threatened suicide. That girl that is with him may be underage. They can ask to see her. We can call the police on a 3 way call, too.

Have you spoken with him?

> No. I tried to text again. No response.

I just tried too. Can you call? I can't deal with this.

> Send me the police number you called.

I called 911. The number of the cop was an unknown caller and I tried to call it and it didn't go through.

Weston just got home from Hawaii. He's trying to text him.

> Maybe he can help?

He's trying to text

Did you call the cops?

Chapter 6: Let God and Let Go

No I'm at family dinner.

Ok- I called. Cops on way

ok. sorry

hang in there.

His car's there. They can't get into apartment.
They said it looked like nobody is there
when they looked in windows. Didn't answer
Weston's text. What's property mgr. #

Ferdinand: 555-555–5432. He's in middle room.

You realize he will be thrown out?

Yep. He needs jail

Trying to hide from my parents right now…my
mom can't handle anymore. Did they get in?

Not that I've heard. We haven't even done
xmas yet. Kenzie is coming over for first
time in 6 months to try and patch things up
with her dad. Way too much drama for me.

Confessions of a Heroin Addict's Mother

Shit

I feel like I should go down there but I won't be able to get in either.

Send Weston. Have them break the door.

Cops won't break door. Already asked. Weston got home from trip a couple hours ago and is at a Christmas dinner.

Tell them we think he is dead

They can call paramedics. They'll break it down

I can call 911 and demand paramedics

Just got off phone. Cop can't do anything. I may have to go break door myself

Let me try my brother Tommy

Good idea

Cop said a threatening message didn't constitute enough evidence to warrant breaking door.

Chapter 6: Let God and Let Go

> Tommy is heading there to break door. Give me address. Can't find it again.

I think they are already gone…have to call dispatch then give message to give officer 162 I street #2

> Tommy will be there in 5

801-555-5555 Case number 16-2349281

Kenzie just got here. We haven't seen her since the wedding.

> I just called 911

Police spoke with him and called me, didn't have reason to arrest. Didn't see anything and can't search without consent. Can only recommend he get help. Tyler didn't want psych counseling.

> They are there with Tommy. They are struggling to find anything to allow entry into his room. RIDICULOUS!!!!!!

I know!!! The officer called me!

We can't even manage to get this kid arrested to save his life! The officer asked what my primary concern was, a wellness check to see if he was alive, or to get him arrested. I said both, but he said there were no grounds for him to do a search without Tyler's consent. His uncle, Tommy, had

173

Confessions of a Heroin Addict's Mother

been there and made Tyler take off his socks to show the officers where he had been injecting into his toes.

I texted him a final message before I went to bed:

Glad the worst Christmas ever has come to an end. When are you going to decide that your lifestyle is not working out for you? Oh… and safety inspection must be done this week and proof brought up to Park City DMV. I'm not dealing with it this time but if it's not done, I'll sell car at end of week as it's in my name and it will be ticketed. And, you're driving high on my insurance! You should have money from that construction project, if you didn't shoot it up your arm. oh…and I didn't tell you I had a bad mammogram that needs to be rechecked this week…Just so you know

Ok listen and think like a normal sane human for a sec. My phone was off. I didn't hear it. And I slept in. I didn't mean to do that. I actually really wanted to spend Christmas with my family considering last year's was not ideal. But sadly, that sleeping in caused worry. Worry which I understand based on my past. But the worry of if I'm alive or not tends to get old. Especially when half the texts I get from you are asking me that very question. It makes me really sad. So when your 18 year old son, who was basically shunned or looked down upon by both sides of the family (at least somewhat), doesn't wake up on time because of his phone for a gathering of people that very well could judge him (although it was meaningful to me anyway), it really makes me feel even more shunned and unaccepted when you guys tell me I am the only one who ruined Christmas. Think about how I feel for one second. None of you ever do and I'm done with it…peace sign.

Chapter 6: Let God and Let Go

If you look back on your texts, my first one this
morning was a merry Christmas with excitement
to see you...the "are you alive" texts came after
multiple texts remained not answered.

> Because I'm tired of it. You and dad are the main
> reason I want to kill myself in the first place most of
> the time because you cause some bullshit like that.

We caused? I was trying to make arrangements
to get you to us so we could spend a nice
Christmas together! What was I supposed to do?

The deal we had talked about on Saturday was that I would
pick you up at 12 to go to Grandpa's. Up until 11:55 neither your
dad nor I knew if you were alive. When you don't answer both
people's attempts ALL morning to call and text on Christmas
we start asking if you were ok the night before? Were you in
good spirits? did you get a wad of money from work and go on
a binge? Are your roommates around? Are you lonely? Every
scary thing for a parent to think...how did you expect us to act?
We've only ever wanted you healthy and happy. That's it.

You can blame us all you want but the only one who can
fix this is you. Take yourself over to LDS and check into
ER to detox. Then you can figure yourself out, off the shit.

Worrying about whether you are alive tends to get
old for us, too. However, it is a valid concern, ...
and your dad's visit confirmed all fears.

175

Confessions of a Heroin Addict's Mother

I finally drift off to sleep and get a call at 11:30 p.m. from Tyler. All of this is my fault. He didn't want me to hang up on him. Wanted me to hear him out. The girl was the only one who listened. She probably just needed the drugs that he provided to her. He said we had ruined his life. He had wanted to spend time with family for Christmas. We had somehow made that impossible. I hung up. I couldn't listen any more to how I had ruined his life. How this was all mine and Chris's fault? How we were not normal people, normal parents.

I lay in bed steaming about his call and texted him:

> And the reminder about avoiding the ticket by finishing car registration was valid, too. You did not do the first part after 20 reminders, and I was pretty sure the safety wasn't gonna get done this week. I have a lot on MY plate and trying to get another diagnostic mammogram done this week before my insurance runs out and I have to pay $400 out of pocket…oh, and worrying about you AND about if I have breast cancer. Oh, but this is all about you isn't it?

I probably did not need to include the part about the mammogram, though it was true. He didn't even respond to that part anyways. The kid was too selfish for a guilt-trip to be an effective manipulation. I text him again, unable to sleep.

> And both families were excited to see you and they were opening their arms to you. They only want to see you healthy.

> Didn't Grandpa Arnold even call you unprompted with an invite?

176

Chapter 6: Let God and Let Go

So what's your plan to fix this?

I'm afraid to ask if you're ok, 'cause
that bothers you. Would you please let
me know what you are going to do for
yourself to get better? We don't need
blame. We need solutions.

No response. I will have to go to bed wondering if he did something
to himself. Exhausted.

At 3:55 am he texts:

> I was in bed asleep. Ya know what gets old? a mom who
> freaks out every morning about if I'm dead. Stop doing it
> please. No more asking if I'm ok. At this point I'm either dead
> or you don't need to worry about it. I love the hell out of ya
> but I'm so done with all of you. If I lose my apartment over
> the bullshit event, that also ruined my holiday that was so
> important to me. Just think about what you are doing to me.

You want a relationship but you want it on your terms.
You can't expect a normal relationship with your family
or anyone else while you are using. Your choice

Ferdinand called me. The kind Romanian property manager. The
stern but reasonable man we had chuckled over regarding his manner-
isms a couple months before, as he had showed us the tiny studio with
the shared kitchen and bath in which Tyler now lived.

"I met you when you and Tyler looked at this apartment to rent, and
I wanted to express a concern. Sometimes young men start to stray like
Tyler's roommate that we just got rid of. They start to smoke pot and

177

things like that. I think Tyler is doing that and much worse, and I just thought you would want to know. I like him. He's a good kid. I'm just worried about this kind of thing following him." He didn't say how he knew, or mention the police calling him on Christmas to get in for a wellness check. He was very kind and didn't threaten to evict, just expressed concern. I really appreciated the call, though he wasn't telling me about something I could control.

The very same day, I had to move a bunch of boxes out of my storage unit and into Matt's as we consolidated our storage spaces into one. There were eight or so boxes still in Matt's storage from one of the times Tyler had been thrown out of his apartment. I'm not sure if it was from the first or second eviction. The boxes held scattered remains of things he had cast off, didn't need, or didn't have room for. Mismatched socks, random dishes, school uniforms, mementos of a seemingly forgotten yet fairly recent life. Self-portraits from before, when he still depicted himself as presentable and handsome, and portraits of friends he had drawn in art class, study hall, or while they were hanging out. I had not seen any recent self-portraits, but wondered how he would depict himself now?

Chapter 6: Let God and Let Go

Matt and I needed a break from a stressful Christmas and from Matt's busy work season, so we decided to head to Jackson Hole for the New Year weekend. Matt drove, and I texted Tyler to follow up with him about my conversation with Ferdinand, and to remind him that the safety inspection needed to be done on his car to complete the registration. Something I had reminded him many times already.

Thursday, December 29, before leaving on trip:

Going to Jackson 'til Monday. Did you get car safety inspection?

Like I've said…you need to get safety inspection. I usually go to place on 3300 S. and Highland…then the certificate needs to be brought in to the DMV…not sure if it needs to be Park City or can be SLC, take that thing from window in with you. You might have to make a couple calls. It's in my name and I'm not sure if you can take it in or if it has to be me. Call and ask. I'm gone 'til Tuesday, and it's due on 31st so tomorrow is it, that's why I wanted you to take care of it yesterday when you weren't working and I was able to help you…your deal. Not mine.

?????

It will be closed Monday. Has Ferdinand threatened to kick u out? He said he made Alex leave cause he was smoking weed and he said he thinks you are doing way worse.

He's worried about you.

179

Confessions of a Heroin Addict's Mother

> No Ferdinand hasn't threatened anything. They're doing a small remodel of the layout of our unit to make Alex's old room bigger because there's a totally useless hallway that could be taken out and it'll make the room a bit bigger. They're also fixing the heaters cuz they do not work at all. I'm surviving with the space heater. Ferdinand was calling today cuz he wanted to see if I wanted to move into the room in the unit next door while they fix the heaters in my room cuz apparently they need to jack up a bunch of shit. Did he say something to you?

> He did not make Alex leave either. He and Alex went into my room together without asking a few weeks ago without letting me know and I'm sure something like paraphernalia was out. It says in the contract that the landlord is allowed to go into the shared space, but personal rooms they're supposed to at least let the tenant know. Ferdinand wouldn't kick me out, I'm pretty sure about that, but Amy would for sure. Alex smoked weed in the house and didn't even open a window or anything, with his door and the door to outside wide open. And then he left, leaving me in the house smelling from his weed and Amy and Ferdinand came into our building. She said if it happened again she would kick us out.

I'm so confused as to why he thinks that getting caught is the only thing that he did wrong. Contracts, protocol, denial, denial, denial. This is all someone else's problem. Someone other than him had done something wrong to threaten his lifestyle. As though he had a right to get away with this because he was smarter than everyone. I mean...the audacity of smoking weed and leaving the windows closed! If Alex was just smart like him and quietly shooting heroin, he wouldn't be doing anything to get them in trouble! He was talking to me like I was a buddy and he needed my help hiding his shit from the authorities. Telling me Ferdinand, "might have seen something," as though I'm cool enough with it to be in on his deception.

Chapter 6: Let God and Let Go

Ferdinand mentioned he was worried you were doing worse than weed. Hate to see you get kicked out.

Yeah I would too. Hmmmmmmmmm

What's your plan for change? This living on the edge has to change

You mentioned NA meetings. Have you started?

No answer.

The Ideal Mother
CHAPTER 7

Friday, December 30,2016, on the drive to Jackson Hole, Wyoming, 11:09 am:

Did your insurance card come in the mail?
From Sunday that is your insurance.

We got a call from Matt's Uncle Charlie on the way to Jackson that Matt needed to call the care center in which his mother lived in North Carolina. Matt called and spoke to her nurse who had no idea that she had a son, partly because of his mother's dementia, and partly because he never called her. Or, at least, he had not called her since he and I met. She had suffered from many health problems for years, and my husband's relationship with her was anything but good. Matt had been primarily raised by his Aunt Brenda and Uncle Charlie. His mother had first sent him to her mother when he was three, but he was soon sent to his mom's sister, Brenda, because his grandmother was unable to care for the spirited, young Matt. He went back to his mom's from fourth through sixth grade, because Brenda and Charlie were struggling with him acting out, and they felt like he needed to be with a biological parent. When he was back with his mother, he had run away a couple of times, recalling that he had slept on the commuter train, and below a stairway. They lived above a bar in Cleveland, and Matt never felt very secure there, with her. He could hear the music, lyrics and all, pounding below their floor. The roof leaked when it rained. I had made the mistake of referring to some place as the "hood" once and was quickly corrected. Matt knew "the hood," as he had

182

Chapter 7: The Ideal Mother

really lived in it. I admit that I had struggled in my life at times, but I did not know what "the hood" really looked or felt like.

His mother had offered him drugs at some point. What kind of mother does that? I've spent the last five years trying to shelter my boy from drugs. This was all of Matt's story about his relationship with his mom that I knew. I was not really privy to much more information than that, perhaps because he didn't want to remember, or because he didn't feel it important to tell me of his memories of his mother. Perhaps he didn't have many to tell. No stories of outings or events. No favorite meals or holiday gatherings. Maybe he is just too private to share. He did tell me that after sixth grade, he had wanted to go live with his dad in Indiana, though he had very little to do with him for most of his life prior to that. I don't believe that he ever found his "place" in that family either; wedged between step and half-siblings that he hadn't grown up with. He left there to join the Air Force at seventeen, introducing him to Utah where he would return to settle; searching for his family in the military, a fraternity, then eventually, through trial and error, with me.

The nurse felt like Matt's mother was nearing the end and that we should come and see her immediately. She had shared the labs indicating that her kidney dialysis was not working, and it was causing her a lot of pain to transport her to get the dialysis. She wanted permission to stop dialysis and start hospice care. We made reservations to fly there the following Thursday. I really wanted to meet her before she passed, partly to have an understanding of where Matt came from, and partly to be more a part of his life. We were to stay through Sunday and visit with his Uncle Charlie who, with his wife Brenda before she passed, had been more of a parent to Matt than anyone.

Friday, 8:44 pm message to Tyler:

How u doin?

??????

Confessions of a Heroin Addict's Mother

> I'm fine!

Ok! It's nice when you respond

Oh…and in case u wondered (I'm guessing not since you didn't ask) my second mammogram was fine yesterday. No cancer

Saturday, December 31, 9:35 am after a tense phone call:

> Mom I'm just so anxious at this point I don't even know what to do. I've got a ton on my mind here, cut me a little slack.

That doesn't change the fact that things need to get done and I can't do it all. Your insurance changes today and u haven't even told me if your card has come and u don't answer my texts so I stay up all night worrying. It would suck to lose your car but I can't do anything about it and parked in the street it will surely get ticketed. I'm trying to help you avoid problems.

I just get so sad 'cause some days you're nice, and positive, and looking for change and others you're just rude to those who care the most

> I don't know what to fucking do about it. My whole life is falling apart in front of my eyes and I'm on the brink of totally losing it.

Chapter 7: The Ideal Mother

I wish I knew how to help…everything I've tried
hasn't been helpful. You need to decide for yourself
to do something and commit to a program. Close
your eyes and visualize who you want to be…

What happened to all the positivity from the other day
when you told me u were starting NA with friend and
helping another dude out that was heading down the
wrong path? Can you go to Odyssey today?

> I'm unhappy regardless of what I do.
> But even more so when I'm trying to get
> clean, I know the bad feelings will still
> be there no matter what

You probably need to give it more time…you
keep defeating yourself by using again. You need
counseling and a mentor to get through hard feelings

> Yeah I just don't want to have to pay for all that
> shit cuz it's so expensive and has never worked
> out. I'm just going to get screwed like always.
> No way my car door not working will allow me to
> pass inspection. I've looked it up a ton.

Don't know what to say about car. Not like we
wouldn't find resources to help with rehab and
like we said Odyssey is sliding scale.

That means it's based on how much you make.

185

Confessions of a Heroin Addict's Mother

Saturday, December 31, 2:59 pm:

And NA is free. So is Refuge Recovery

What happened to New Years being a clean start?

Not sure why you don't answer?

Saturday, December 31, New Year's Eve, 5:01 pm:

I don't text much. I'm alright. I do want to be clean this next year. It's my goal. It's just going to be very, very difficult

It is going to be very difficult. But possible. I'm behind you and will do what I can to support you staying clean. I love you more than you can know and want you to be happy more than anything. Surround yourself with those who will make it easier. You have a lot of good friends and people who care.

Thanks mom. I love you more than you know as well. I really want this

<3

Chapter 7: The Ideal Mother

If you REALLY want it...the finances, friends, and other struggles will fall into place. Maybe writing down your goals and plans for this NEW YEAR would make it a good resolution. There is a comet passing right now, to the left of the moon. A sign of a good year to come!

Monday, January 1, 2017:

How's it going?

> Going just fine mother how are thee? I'm really glad you don't have cancer. That sucks about Mike's mom being near the end though and my grandpa with Alzheimer's has me thinking I could likely be in the same boat down the road. My health problems I have at this age are terrifying. I can't imagine what they could be like when I'm older if I continued fucking with this stuff it'll be not good.

For sure...glad you are coming to that realization. I think I'm gonna start going to Sunday Refuge meeting instead of church if you're interested in going with. I have a bunch of goals and resolutions this year. Finding some peace is one of them.

Tuesday, January 2, on the drive home from Jackson:

We got word on the way home that Mike's mom passed away

> I'm so sorry

187

> He had a pretty strained relationship with her as
> she was far from an ideal mom, but still his mom.

I don't know what an ideal mom is though I'm certain that I am far from it despite having made an effort at conscious parenting. I wonder how someone could have turned out as wonderful as Matt. Do we turn out great because of, or in spite of, our parents? Despite being bounced around between various family members, Matt was an overachiever. High school student body president, Airman Of The Year in his Air Force squadron, President of his fraternity, night school during the Air Force, business school, MBA, and now, a successful business owner in Park City.

He did not have the private schooling and supportive family that Tyler had. Tyler had had everything. Is parenting a crap shoot? Had I perhaps done too much? Was I a helicopter parent who meddled too much? Would letting Tyler raise himself have provided a better outcome?

I had my phone playlist connected to the car and the old Irish tune Peggy Gordon came on. It reminded me of the person that has been most motherly to me in my life. My dear friend Kate had been in a little bluegrass group with me when I lived near Jackson so many years ago. She was a thoughtful listener and a writer. We had a connection far greater than I ever experienced with my own mother. For the first time in my life, at the age of twenty-seven, I could feel that bond that I had never felt before. She was the mother I wanted to be, and had wanted to have. "Peggy Gordon" was a song that we usually finished our Thursday night potluck and music nights with. Her husband Alan would sing it and Kate would play the sad fiddle part.

Peggy Gordon (Traditional)

"Oh Peggy Gordon, you are my darling
Come sit you down upon my knee
and tell to me, the very reason
that I am slighted so by thee" …

Matt was solemn after the news, and he shared stories he had not told me before about his mom as we drove in the snow back toward home. In the way that music touches the soul at just the right moment,

Chapter 7: The Ideal Mother

Townes Van Zandt's "To Live is to Fly" came up next, the lyrics so poetically describing life's struggles by an artist so gifted yet painfully challenged in life. Townes suffered from addiction and bipolar disorder and died at fifty-three, from complications of a troubled existence. Perhaps his pain helped our souls connect on some level.

There were a couple days between getting home from Jackson and leaving to North Carolina for Matt to make arrangements for the cremation and for our visit. This would be the first time I would meet the uncle who had been the most influential in raising him, as well as Matt's cousin that I had never heard of, though they were raised together. We stayed in his uncle's guest room, in his comfortable home in the suburbs. I regretted that I never did get to meet his mother.

I was trying to gain an understanding of Matt's family...pieced together like a worn, old, crazy quilt. Some parts threadbare and missing, others parts consisting of beautiful, rich, threads of colorful embroidery, holding the pieces of fabric together for dear life.

We drove to the funeral home and picked up the ashes contained in a beautiful mahogany box. Matt was clearly emotional, which was rare. I never asked if he was sad that she was gone or sad that she was never really there for him. It was probably both. We then went to the nursing home to collect her belongings. Everything was contained inside two medium-sized cardboard boxes that the orderly pulled from the back room. We drove back to Uncle Charlie's house and Matt slowly went through the contents, as though moving slowly would make them seem more grand or sentimental. It mostly contained comfortable clothing and a couple of ugly straw fall decorative scarecrows that Charlie had said were adorning her room when he had visited her recently. There was some loose change. I watched Matt slowly count the pile of pennies on the floor. His inheritance: ninety-three cents.

Universally, people save the photo album when they have a short time to vacate a house in an impending disaster. Happy reminders of time well spent. At Charlie's house, there were many hours of pouring through photo albums to find those reminders for Matt, followed by a trip to Walgreens to make copies of the pictures. Which will we copy to keep? The decision was easy, as there were only about five of Matt's mom. None with both her and Matt together. We did find her high school senior portrait with her beautiful, sultry, over the shoulder gaze. I could

189

see her in Matt's daughter, Kenzie. The picture was from 1962. We had it restored and put on the pretty box with her ashes, which flew home with us amongst our carry-ons. The ugly straw dolls would sit next to the box on our fireplace mantel at home with the pennies that were put into a roll. A tribute to distant mothers and ugly dolls.

We braved the weather in North Carolina. Matt's uncle was lovely, but after a few days, we needed a real cup of coffee and a little alone time. There was an inch of snow one day and the state practically closed down and was sent into a state of emergency. That was ok. It made the coffee shop really quiet as we caught up on emails, Facebook, and a little work. I was interrupted by a call from a Utah number that I didn't recognize. That always sends a little panicked flutter into my heart. For good reason. It was Tyler's property manager, Amy. She worked with Ferdinand, the Romanian landlord. She wanted Tyler to move out of his apartment. She was aware of illegal activity that was going on in his unit and they wouldn't have it. Other people in the building had complained. She said he had until the end of the month, but hoped it would be sooner. I told her that he was an adult and he was on his own for this one. Thank God I didn't put myself on the lease. I had known better at that point. This would be his third eviction this year. Four treatment centers and three evictions. I had told him I would not move him if he lost this apartment, and I planned to keep my word.

Hallmarks
Hallmarks of a caring mother;
Acts selflessly
Puts others first
Is helpful
Offers advice

Hallmarks of a codependent mother;
Acts selflessly
Puts others first
Is helpful
Offers advice

Eva Summerhill

To Help or Not to Help
CHAPTER 8

I've always been a person of action. Busy. Productive. I don't like states of limbo, unfinished business, or gray areas. I don't like waiting or wondering what's going on. Patience is not one of my virtues. But mostly, I don't like not being able to fix something, or feeling ineffective. Why the hell can I not fix this? Be more influential? Say the right thing? In a group, I usually become the leader. I set the tone, rules, and policies. When I am interviewed, I usually get the job. But I have to sit back and watch my kid slowly kill himself. I'm told if I do anything I'm enabling him, taking the ability to realize he has power to change away. I'm thinking this week will be it. He can't sustain this much longer. It's a waiting game to see when he has reached HIS bottom. Not mine. I'm sitting here in the same restaurant, the same seat, where two Novembers ago we were planning his kidnapping, when we were still thinking we had some ability to change him. Nothing's changed, it's only gotten worse. I have lived in a suspended state of grief for nearly two years. When someone dies, you grieve. You never fully get over it but it does not disable you for years the way watching a serious addict does. You try to hold on to hope but it gets dashed with every relapse. I came across a poem that explained it perfectly;

I had my own notion of grief

I thought it was the sad time

That followed the death of

Someone you love.

And you had to push through it.

To get to the other side.

There is no pushing through.

But rather,

There is an absorption.

Adjustment.

Acceptance,

And grief is not something you complete,

But rather,

you endure.

Grief is not a task to finish

And move on.

But an element of yourself-

An alteration of your being.

A new way of seeing.

A new definition of Self.

Gwen Flowers

I watch the high school kids from Skyline stream in on their lunch break. Healthy, bright-eyed, smiling. What if I send Tyler my journal on all of this? These notes? Our letters back and forth from his time in the wilderness? The things he said. The pain and worry we've experienced. That's not enabling is it? To let him see how we are consumed and obsessed by this? Guilt trips absolutely don't work. But maybe seeing his own words will? Seeing the promises, the gratitude, the desire for change?? He knows I'm writing a book and is angry about it, though I'm changing the names. There is no risk of exposing him, except to himself. Anyway, to change the names is only a formality. All of our reputations

Chapter 8: To Help or Not to Help

are shit at this point. Damn autocorrect. Changed "shot" to "shit," but I'll keep it...It's more accurate.

I need to write this book for my sanity. For me, putting my thoughts on paper invites a different kind of scrutiny or inspection. Objectifies things. I can form an opinion of what's going on as though my own actions are someone else's. It takes me out of myself and transforms me, into the observer, documenter, and finally, narrator. It's much easier to inspect another person's life than one's own life, and in writing about this, it's as though I'm looking at another person.

At some point, I have an epiphany. My ENTIRE happiness has been based on my saddest child's happiness. I am the very definition of codependence. I have failed to connect to any kind of higher power that might take this burden from me. My pride has taken my ability to give my child the freedom to do for himself what he is fully capable of. I have robbed him of that by shaming him, and holding on to the false assumption that I have the ability to control his actions. I have robbed myself of my ability to feel joy outside of this horrible cycle of dependence. I have robbed my husband, other family, and friends of my full availability to them. I have held back my commitment to them out of my unnatural addiction to feeling like I can control Tyler.

Confessions of a Heroin Addict's Mother

Texts to Tyler after seeing John, and going to my first Renaissance Ranch meeting;

I just wanted to tell you I went to a parent support group (like an Al-Anon meeting) at Renaissance Ranch last night. Pretty "Mormony," but not in a bad way at all. I went with the attitude to just take what I could use (which was a lot) and leave behind what I couldn't (which was a little). I just want to tell you that I'm so sorry if I've ever made you feel ashamed. I know that addiction makes you feel enough shame yourself, and I regret it that I have added to that. As far as MY boundaries go...I have to have them, which means I will support your RECOVERY in any way I can, but I will not support your addiction. I will also not take away the ability you have to help yourself by doing for you what you are capable of doing yourself, which is so much more than you think. Let me know how I can help you in your recovery. I was encouraged last night, as the couple that owns Renaissance led the group. Their 2 sons run the place. Both of them are recovering heroin addicts, 7 and 8 years clean. One of them was in jail 13 times before getting clean. There is HOPE! I believe in you.

Also, John my therapist told me about a treatment place called the Haven on South Temple and 10th East. You would need to detox first but it is based on income like Odyssey.

I don't know Mom. I'm so stressed out about everything. I have no idea what to do.

Maybe start by detoxing at LDS. You may need to get on a list for Odyssey or the Haven. Why don't you find out details and go from there. You can't continue living like this

Chapter 8: To Help or Not to Help

I received no response from this text for days, which felt more like weeks. Then I got a message from Chris, that Tyler had divulged to him that he had been arrested in Pioneer Park for heroin possession a while back, and was given a court date for February 14. It was strange that I felt some relief from hearing this. All I had heard from Chris for the last week or so was that Tyler was communicating with him, but he was very down and sounding suicidal. He had no hope. Perhaps some jail time would do a couple things: 1) get him detoxed, and 2) give him a safe place to live and some supervision, as well as, hopefully, some kind of AA groups or other counseling. A low, low bar had been set when jail looked like a hopeful option.

Tyler finally texted that he needed his data turned back on. He had not been receiving messages from me because they were coming as i-messages. I had mistaken his lack of response to my messages as something completely different. I re-sent a weeks worth of messages, including a reminder about The Haven, which he said he would check out on their website. I encouraged him to just go in and talk to them. A website doesn't give anyone a real picture. He needed to engage.

A New Year
CHAPTER 9

January 25, 2017

When I'm having a difficult time within my own family, I find that I'm unable to focus on anything outside of that. Politics, disasters, and current events are all dwarfed by my obsession with controlling what's near. I can only move outside of my circle when my circle is round and smooth. This era was different though. "The Year of the Woman." "#MeToo." With pussy grabbing politicians and the makers of Hollywood being flipped on their misogynistic dicks, I couldn't possibly stay home. I marched with my sisters. Marched with my husband. Marched with my dog. Knitted lots of pink pussy hats. Wore a pussy hat, and lamented the election of someone so crass and corrupt to our highest office. I was deeply disturbed by where this country was going. Backwards.

Chapter 9: A New Year

Earth Mother

I am only a vessel
My body bound to the Earth Mother and time
My hips rounded like hers for carrying

She tells me every twenty-eight spins when I have not fulfilled my duty
Bleed Dear, with the pain of seeds wasted
Lost children along with part of you
Your lining

I fulfill my duty
Succumb to the intrusion
Carry the seed deep within my mother hips
Three quarters of my mother's journey around her sun

Cord severed, I hold him outside rather than in
Still connected at my breast
Nourishing him from my body
My soul

Weaned but yet I yearn to nurture
My very reason for being
I'm told to deny my connection
Let him find his way

Fifty times around her sun
Earth Mother reminds me that I am no longer useful
At night, by the witness of her moon
She tries to burn me

I feel the heat and sweat
My body shape left in a puddle where I had slept,
along with a little of my soul
Reminding me that I am no longer needed
And I should just let go

Eva Summerhill

197

Confessions of a Heroin Addict's Mother

How you doing?

Good Mom how are you?

Great. Had a fun day at the Capitol. You would have enjoyed it...thousands of women screaming from the rotunda at the Capitol all the way down to State Street!

My friends drove by it and said it looked cold!

Let's talk tonight or sometime tomorrow. I'd like to let ya know how good I'm doing at the moment. I've got some true friends right now who are the definition of supportive and trustworthy. I think that I'm realizing that in the past, I had a lack of support with my friends, and people abused the fact that I'm always a nice and giving person towards everybody. I always support others and help them out but It's been a long time since I've really gotten that in return with any amount of significance, but I met my buddy Carlos at a party about a year ago, and we kept in touch somewhat to help each other with hopelessness issues, but had never really spent any time together. He and his best friend Sammy who I've known for a bit came over, and it was the first time in such a long time that I was able to fully open up about what I've been going through and have a totally meaningful responses. On top of having intelligent conversations, it made me feel better than counseling. On top of that we had a ton of intelligent conversations about cool stuff that nobody else seems to give a fuck about. He's so supportive of me getting off of drugs but he doesn't judge me and neither does Sam or his girlfriend. We've become best buds now pretty much and my positivity towards life has completely flipped around and has my motivation. It's so nice to have friends that are like this. I really think I can do things in my life without drugs, having these kinds of people who are generous and intelligent and always there for each other.

Chapter 9: A New Year

Sorry I fell asleep before you sent message.
I'm happy you have found some supportive
friends. Talk Later.

We did talk later, and had one of many conversations that I would regret. I had heard all of this before. "I finally found supportive friends. Friends with whom I can have an intelligent conversation. Friends who support me staying clean." I could count five or so times when his hopes had been dashed by such friends, or his addiction, or their addiction, destroying the tenuous bonds that constituted "friendship" in his eyes. I told him that this was a familiar story. I shamed him and highlighted just how much his life really sucked by reminding him that his friends had always bailed. I dashed his hope. Reality was not what he wanted to be reminded of.

DIY Detox, January 27, 2017

I was waiting to hear about boxes and cleaning supplies needed. No response all day, with the detox supposedly happening tomorrow. I was once again going to have to face the task of cleaning up his shit after saying I wouldn't. I'd told him he would need to at least box up the stuff he wanted so I knew what needed to be stored. I was so tired of moving/storing/washing/sorting his stuff. I laughed in college when a professor in one of my psychology classes was describing co-dependence, and gave an example of a woman who ironed her husband's shirts as he was packing up to leave her. I guess it's not funny anymore.

I tried to get ahold of Tyler most of the day, and finally reached him by phone. He was extremely agitated, but said I could bring down the moving boxes so he could pack to go to his dad's the next day to detox. I had a few errands to do in Park City on my way down. I was trying to group my trips, as I didn't want to head to Park City, go all the way home, then all the way back down to Salt Lake, when he finally consented to letting me help him out. He texted me that he was hungry, and I texted back that we could get something. He sent a few more texts to me that

199

suggested he was anxious for me to get there, for some reason. He called a few times to see where I was, after I had waited all day for a response. When I did arrive, he unleashed on me, telling me he saw no hope, and it was because I had sent a warning message about trusting friend's intentions too much.

He said he was starving, and we went to Café Zupas to get some soup and sandwiches. He was angry and felt like antagonizing me. Looking at the time on his phone he said,

"Look, it's 4:20."

Button-pushing little shit. 420 is the code for marijuana arrests with the police department, but April 20th has become the day to celebrate getting high on pot. A code word for the counterculture. He was just trying to piss me off, and he did. I drove him by the Haven after dinner to try and talk him into going to see what their program was about. I felt like he needed to be informed as to what his options might be. We argued for twenty minutes outside of the Haven, getting on conference call with Chris so that I might garner his support in convincing Tyler to be proactive in finding a place for his recovery. It would look better to the judge if he was already on the right path. After a lot of tears and anger, he consented to go in and check it out. I was twenty steps ahead of him and I looked back to see what was taking him so long, not trusting him to follow me, when I saw that he had slipped on the ice in his stupid skater shoes, and had slid all the way under my truck from the snowbank that he had stepped out on. He was a total mess at that point. Tears, swearing, and uncontrolled rage forced an end to our outing. There was no way he was going in and he didn't. What happened to my epiphany about control? Had I learned nothing? Why would I try and shove this option at him?

I drove him back to his apartment and grabbed his car so I could help him get gas, as he was close to running out again. After he filled up, he sped away from me at the service station without turning on his lights. I had to call him to tell him to turn them on. A couple hours later, he texted that he was hungry and needed a little money to get a few groceries. I reminded him that he had just eaten a huge dinner, and that Chris was going to pick him up early the next day. Then he said he needed a toothbrush. I told him his dad could bring him one. Then he told me he needed money to pay off an overdraft for an Uber ride so he could get his Suboxone the next day. I know when I'm being worked. I asked how much he was overdrawn. I told him I'd put money in his account for the overdraft right before the Dr. appointment, along with his co-pay for the appointment. I knew he just wanted cash for heroin. I wasn't giving it to him, but he found a way to get money anyway. If someone could bottle the ingenuity of a heroin addict, they might be on to something.

The following day I met Tyler at his apartment. This was the big day. He was to drive his van to the mechanic for maintenance. Chris would meet us there, and would be taking him home to detox him. My nerves were trashed. He was violently ill already when I got there. I doubted his ability to drive but I just had to get him a few miles so his car could be fixed. I drove closely behind him, and I could see that his head kept bowing down, as though he were nodding off. This was a horrible idea. I should have figured something else out. How was I to know he would be in such rough condition? How could I have not expected it, at this point?

We rolled into the shop, and I looked inside the van, as Tyler stumbled to Chris's truck. The state of the van was beyond belief. He had quit even trying to hide anything. There were syringes and black shit dripping down from the cup holders. Garbage, candy wrappers, smelly clothing. This had been party van central, and I could only imagine what had gone on in there. Regret for ever buying him the damn thing washed over me. We'd been so foolish. Chris and I crammed garbage into bags and suitcases so that the mechanic wouldn't see it, and in doing so, we found a note with his rudimentary drug-deal accounting on it. What kind of immature novice leaves crap like this?

Money Owed

Kevin: 200+ It's been almost a month...interest?

Matt: to be discussed...50

Double D: Countless. Talk to

Jeff: 30 for white

_____ for black

Asshole: 40-50 + Speaker or ass whooping

"His stupidity will, and should, get him locked up." I thought to myself

I tucked the note into my purse to steam about later, and sent Tyler off with Chris, relieved that I might get a break for a couple days. The week had been an attempt to do all and be all to everyone in my life. In just a week's time, there had been two women's marches, one at the beginning of the Sundance Film Festival, and the other at the Utah State Capitol building, in conjunction with others held across the country after the dreadful inauguration. I have my own "#MeToo" story, but had too much on my plate to do anything besides march in support of my sisters, who were ready to tell theirs. I couldn't fight that past battle when I was currently living in a war zone. There was an Al-Anon meeting, a parent support group at the Renaissance Ranch, attempts to work, and five Sundance movies at crazy-ass hours, because Matt bought a ticket package, and I was trying to not let my obsession with helping Tyler overshadow my ability to do things with my husband. I knew I was overwhelmed. Then, the car transfer, trying to get Tyler ready for a move, and a detox, a $704 phone bill for Tyler, and then, a bad cold. I couldn't sustain this insanity.

Friday, Jan. 27, 2017, so this is what a homemade/do-it-yourself intervention/ detox looks like:

He was sick all weekend long. Coming off of the dope makes you have flu-like symptoms times ten. Vomiting, chills, congestion, constipation, nausea, fever. Chris had tried to take him to a Refuge Recovery meeting, but they had to turn back when he had to puke by the side of the road. Most people don't get past this stage. It's just too horrible and they'd rather stick a needle in their arm, if it means the dope-sickness will end. Five days. That's what he needs for us to get him through this stage, with Chris by his side twenty-four/seven to make sure he doesn't slip. He would sleep by his bedroom door and make sure that nobody came to his window to bring him anything. I just don't know if we are doing the right thing, but my counselor, John, made a good point that it's hard for someone to feel any hope when they are homeless AND going through this sickness hell.

Chapter 9: A New Year

I would try and plan a camping trip to get him closer to his court date and further away from his influences and triggers. I had limited funds, so camping was a good option but even more, I still believed that the connection to nature, once he remembered it and embraced it, would be what ought to bring him back. To that mission, I messaged Wes and Jennie:

Hey Jennie, how are you and Wes doing? I loved seeing your trip pictures! So I don't know if you have been keeping up with Tyler and Chris, but Tyler did in fact get arrested, and has a Feb.14th court date for charges that could land him in jail or rehab. I'm seeing this as a good thing. Chris is detoxing him at his house (Dee finally consented to him being there). We are trying to clean him up for his court date, hoping that he gets a glimmer of hope back that will make him want to work hard at staying clean...when you are coming off the dope, you are really sick for 5 or 6 days, and most people just go back to using to stop the sickness. Chris is with him 24/7 until next week, when I'm thinking of taking him on a trip to get away from his life here, collect himself, and meditate. We are looking at possibly camping down in New Mexico or Arizona... or somewhere else. We are open to suggestion if you two can think of anything. I want to make it a mini-retreat for both of us, and I need to work hard at not "shaming" him. He has enough shame. Any suggestions would be great!

Good News! Wes and I conferred and think that Saguaro National Park outside of Tuscan is your best bet. Most places will be too cold to have fun camping, but it should be pretty good there. The desert museum is there, which is great, coyotes and good birds in the monument, and some nice rocky trails through the cacti. We love it there. Plus, near enough to Tucsan to go on a Mexican food run. The area around the U AZ campus is a great hang out - pretty area (west side of campus), and there is a fav nursery here - desert survivors with native plants, run by, and for, disabled folks. Also, Gary Nabhan has some cool garden thing going on there - Google it, it has to do with sustainable gardening in a desert native style.

These guys really knew us! She had me at "garden," and I hoped Tyler would enjoy the birds as he used to. These are the professors at UC Davis that love Tyler so very much. I believe Tyler loves and respects them in return, perhaps more than anyone else.

That is awesome! I will definitely consider it. I think there might be Refuge Recovery meetings in Tucson (Buddhist AA). A mini retreat. Tyler has always loved ornithology, and the natural world in general. I keep hoping he will connect to something…and remember who he is. Thanks so much!

Look around the U AZ campus, good place for him someday. There is a junior college called Pima Co. in so. Tucson as well. I think the Buddhist meeting area is right near campus, that would be such a good thing to visit!

Great! Sounds like a plan. Love you guys!

Love you too, spring is in the air here, and will be in Tucson as well. We always thought that is where we would end up!

Monday, January 30, move number four

We met at Tyler's apartment on the tail end of his detox with Chris. I was going against what I said I would never do, move him and clean, for the fourth time this year. At least I had insisted on Chris and Tyler's help. As we worked, I thought back over all of the places he had lived in the last year, trying to figure out what had happened with each. Move one had been from my rental house to his first apartment, with guys that he had found on Craigslist. I had set him up with the dishes and housewares that I would not need when I blended my life with Matt's. His first apartment. I remember that he had an anticlimactic look on his face. That was odd, after he had been asking for emancipation for a year.

"So...I'm sleeping here tonight?" he had asked me after I dropped him off, moved his stuff, and hugged him before heading over to clean my old place. I was hurrying back to my place, because new tenants were arriving shortly behind me. That first place had ended with an informal eviction. He had partied too much. Even his college-age roommates had thought so and had been alarmed by his behavior. The clean-up that time had been typical party crap. A broken coffee mug, one of my old set, that would leave a sliver in my thumb that remains. I was picking up the mess of a kid too young and immature to be on his own, and without a lick of impulse control. I packed up a strobe light that he had seemed to find money to buy, though he never had enough for food. Clothing and personal items were strewn around the room, but nothing terribly atypical for an eighteen-year-old, I guessed. The roommates had talked me into leaving the couch, an outdoor table, and chairs, as well as other items in an exchange for being "inconvenienced" by having taking a chance on him.

I then moved him to Taylorsville, in a shared house. The owner lived in the basement with her boyfriend, and rented the upstairs three bedrooms to others. At the time, it seemed the ideal set-up. There were adults that would live there, common areas that needed to be kept clean, and house rules that would need to be respected. The move away from this place had been much more difficult. At that point the heroin use had just started. Tyler's housemates had found things missing and went in his room to see if he had them. He did. They also saw all the drug paraphernalia. That's what got him evicted. I received a call from his landlady while Tyler was in the hospital with sepsis. The landlords always call me. Chris had gone before us to clean that time and was mortified. Needles. A total mess. I reminded him to be careful checking the pockets, so he didn't get pricked. I would finish boxing everything else up with Tyler, after Chris removed what he didn't want me to see, while being stared down by the owner of the house, her friend, and her boyfriend. A kind but stern lecture came from his landlady following the completion of packing, as we left her house.

I had tried to mentally prepare myself for the fourth move, just months after the third. I thought I was ready, but you are never ready to see the total demise of someone that you love. I had promised I wouldn't help if he were thrown out, and here I was, helping. Mad at myself. Mad at him. Mad at the world.

The scene was so shameful that I did not need to say anything to Tyler, and tried my hardest not to. I had been told that shame was the worst thing I could throw at him. I felt like a chump for being there. Piles of dirty dishes, weeks old, stunk up the kitchen. There was no garbage disposal, so when I tried to wash the crusty dishes, I had to pick the chunks of rancid, curdled milk out of the dish strainer so that the sink could drain. Garbage was overflowing from the can. Tyler had long since blown through the clean dishes, and instead of washing them, they were using paper plates. How long had he lived here? Four months or so? It reminded me of a scene in Breaking Bad, where everyone in the meth house had just given up hope and was living in total squalor. I don't know how a place could get so filthy in that period of time. I went to the front bedroom, which one of his roommates had recently vacated in some sort of dispute with Tyler. One of many friends that Tyler was sure, at first, was his "soulmate." It had become the party room. Hookahs, syringes everywhere, empty pizza boxes, garbage, incense. I went in and told Chris that he needed to see the front room. Tyler admitted that it had been the party room since his roommate left the month before, and it was all his mess. Chris told me to stay out. I was thankful that he took it upon himself to clean it with Tyler. Tyler's job was to put all of the caps on the syringes, so we wouldn't get poked by them, and throw them in the waiting dustpan. I finally had to go in the room to help Tyler put the blood-stained mattress in my truck. I could haul it to the dump while they boxed up the things that he wanted to keep, and throw away the nine large garbage bags of junk in the dumpster. When I went in to help Tyler with the mattress, I saw splattered blood on the walls. Images of him injecting ran through my head. A daytime nightmare. I couldn't imagine what my nighttime nightmare would be tonight, the dark, magnifying the horror we were living.

Chapter 9: A New Year

The T.V. was gone. Chris had told me that Tyler was trying to pawn it a couple of weeks prior but hadn't been successful. It was a forty-six-inch Vizio that I had purchased for Tyler's tenth birthday. After the divorce, I didn't bother purchasing a television. We didn't watch it all that much before the divorce, and money was really tight. It seemed like a frivolous expense. This was around '08, in the height of the housing crisis, and I was a property investor. At that point in time, it would have been an enormous sacrifice. Tyler had begged and begged for me to get one. We had not had one for a couple of years, and we were having a huge sleepover with fourteen or fifteen kids for his birthday celebration. What chaos. What fun! Countless pictures from that party of bubbly ten-year-olds resides indelibly in my head. That was also the year I bought him an electric guitar, a picture of which was emblazoned on the cake in frosting, decorated beautifully by my friend Sydney. I had purchased the television right before the party, so that we could watch late-night movies. He was so pleased. But now it was gone. Probably traded for twenty dollars' worth of smack.

I came into the apartment for the last load, to be taken and stored somewhere, I still didn't know where, until sometime, I didn't know when. Tyler and Chris were arguing. I had seen the bandana hanging out of Tyler's pocket earlier, but was trying hard not to say anything. It was his symbol of revolution against the norm, of being his own person. Bandanas around the head, a bandana around the ankle, bandanas pinned with thumbtacks all over his bedroom. I think he thought that it signaled to the world that he was a "badass" for some reason, which I'm convinced was his objective for years. He told Chris that he didn't care about that stuff when he was on dope but now that he had been clean for a few days, he felt like he needed to care about his image again. And the image he cared about was being a badass. We were so angry. Not just about the bandana, to be sure. I finally unleashed, and asked him to imagine what it was like for us to have just witnessed the mess that he had made. He looked sincerely apologetic for a glimmer of a second, then begrudgingly pulled the bandana out of his back pocket. He gave me a long hug and thanked me before Chris drove back to his house with Tyler.

"If we could just get him feeling better, and get him to the court date, we could just let the repercussions happen. If he got sent to jail, he might finally admit, to himself, that he had reached his own bottom. If he got sent to Odyssey House, he might actually recover this time, if a judge mandated that he stay clean, rather than his parents. But if he keeps going like this, he will surely die," I thought to myself as I drove home.

A ray of light shown through after the despair we were all feeling from cleaning out the apartment. I had decided, actually, the day before we had cleaned the apartment, that I would take Tyler on that road trip, mostly because we needed a place for him to go, now that he was essentially homeless, and Chris wasn't sure how long after the five day detox he would be able to have him at the house, already skating on thin ice with Dee. Chris also needed to get back to work, and I thought it would be a good chance for us to spend some quality time together. Matt and I were in the process of purchasing a business that would have me really busy in a month or so. Actually, the timing was perfect for me. After seeing the apartment, I was worried that keeping Tyler out of trouble, keeping him busy, and in good spirits would be more than I could handle. Except for the bandana argument, Chris and I had done an exceptional job at not shaming Tyler. There would be no need for that once the dope sick phase was over, and it almost was at that point. Anyone, even a junkie, could see how deplorable the situation was. We didn't need to say a thing.

I really had garnered a lot of wisdom from my meeting at Renaissance Ranch. I had heard that shame wasn't good for addicts, or probably anyone else, for that matter. I'd heard it from Rick when he spoke of his recovery, and I'd heard it in various programs, but an example had been given at Renaissance that was like a script from our story. Upon exiting a rehab program, a kid's father proceeded to tell him, "This better have worked. I just spent my retirement trying to fix you."

Tyler knew exactly how much each rehab had cost us. He had heard it enough. He knew I didn't have it and had incurred debt to help him. I've always felt that kids need to hear the reality, but I had been inadvertently shaming him, to the point that he just wanted to hide in the hole that he had dug, anything to not face the guilt that I threw at him. How could I have let him know the impact he had on the family without feeling some sort of shame?

I softened my approach and made a conscious effort, so did Chris. I spent the day after the move washing load after load of laundry in

Chapter 9: A New Year

various states of being. School uniforms, still crisp and new, the tan khakis and light blue button-down worn by the high school students. The navy cardigan and the chamber orchestra Ireland shirt from their trip... all still clean, but I washed them anyway. Everything had felt tainted by the atmosphere of the place, the very air. I had to wear gloves, and make sure no needles were in his pockets. I didn't find any, just little pieces of foil with burnt stuff on them. There were clothes with blood stains I just tossed. Pants with anarchy signs and drawings all over them in ballpoint pen. Garbage. The really cool sixties shirt I had found in the vintage section of a store in St. George that I thought he would love, and he did. Keep. More single socks than any human should have. Match up. One of the single unworn socks was from the pair that I had so carefully knitted him while he was in the wilderness. The ones he had felt were too nice to wear. I never did find its mate.

On day five of Tyler's detox under Chris's supervision, he went to an alternative therapy session with someone who specialized in Craniosacral Therapy. Chris had heard about her through a couple of friends to whom her help had been enormous. We were willing to try anything at this point, grasping at straws to find an answer. I am one of the bigger skeptics of the world, and I had never known Chris to "fall" for anything on the fringe as far as therapy or religion, but here we were, at a crossroads, with no sense of direction. Tyler had liked it, and had felt fantastic afterward. I did some research after he went, and read on Wikipedia that there was little proof that it did anything but relieve tension and anxiety. That was good enough for me to be considered positive.

My experience with fringe therapies previous to this was limited to a sweet lady that I had befriended, who lived in a building in Park City where I was remodeling a condo. She was an energy work therapist. We had talked about my struggles with Tyler many times, when she would poke her head into the condo to see how the project was progressing. She had told me that she thought that I might benefit from a little mini session. I really didn't have time. I had three projects going on at that time and was under a tight schedule to finish this condo. I did eventually consent to her energy work session, mostly to have her leave me alone about it. I went to her condo and she had me lay down on her couch. I felt totally strange and uncomfortable, and I was worried that I would get her couch

209

dirty from the mortar all over my clothes, from the tile-setting that I was doing. The fact was, I felt surprisingly relaxed after I left.

Again, I saw the connectedness between people and things and the God that lies therein. If someone wishes you well, gives you some kind of blessing, in whatever way they know how, that, to me, is God. I received a Mormon blessing from a good friend of mine who knew what I was going through. I don't believe in his church, but the fact that he wanted to impart some peace to me in a way that he believed would work meant a lot to me. The energy work that the lovely lady in Park City did for me was like that. There is a kind of connectedness that happens when someone shows some empathy, or even just makes eye contact and smiles. Perhaps this is what Tyler had felt in the Craniosacral therapy. His therapist was also a dog-healer and once, when I went to pick him up from her house, he had about an eighty-pound rescued pit bull comfortably draped over the top of him, and nuzzling up against his neck on the table where he was undergoing his therapy. She had a gift for evoking trust.

Two days after the move, day six of the detox, I texted Tyler to see how he was doing. He texted back that he was working with Chris! With an exclamation point! He had been without anything to exclaim for some time so I left it alone, and just allowed myself to feel good about it. Chris's career sometimes had him operating a camera, sometimes acting as director of photography, and sometimes producing. He had done everything, from shoot segments about Utah for the Olympics to documentaries, and had a true gift for his craft. For two years during the Salt Lake City Olympics, he filmed the features on Utah for the world broadcast. This allowed us to travel around the time when Tyler was four, visiting the best places that Utah has to offer, which are many. As Tyler had grown up, he had been given the opportunity to work as a production assistant on many productions, but he had become more and more unreliable the last two years, and Chris could not trust having him involved with a production. Chris's original plan had been to stay away from work, and with Tyler constantly, until I took him on the trip. However, he got a call from a program that he had been shooting for, and they were desperate for him to work. There was some sort of legislation pertaining to the issue he was filming about being discussed in the Utah legislature, and they needed him to be there. He had no choice but to take Tyler, so as not to leave him alone. Everyone on the crew was well aware of Tyler's struggles as it had dominated Chris's life and affected his work. They had overheard phone conversations, seen the crises, and been part of the cancelled work or shifted schedules, just as most of our close friends and business associates had.

They worked a fourteen-hour day and Chris called me, tears of joy choking him up. It was beautiful. Tyler was engaged, listened to four hours of legislators talking, worked non-stop, was respectful, awake, and helpful. He just wanted me to know how incredibly positive it was. I cried too. Tyler had even called the court to find out specifics of what to expect on his court date, in front of the crew on the way to the shoot. He was owning it. He called and texted me the next day with the first positive messages I'd heard in some time.

I was so excited about the trip now. We had enjoyed many great road trips together, just the two of us. Trips that looped through Colorado to visit three of my siblings in different towns, Salida, Ft. Collins, and Loveland. With or without the dogs. Trips to bluegrass festivals. Trips with Rick and his kids to Southern Utah. Trips to go birding or find insects for school projects.

Best of all was our trip three summers before. Tyler had flown out to visit Jennie and Wes, and to spend a few weeks with them in Davis. He was supposed to be helping them with a research project that had to be cancelled because of the intense heat in Southern California at the time. The project had been something about collecting bugs, or something entomology related. He had a blast with them, despite the project's cancellation. I drove solo in my dad's Alaskan camper that popped up on hydraulic lifts over a utility truck, slowly making my way through Utah, Nevada, then finally California. My first night I camped on some old mining road in Nevada, pulling out my fiddle in the middle of nowhere and playing for myself. The next night I set up camp in Washington, CA, a time-warp mining town, in a campground that, I believe, was called Gene's PineAir. It had taken me some time to find a place to camp, as I had become too accustomed to BLM camping in Utah, where you just drive off the road and set up. I was glad I found it though. It had a great swimming hole on the Yuba River, in which I happily indulged. The quaint old town was just across the river, with its old Washington Hotel, that had accommodated the likes of Wyatt Earp. I had a delightful conversation with the eighty-year-old camp host, who was surprised that I was solo camping as a woman. She seemed like an adventurous old gal herself, so her interest surprised me. It was humorous to see the tipped over trash cans from bears, rummaging through leftovers at the camp during the night, and the dog who had to move from laying in the middle of the main road in Washington when I came through.

The following day I picked up Tyler in Davis, and we enjoyed absolute bliss in camping up the coast, into Oregon, marveling at each beach we camped at, for its uniqueness and beauty. We collected driftwood, polished rocks, and a beautiful green beetle that we thought was dead until it came back to life inside my pocket. We had our Dutch oven, this time, a sea food feast, and the obligatory cherry Twizzlers that always accompanied us on every road trip. Best of all, we listened to *This American Life* podcasts made possible by some sort of tuner that had to be streamed through the radio, which meant you needed a good signal. We would get completely wrapped up in a story, and it would either stop because it was buffering, or we'd lose our radio signal and have to find a new station to go back to where we left off. Oh how we loved the stories though, mutually gripped as we drove up the Oregon coast.

Chapter 9: A New Year

In retrospect, I think Tyler may have been experimenting with drugs on the Oregon trip. He sought alone time more than I was ok with but, at the time, I just thought he needed a little space from my constant companionship. It seemed sometimes he was even trying to "lose me." His dad had taken him on a fishing trip to Alaska that same summer and noticed the same thing. Teenagers are strange beings. With so much going on with them socially, as well as hormonally, it's hard to know what behavior is odd or unusual.

This trip would be epic...like old times. We would drive to St. George and stay a night with my mom. I'd told her to hide any pills, and not to shame or lecture. We were trying a new approach. From St. George, we would go the route that would take us to the Grand Canyon, then south toward Tucson. It would be a retreat on our own terms. Yoga, hiking, meditation at a Buddhist temple, a Refuge Recovery meeting, Mexican food, and of course, the Grand Canyon, where he had never been. I'd let Tyler tell me if he'd like to go other places, and give him the map. Let him get excited about the adventure. There was so much to pick from. Monument Valley, Canyon de Chelly, The Biosphere, the Observatory. There was a Frida Kahlo exhibit at an arboretum, which I found interesting, but I did not know if he would.

I was sure Tyler would tease me if I brought up long lost Everett Ruess, the romantic story of a young poet, artist and wanderer who had been lost in the Southern Utah or Northern Arizona area in November of 1934. I had been obsessed with the romance of his story and the mystery of his disappearance for years, and had even journeyed once to the very remote canyon that was his last know camp, where his burros and some of his gear had been found, near Escalante, Utah, now half drowned by the damning up of Lake Powell. We would be going through Everett's beloved canyons. The steep red rocks that had always drawn him back, until they consumed him somehow, at the young age of twenty-one. His joy was in these canyons. I see Everett in Tyler. Battles with mental health issues, depression, belonging and exclusion, teetering on the edge of a cliff or precipice, trying to find a path. Both of them artistic, beautiful, misunderstood. We would take Everett's journals and letters with us, along with other travel books, recovery books, and our own journals.

Anticipating the trip made me more excited and optimistic then I had been in a long time. I was riding the spin bike at the gym, while my brakes were replaced on my truck before the drive the following day. I turned on a TED talk. If I'm in the gym, instead of being outside where I prefer to be, I need some serious mental stimulation, or entertainment in the form of music, *This American Life*, or *Ted Talks*. I picked a talk on addiction this time. It felt like something guided me to turn that on. It was EVERYTHING that summed up our experiences with the last break-through. Addicts don't need shame, they need connectedness. Precisely where I feel that my God resides. The talk was by Johann Hari titled "Everything You Think You Know About Addiction Is Wrong." Hari had embarked upon a search to find out why our current methods of treating addictions had failed, and if there might be a better way. Hari contends that in order to avoid addictive behaviors, a person must have bonds and relationships with society. He discussed the rat experiment done in the late nineteen seventies, by Canadian psychologist Bruce K. Alexander and his colleagues. A rat is put in a cage with a choice between regular water, and a water bottle that also had drugs in it. The rat would drink the drug water until it died, which fits our narrative of what we think happens to an addict. But a later experiment was done where a rat was given a "rat park," with loads of friends, food, bright colored balls and tunnels, but the same water bottles. However, in this study, the rats rarely drank the drug water, and almost never compulsively. Having a connection, something to live for, was more significant in helping or preventing addiction. We have created a society where life looks like an empty

214

Chapter 9: A New Year

cage, without connection, because of technology, and added floorspace, creating distance between us. Threatened connections, and tough love, exemplified in shows like *Intervention,* do little to help an addict. When we have unhealthy connections to things, we need to deepen positive connections. With addicts, we need to take the approach, "I love you, whether you are using or you're not. I love you whatever state you're in. If you need me, I will come and sit with you."

I sat in tears on the bike. This was it. It was all intertwined with what I was learning about Buddhism and unhealthy attachments versus connectedness. Freedom from attachment equaled freedom from suffering. That did not mean I could not have a connection. There was a difference, and I had to learn the difference between the two. If I attach myself to an outcome, that's when I can be disappointed. This kind of attachment can be extremely addictive, as sometimes, you are not disappointed! In college, I learned that it is much harder to break a habit when you are rewarded sometimes, than if you are rewarded all of the time, and then the reward suddenly stops. In the later instance, a rat will just walk away if the reward ends. But if a rat is rewarded on occasion, just like a gambler, he will keep trying and trying to do a task, because he might have a jackpot on the next pull of the slot machine handle, or a rat treat dispensed in a bowl.

"Expectation is premeditated disappointment," I heard in an Al-Anon group one day. To take it a step further, from Buddhist thought on detachment and connectedness:

..."When we reject the illusion that we have a "self" that exists separately and independently from other people and phenomena, we suddenly recognize that there is no need to detach, because we have always been interconnected with all things at all times." (ThoughtCo)

I never saw the wilderness experience as tough love. To me, it was more like getting away from your dysfunctional friend or home situation, long enough to reassess your life and your connection and relationships to others and yourself. There were a great deal of experiences that the campers had with each other, that helped create strong bonds, as well as an understanding of one's feelings. It was also a massive metaphor for struggling, and then finding the power to overcome difficult situations that you thought you could not achieve before an experience in the wild,

215

such as busting a flame. Tyler said that he did not get anything out of it, but I disagree. I think it might take him a while to understand that he did in fact learn that he had the capability of being self-reliant, and he gained a better understand of his responsibilities. There have been a number of instances where he has used the verbiage about communicating and advocating for himself that he learned at Second Nature.

My soul is calmed by the little quotes I find on Pinterest, things I jot down from Al-Anon, and poems my recovery friends send me. It's funny how a few words can bring hope in a painful situation; bring light where it seems so dark.

"Attachment is the origin, the root of suffering;
hence it is the cause of suffering,"
- Dalai Lama -

The Trip
CHAPTER 10

Chris called to give me the heads-up that he was really elated at Tyler's progress, but was concerned. He said I would see why when I picked him up. I hated it when he did that. Why couldn't he just say what he was thinking, and not create a bunch of drama and worry? He liked the suspense I guess. I did appreciate his push to organize the detox, and I was ecstatic that Tyler was doing well and had a positive attitude. I could put aside my disdain for his approach if the approach seemed to be working.

I drove to the curb and texted Tyler that I had arrived. He came bounding out of Chris's house with his bags and off we went to tank up on gas. He was clearly excited, and non-stop talk started to spill from him in a rush, as though he were catching up after a long period of numbness and silence. He wanted to go back and get his cello. His cello! It was a bad idea to take it on a camping trip because the temperature extremes were not ideal for a string instrument, but I felt like he wanted to find a pathway back to who he once was. On the drive, I could see what Chris was talking about. Tyler couldn't get the words out fast enough. It was difficult to be too concerned though, because he had been closed off for so long, and it was what I needed so much. He was alive, my Tyler, not the kid I had tried, and failed, to connect with for so long. We talked about addiction and how much it sucks. We talked about music, friends; what he missed about his old life. We talked about the future, and things he dreamed about, like going to Europe, like a buddy of his, who was going from place to place, working jobs he'd found, and then moving on. We talked about him learning to fly drones, and forming a company with Chris. About leaving Utah, and starting fresh somewhere new. I had seen manic episodes, and it felt like that was what I was witnessing here. Perhaps it was just so different from his demeanor the last few years that it caught me off guard. I really did not know what to make of it, but

I wasn't unhappy about it. We had always communicated wonderfully on our old road trips, but this seemed different. It was though he had some kind of deadline by which he needed to tell me everything. Like he wouldn't get a chance if he didn't live it all and say it all, right here and now. Later that night, I did a Google search to see if his new antidepressant, Lexapro, could cause a manic episode, and found out that, indeed it could. I'd have to watch him for a couple of days, and see if it was just excitement, or something more. I was hoping it was just excitement.

When we arrived in St. George, immediately upon hearing that Tyler had his cello, my mom wanted to hear him play. I had to stop my Mom from talking though, her obvious excitement at having visitors, so that he could actually play for us. I had to explain that I had not heard him play except once in school, since she had, two Mother's Days ago. I had actually started to believe that I might never hear him play again. He played the Bach Cello Suite in G Major. My favorite. His face bore the love of playing again, unlike anything I had seen in a long time. Buying himself back into good graces with his sweet notes. The best offering of all for a mother and a grandmother.

As Tyler played, I thought about how we had come to know Ellie, the homeless cellist, on our outings in Salt Lake. He was always in front of the theater on Broadway; the theater that played the independent films, like clockwork, before the seven and nine o'clock shows, busking with his cello for the moviegoers. We had also seen him at big events in Salt Lake, like the Greek festival, playing in front of the big tent at the Greek Orthodox church, down on Third West. He was smart about where the crowds would be, so he must have been together enough to plan his performances. I had inquired about him through my musician friend. He was a curiosity to me, not only because Tyler was a cellist and it was fun to watch another musician perform, but because he was so unpredictable in his performance. Some of the times that we would watch him, he showed us a glimmer of his virtuosity, hidden underneath his dingy street-person clothes. Other days, he could barely hold his bow and acted completely lost, his eyes glazed and nearly shut. I heard that he had been in a famous quartet in Europe and had come here to work at one of the shops that builds instruments and had somewhere, along the way, fried his brains with drugs. I heard he would play for money for his drug fix.

Chapter 10: The Trip

Friends once wanted to repair his cello for him, but he couldn't part with it for long enough for it to be repaired. I had asked him if he was ok. He said he was where he wanted to be, as he sat in the drizzle, with his cello exposed. Today, Tyler was like Ellie on a good day. The curiosity I once held for a homeless cellist; turned toward my own child.

Our connection through music was one of the most beautiful things about our relationship. In second grade, he made a Mother's Day card for me in school. It was an answer to the question,

"What is your favorite thing to do with your mom?"

"Play music," was the adorable answer that made me tear up. I had always accompanied him on the piano when he practiced, until he became more advanced, and sight reading the accompaniment was too difficult. I couldn't always find the time to learn my part. Now, I dream of playing an amazing piece with him. One that requires a great deal of time together to polish. A sort of auditory affirmation of our bond.

Our couple day stay in St. George was joyous and busy. We stayed up late the first night, invited by the next-door neighbor, a retired astronomy professor, to come over and look through his impressive telescope. He had it set on a permanent mount in his back yard. My mom lives in Kayenta, a community committed to preserving a dark sky, which made it perfect for viewing the stars. Tyler seemed pleased to be doing an activity that we used to do when he was younger, dragging the telescope to Jackson Hole and freezing our asses off, waiting for the right moment to view, usually late into the night. He also seemed a little surprised at the time the neighbor, Ron, took to find and explain what we were seeing.

We hiked on Land Hill, taking the Anasazi Trail up to an area called Temi'Po'Op', which means "rock writing." It contained a rich collection of petroglyphs carved into the blackened rock, or desert varnish. It was a massive collection of ancient art overlooking the Santa Clara River, sitting high above the fertile river valley where the Anasazi, and those who came after, had farmed for millennia. It was a beautiful, crisp, clear morning for a hike, and Tyler and I walked up the incline effortlessly. I couldn't get enough of the time together, and it seemed that he couldn't either. We looked in awe at the ancient beautiful writing, displayed before us, as we contemplated their meanings. We felt like going beyond the largest collection of petroglyphs, where most people stop, both of us

219

full of energy and fueled by hope. As we made our way up and over the mountain, we could see three people down the scrubby mountainside in the distance intently gazing at something. Intrigued, we went over to see what it was. An elderly man was showing the other two a rock where he claimed mothers went to give birth. The man took great pleasure in recognizing Tyler's interest in what he was saying, and went on to tell us some intriguing theories on what some of the other rock art depicted. His name was Boma Johnson, and he was a professor at Dixie State College. Again, I savored the connection that he, like Ron the night before with his telescope, made with us. It was as though Tyler had wakened from a really long sleep, and hadn't been aware that all of this wonder was out here, to be had by those who sought it out.

Tyler had confessed on the drive that he had tried to overdose once to end the pain, but felt like he had an unusual tolerance. He spoke with a touch of grandiosity that I had always been uncomfortable with, frequently too confident in himself and his abilities. I was glad that he had an unusual tolerance for heroin, but was painfully aware that attitude might kill him one day. He blasted Pink Floyd, one of his favorites these days, following up with an explanation of what that music meant to him. *The Wall* represented what it felt like to be trapped in a life of heroin use, unable to break through the wall. The loneliness and desperation. The disconnection. Tyler had thought that the life of drugs held an excitement that he could never experience in a normal existence, like I led. He had frequently told me that he would be bored stiff if he lived like me or his dad. To his dismay, what he had found instead, was the desperate loneliness that came from sitting in the dark by himself, disconnected from friends, family and everything else, trying to figure out how to get twenty bucks for his next fix that he would need in four hours. He admitted there was nothing exciting about that life. It was monotonous, redundant, and sad. He felt trapped.

The Wall is a semi-autobiographical story about a young boy who loses his father in the war and is raised by an over protective mother. When I was a teenager, like most kids my age, I loved Pink Floyd. Some naive adult even let us use the song "Comfortably Numb" as the theme for one of our junior high dances. But listening on our road trip with Tyler explaining the significance of the lyrics to him shed a whole new light on the album that I had listened to so many times. This time when I listened, I understood his crippling loneliness, the empty life which once was full and connected, and the need to build a wall against the shame felt from the outside world, while simultaneously missing the connection to it. I saw myself in the overbearing, overprotective mother. The need he had for my approval, and the despair he felt in disappointing me. I will never see this album the same again.

Leaving St. George, and making our way toward the Grand Canyon, we took the northern route, heading through Hurricane, UT, north of the Grand Canyon, and around toward the South Rim on Highway 89, through the Navajo Reservation. It was still really cold in early February and I was starting to feel an awful cold coming on before we even left Salt Lake, but I would not be deterred. As we crossed the Colorado River and onto the reservation, we felt inclined to stop at a bridge, where vendors had booths set up selling Navajo jewelry. I bought some broad, silver hoop earrings that I was told had symbols delicately stamped into them, indicating a journey. And what a journey it was! I wore them the rest of the trip. I thought about the Wes Anderson film *Darjeeling Limited*, one of mine and Tyler's favorite movies. In it, three brothers travel through India on a train, trying to create a religious experience, only to find that it would happen naturally, when they weren't desperately trying to create one.

Driving through the impoverished area of ramshackle houses on the reservation made me appreciate what we have. Music blaring, with my sidekick curating the tunes. We saw a homemade-looking sign, painted on plywood, somewhere near Tuba City, Arizona, pointing us toward dinosaur tracks. We had no schedule really. No pre-planned route or expectations. We could cater to our whims and curiosities. Tyler insisted that we turn off and check them out. The only way you could see the tracks was by having a Navajo person lead you to them, so then you felt obliged to buy something from them at their jewelry booth. An ancient-looking Navajo grandmother named Isabella showed us the tracks. She was affable and informative as she slowly moved toward the tracks, delicately outlining them with her fingers. Then, she led us back to her booth where she showed us the jewelry that she said she and her children and grandchildren had made themselves. I tried to erase the skepticism from my head as I thought about all of the "Made in China" souvenirs that you see in so many tourist shops, in so many places. Tyler was studying some beads, two strings of them, one red and one blue, which I bought him. I'd never been one for souvenirs, but there was an interesting necklace made of a turquoise circle with a hole on a leather tie that I was drawn to. Isabella said it was for protection. Sold! I still wear it frequently and think of her, and hope that it works, though I like it even if it doesn't. Why can't I just have some trust? For someone who doesn't trust, I sure wear it a lot! I always felt like some sort of poser around most things sacred, like those people who go to the church called "the Church of the Just in Case... Just in case there is a God!" We drove away toward the Grand Canyon, laughing about the John Prine song "Souvenirs," that Tyler knew I really liked, because I played so much John Prine when he was younger. The song is about the melancholy brought on by some souvenirs. I wrote a poem about what souvenirs meant to me:

Chapter 10: The Trip

The Necklace

I save the odd stuff from trips-
From the connection I felt

Things that represent a hope, or feeling
From that place

A smooth, polished rock and a green iridescent beetle
From the beaches of the Oregon coast

Beautiful origami-like packaging wrapped around a book
with Japanese recipes
From the kind clerk in the Osaka bookstore

Hand written recipes stained with juice from the meal
From my friend's gathering

Photos of stacked vegetables and hanging eels
From the market during my visit to Japan

A necklace for protection from the Navajo elder
From her knowing eyes that warmed my skin

Eva Summerhill

At the Grand Canyon, we stared in awe at the splendor of it all. Snow was still on the ground around us and it was really chilly, but it didn't matter. Tyler wanted to find a perfect place to play his cello. It was the most amazing gift he had ever given me. He played on a rock bench, perched on a lookout jutting out into the canyon. A small, curious crowd gathered around to watch him, moved by the unusual concert spot, and the sincerity in which the soloist played. It was one of the best days of my life.

The plan had been to camp the whole trip in order to save money, but I really didn't feel well. The elevation near the Grand Canyon South Rim is about five thousand feet, and it was early February. My sleeping bag was a desert weight bag and I felt lousy, so we decided to get a hotel in Flagstaff instead. We found a quaint Italian restaurant near our cheap hotel, and I watched as Tyler flirted with the cute college-aged waitress. I enjoyed a little glimpse of normalcy. I had recently begun to feel as though I might never have any grandchildren; as Weston didn't want children and to this point, I couldn't imagine that Tyler having children could be a good thing.

We continued through Sedona. I thought I could definitely live there, as we went in and out of the new-age shops, bought books on Buddhism, and wondered if there was anything to all of the crystal stuff. Maybe I couldn't live here. The pretentiousness might get to be too much. I could perhaps live on the outskirts though, as it certainly was breathtaking.

Finally in Tucson, we found a perfect camping spot just outside Saguaro National Park, very near the Desert Museum that Jenny and Wes had recommended we visit. The tall grand Saguaro Cacti were amazing. I was still coughing horribly, and worried that I might keep people up in the campground. The zipper was broken on our tent, and I felt slightly vulnerable when the coyotes howled at night. It sounded as though they were feet away from our tent. I clipped the tent door closed with a hair clip. Everything seemed mostly perfect about our trip. Though I was nervous when Tyler's bathroom breaks would take too long, I reassured myself that it was a long walk to the restroom. I felt that danger lurked in gaps of time away, and in the wild, untamed, hungry coyotes.

We spent our time traveling into town and found an oasis in the desert called Mercado San Agustin, with a coffee shop, a few fabulous restaurants, and some artsy shops, all built around a courtyard, where we basked in the early spring sunshine and drank coffee. We went to a Refuge Recovery meeting, where Tyler openly shared about his struggles and about how much he appreciated me, and this trip. It may have been the first time that I heard him talk in words of appreciation of my struggles, and it felt great to hear him sort of "make amends," in his words. We spent a number of hours at one sitting meditating at the Buddhist temple, and though meditation is often difficult for me, it felt wonderful this time.

We had a wonderful visit to San-Xavier Mission, which was the historic Spanish catholic mission south of Tucson, considered the oldest intact European structure in Arizona. It was awe inspiring, though its lack of completion, with one tower left unfinished; fed into my compulsion to fix things and make them complete. I hate unfinished business, mine as well as others, so the almost done towers bothered me a little. Symmetry. Balance. Completeness. I guess I am a Libra.

We went to the Desert Museum, which was as great as we were told it would be, then spent a day at the University of Arizona. I commented constantly about what a great place this would be for college. I pointed out all of the beautiful buildings, the hip shops catering to people his age, and the great mission style bungalows clustered within walking distance to the school. I got irritated when he tied a bandana around his head as soon as we got near the campus and people his age. We had a discussion about him only liking "edgy girls." He told me they were the only interesting girls out there.

We visited Kartchner Caverns, taking a guided tour through the cave past massive stalactites and stalagmites, then, we headed down to cheesy Tombstone, where we drank sarsaparilla and decided we were underwhelmed with the town, considering all of the other amazing things we had seen. At night, before dark, Tyler would perform with his cello for the campers around us, mostly old people escaping winter somewhere, who encouraged him with their kind words. Inside our tent with headlights after dark, we would read poetry by Rumi, our book on Buddhism that we bought in Sedona, and a Refuge Recovery book.

Back to Reality

Eventually we had to return home and back to reality. The trip had been a way to keep him busy until his court date, as well as give him a place to go, as he was now homeless. The date was almost here. February 14, Valentine's Day. My first Valentine's Day married to Matt. I hadn't told him yet, but for a gift to him for Valentine's Day, I was finally taking his name. I had been to the Social Security office last week to get it rolling. He had teased me that I really didn't want to get married, or was, in some way, preparing for an exit. The truth was that I was so overwhelmed with all of the chaos with Tyler, that I was having a difficult time even thinking about the fact that I was now married.

Two left dress shoes. One right one that didn't match either of the two left ones. There is a chaotic disarray of life's stuff strewn about as Tyler swings back and forth on the recovery pendulum. I don't know where the pairs to any of his shoes are. The clarity of the timeline of what has happened eludes me, as the sustained turmoil brings a brain fog that I'm not sure will ever clear. The sequence of events is so unbelievable that it makes more sense shrouded in fog. He would need a pair of dress shoes for his court date, and though I didn't know it yet, he would need them for the second, third, fourth and fifth.

Chapter 10: The Trip

I have to wait to hear the verdict of the trial in which I have no role but to anxiously watch, and hope for a positive outcome that will determine my son's future. My role as a mother stripped down to observer. Through the parking garage, through the metal detectors, through the hallway, through with all of this. I never wanted to know how the justice system works, except superficially. I passed by an old student of mine in the hallway from when I was teaching juvenile offenders how to build houses. Here I was with my son, now.

We sat for hours hearing one case after another, fidgeting while staring straight ahead, watching one person after another either lead in, if they were coming from the jail, hands cuffed behind them and shackles on their legs, or walking up from the benches where we sat, if they weren't already incarcerated. This day was to read the charges. The next court date, he was put on intensive supervised probation. If he could stay out of trouble, he could avoid going to jail. All he had to do was stay out of trouble. It seemed simple enough to me. But it wasn't simple. Nothing about addiction is simple.

This book...sometimes a journal, sometimes a memoir, a place to vent, a forced look at myself and my situation, a place to project, Groundhog Day. A study of dysfunction, healing, hope, despair and grief. A good portion of this book was written in the moment, during or shortly after a crisis, as therapy so that I could try and make sense of what was happening, without completely crumbling. Things were to become so chaotic over the next year that often I only jotted notes down to be worked on later. Now is the later, but I don't know how to put it all together. So much has happened. So much hurt. There was some novelty, lots of painful predictability, and horrible, horrible redundancy. Like a script being read over and over and over. There were feelings of both love and resentment toward Tyler, and toward the situation. I can't tell you if I have had two Al-Anon birthdays or three, or even what time of year my first meeting was, or what made me finally decide that my life was unmanageable. I remember who was there. I remember sobbing inconsolably. I remember the pain overflowing, and the comfort from those present.

I'm trying to apply what I am learning at Al-Anon. I think about the letter that I cry through every single meeting, as I contemplate what I need to do (or not do, as the case may be).

Open letter from the Alcoholic (from the Al-Anon Pamphlet "Three Views of Al-Anon")

...Don't cover up for me or try in any way to spare me the consequences of my drinking. Don't lie to me, pay my bills, or meet my obligations. It may avert or reduce the very crisis that would prompt me to seek help. I can continue to deny that I have a drinking problem as long as you provide an automatic escape for the consequences of my drinking...

I love you.
Your Alcoholic

I kept this letter nearby for strength. It is written for parents of alcoholics, though this letter works for friends and family of someone with any addiction, and is a good reminder for me of my role in all of this. I want to believe my child. Believe that what he says is true, this time. That he really does want to change and get clean. That he really isn't lying to me, stealing from me, or taking advantage of me. I know by now that none of these things are true. It's painful, but true.

There were more court dates, fights with Matt over Tyler and how I was dealing with him. I usually didn't let Tyler stay at the house, because Matt didn't approve, and Chris and Dee wouldn't let him stay at their house either. He, and sometimes we, had many hotel stays to relieve the tension at home or to give Tyler a bridge between detox and treatment, or treatment and sober living. I don't know how many detoxes happened that year. Maybe twelve? Sometimes the detox happened and he would get out of the hospital and use again. I learned the rules of different hospitals. You had to go to the ER before you were admitted to detox. You couldn't go to LDS hospital detox more than twice in thirty days. UNI didn't take his insurance, so if he ended up there, he would have to Uber or hitch hike to LDS Hospital. Heber Valley was great, but they couldn't take difficult cases that might require an infectious disease doctor. No rehab will take you until you've detoxed. Ogden Regional will only give you about an hour's notice before turning you out on the street if they get another client that needs services. You will be given a sales pitch from competing rehabs while in any detox. No doctor seems to look at what meds you are taking before prescribing new meds, all which can, and will be filled and taken. It's best for me to keep a bag packed with extra

Chapter 10: The Trip

clothes, toothbrush, and a contact case in the event that something happens to Tyler during my work day that necessitates a stay in Salt Lake or Ogden. A hotel was the only choice if there was three or four days between places. The best hotel for cost, and location, was the Quality Inn off of 5300 South, where Tyler stayed a number of times. A few times I acted like I was staying as well, when checking in with the stern Indian man at the front desk, afraid he wouldn't approve of the young, edgy-looking kid staying alone. After the first few stays, he didn't seem to care. I witnessed gut wrenching illness and misery for days on end. Tyler puking in bag after bag and crying in pain. Promises to stop and calls for forgiveness. Case worker after case worker tried to talk to us. Months went by in this wretched cycle.

One Voice Recovery
CHAPTER 11

By this time, Tyler was wandering in and out of my life. Sometimes he stayed with friends, was in detox, or found himself running back down to the park to sleep on the lawn. He preferred that to the shelter, which had more rules than he was comfortable with, and where he was less likely to get robbed. Sometimes his park stays were brief and sometimes he was homeless for weeks or more. He had said that "the block," as the area was referred to by those who hung out there, was like a vortex sucking him in. Pioneer Park was the place where the highest concentration of addicts congregated in the Salt Lake Valley, like some cult of radical followers of the Opioid God, where they were sure they could connect to Him, and have camaraderie with other followers.

It was interesting, because my Mormon pioneer ancestors stayed near there when they first immigrated to the Salt Lake Valley, until they found permanent residence. We had family history books compiled by my grandfather telling us this story. Tyler had made up a funny little jingle about them when he was young. It went, "I've got no home and I've got no money...now I'm living in a box in Pioneer Park." I don't remember how he came up with the song. Would he remember that, I wonder?

There were times that he called from someone's phone from the park because his had been stolen, or sold.

"Can you please come and get me? I can't live like this anymore."

"Of course I will." I'd meet him in a designated spot, sometimes driving late at night, alone, in a less than safe place. There were times when I couldn't reach him, but knew he was down there, somewhere. I just sensed it. I walked around the park and asked people if they had seen him, showing them his picture from my phone.

"Yea, I've seen that kid. I told him he didn't belong here and to go home and not do like I've done."

I asked a cop near the shelter once.

"Yes, he's been around." Tyler had a way of making himself known... wherever he happened to be.

Pat dropped into our lives like some kind of super hero, and with his own history. Like all superheroes, he had his kryptonite, and he knew all about addiction. He had been to rehab something like eighteen times, and he probably knew the force that could pull someone back to the left on the recovery continuum better than anyone. He was the king of harm reduction. "Keep them alive and as healthy as possible until they find their way to being better than they were the day before," was his definition of recovery.

I found Pat's card a few different times as I washed Tyler's clothes to take to detox, to his friends where he was hanging out, or to my storage until he needed them again. Pat's card would be attached to condoms, just loose, or with used needles and old orange caps from the syringes.

Tyler had told me he met someone with whom he felt a strong connection, and who had encouraged him to try inpatient, through his outreach efforts on the block. Pat and a few others in his group had been handing out condoms in the park, and had taken the time to have a few in-depth conversations with Tyler. There was some relief in knowing the condoms came from him for many reasons. Chris had found the condoms and feared that Tyler had turned to sex to pay for drugs. The thought that our germophobic child could have sunk this far was more than we both could imagine. Though I still worry, Tyler claims he has never done that.

Finally, Tyler chose to go to an inpatient treatment center with the encouragement of Patrick, who had made recommendations for him. We went to visit Brighton Recovery, the St. Benedictine Monastery turned rehab that almost had me wanting to be an addict, to enjoy some peace and quiet there. The first time we visited, a fawn ran through the yard as though planted there for effect, and released on cue. I had gazed up Weber Canyon, hoping Tyler felt the inspiration for recovery that I felt in this beautiful place.

He did, though there wouldn't be a bed for weeks. I didn't know why that came up after we were sold on it. Maybe they didn't like my inquiry about insurance, deductibles, and out of pocket maximums. Maybe I shouldn't have told them I wouldn't help pay again, and that this was on

Confessions of a Heroin Addict's Mother

him. This was the type of place that was in demand, where the "self-pay" types could and would drop a ton of dough to fix their loved one. We had done it before. Anything to fix the problem. Tyler needed to get into a place within five days of detoxing, as stipulated by insurance. Phoenix Recovery could get him in.

Hello Patrick,

I just wanted to thank you for the positive influence and impact you are having on my son Tyler Watkins, who is currently at the Phoenix inpatient program. He told me that he decided to go into inpatient treatment after meeting you on the block when you were handing out naloxone and condoms along with your card. In fact I got your card out of a condom pack that he had in his backpack. I can't tell you how much this means to me. As a Mother, I have been devastated by my feeling of helplessness in all of this. He also has mentioned a number of times that he gets a ton out of your workshops at the Phoenix. He probably told you also that the Naloxone you gave him saved someone.

He has indicated an interest in continued contact with you (or involvement in One Voice in some capacity), when he does leave inpatient, and I think this is a great idea for him, to have a strong recovery community in which to become involved.

I would also like to volunteer in some capacity with One Voice. I am impressed with you, your mission, and your website. I live a little far away (Oakley) but I work in Ogden every day if you do anything up there that you might need help with.

I have been attending Al-Anon groups in Park City as well as encouraging (and attending) Buddhist Recovery Groups with Tyler when I can. My husband and I have tickets to see Noah Levine at USARA on the 9th. I'm hoping that Tyler can go also. Tyler really connects with the Refuge Recovery program and I strongly encourage him to get more involved. I also believe that there are many possible paths to recovery.

I just wanted to reach out and say I appreciate you and all that One Voice does.

From my heart,

Eva Summerhill

Chapter 11: One Voice Recovery

I left my contact information on the email, and received a call a couple of weeks after that. Pat called with a flood of information. I found this refreshing, because most of the contacts we had made on our journey were from those who stood to profit from Tyler's addiction. Rehab places, counselors, educational consultants, wilderness programs, addiction doctors, and hospitals were all benefactors of my child's addiction. Blood money. I sometimes believe that addicts are held in this hell, this suspended state of agony, because it's extremely profitable for so many people. What would be the harm of Suboxone, or Vivitrol treatments, or rehab that was long enough to work? Why can't there be more medically supported recovery options? This bounding in and out of rehab, detox, inpatient, trying to find a bed that insurance will pay for, for as long as they will pay, which is never long enough, just ensures a try again, try again approach that is ineffective and expensive. Society pays still, through higher premiums. In addition, rehab is mostly just for those lucky enough to have coverage, or who qualify for Medicaid. And for those on Medicaid, a single person getting Hep C from a dirty needle costs taxpayers eighty to ninety-four thousand dollars to treat! Why is it so hard to get these people some help? Get them some clean needles, some medicine to reduce cravings so they can kick this demon? That has to be less expensive.

Patrick and I spoke for around an hour. He asked if he could use my letter on his website. Of course he could! He told me about the substantial grant that his group received from our very conservative Utah governor. He wanted Tyler to possibly become a recovery coach, and me to be part of some discussion groups for parents, and help make up Naloxone kits, given out to reverse an overdose. I wanted to help in any way I could. It was like those early days of Tyler's life when he was at the NICU in the hospital, too premature to bring home. My only motherly contribution was to pump milk to give to the nurses to give him. I pumped with a religious fervor, every two hours around the clock. My contact was otherwise limited, so I had to take and accept a peripheral role in his care, both then and now.

Many text messages later, when Pat was checking in on how Tyler was doing, he had asked me to be on the board of One Voice Recovery, his harm reduction group, to lend another perspective; that of the parent.

233

Confessions of a Heroin Addict's Mother

We had arranged to meet over coffee, but a hearing came up with the State Health Department that interfered with our plans. The hearing was to determine if more needles would be allowed to be distributed with needle exchange kits, and whether or not other items in the kit would be allowed, in order to promote cleanliness and safety; or, whether this would be considered a distribution of drug paraphernalia. We were both running late to the meeting with bad after-work traffic. Walking in late to the hearing, we exchanged a quick hug and he introduced me to the beautiful girl that was already there waiting for him. Though this was our first meeting, I knew who Patrick was from a taped interview he had given from the Brighton Recovery Center that I had watched when trying to see what Patrick was about. Introducing me to his friend, he said,

"This is Tyler's mom, remember him? Handsome, outgoing kid at the park?"

"Of course!" she said.

I had not planned on speaking. My name and info were not on the list. The Health Department was not necessarily hearing from addicts or family, only those involved in the harm reduction and recovery world, as well as a few politicians with an interest in the subject. Choking back tears, I shared the mother's perspective. I shared how influential One Voice's outreach and harm-reduction tactics had been to Tyler. So few people hear the beginning and middle of the story. They are present and attentive to the end result, the overdose on the street, the arrests, the robbery, the hep-c diagnosis, the jail sentence.

Tyler had a relapse while in inpatient at the Phoenix. He left one day and was lured, in a weak moment, back downtown. He called the Phoenix the next day, saying he'd "fucked up," then he fought his way back in, telling them that he would abide by a strict behavioral contract and it wouldn't happen again. He was joking around with some of the guys on an outing, and said something deemed inappropriate, which caused him to be expelled. I had an hour to pick him up and find him a sober living facility so that he didn't end up on the street again. I was an hour drive away. We were both now seeing sober living as his only option. I was hopeful that he was going to be better, having been through a program. After a week, he stopped communicating. He had pawned the computers, tablets and phones we had lent him so that he could find a job. Then he was homeless again.

Harm Reduction
CHAPTER 12

Fifteen containers of mustard. I don't remember any more details from all of the moves, but I have probably bought fifteen containers of mustard for him, so he's probably moved fifteen times. Into new apartments. In with friends. Into sober living. Into rehab. Into his van. Into Extended Stay America. Into one place or another. Every time, we went shopping for staples so that he wouldn't starve. Bread, ham, drinks, fruit, toothpaste, deodorant, milk, eggs, mayonnaise, mustard. He had complained at some point about the cheap, over-processed ham that I had bought him at Rancho Market, the Mexican market on 33rd South.

I asked him, incredulously, "You inject heroin into your veins and you are complaining about processed ham?" He just laughed.

He couch surfed with acquaintances for a while. Jobless. Homeless. Hopeless. He went to another sober living and started using there. Then, a naive friend named Tyson let him stay, telling me on the phone that I was parenting him all wrong. He was sure that Tyler would be ok if we just listened to him and gave him a bit of encouragement. He would provide that encouragement and support that we apparently didn't provide, and Tyler could stay with him in the nice apartment that the kid's parents paid for. I warned him not to trust Tyler too much. Tyson stayed at his parent's home most of the time because it was closer to his work, leaving Tyler alone in the apartment. He was there for a couple weeks when I got a frantic call from Tyson that Tyler had to go immediately. He had invited a bunch of homeless guys into the apartment, and they had ransacked the place. He was furious. He said Tyler had fought with him and was totally belligerent. He had told Tyson that he was going to shoot up in front of him and kill himself. Call after call was unanswered by Tyler. Chris rushed over. When he arrived, the door was unlocked, so he went into the mess. The shower was running and just Tyler's feet were visible

235

in the hallway as he lay on the floor. A used Naloxone kit was next to him, yet he was alone. We didn't know who had received or given the overdose reversal drug. Chris had never seen him so out of it. He made no sense when he spoke. Another ambulance ride. Another detox. Another near death experience.

Tyson insisted that I meet him at the apartment to move Tyler's stuff out. He was so irate that I was afraid of him, but took responsibility for Tyler's actions, and cleaned and packed his stuff, with the kid berating me and Tyler the entire time. I just agreed with everything he said about both of us being pieces of shit. I understood his anger. I was completely angry myself, as I cleaned up what was once a nice apartment. They had used screwdrivers pounded into the wall to hang up a sheet in the window to conceal their activity. The tub was clogged and full, and the towel bar was ripped off the wall. The frame of the bed was broken, though Tyler had no recollection as to why. Blood was splattered around the sink. My brain was numb as I mechanically cleaned and disinfected everything, rehung the broken towel rack, stuffed his belongings in plastic bags, and hauled them one by one down the stairs from the second story to my truck. I was exhausted. I told myself that I shouldn't have taken responsibility for Tyler's mistake, but I felt really sorry for Tyson. He shouldn't have to bear the brunt of the cleanup. He had just been trying to help Tyler, and I was doing it for his sake. I gave him some money for the damages, and some for rent, and left. I hated Tyler at that moment.

Tyler finished his detox at the hospital, then ended up at Brighton Recovery, where we had tried to get in before. But there was a four- or five-day period where he had nowhere to go until a bed was open. We resorted to the Sandman Motel, where a diminutive lady who owned the place and lived in the home sandwiched in front of the motel and State Street, shook her finger at Tyler and told him that she'd be watching him. No guests, no parties, no excuses. Tyler befriended her and was unruffled by her finger-shaking, and he did comply with her rules.

Brighton Recovery was wonderful. The family involvement opportunities were really helpful for me. There were role playing exercises, family meetings, and phone meetings. I'm not sure Tyler was really invested in it though, his participation seemed half-hearted. After he graduated, he went to another sober living. Then, for whatever reason, went homeless

Chapter 12: Harm Reduction

again. I saw him a couple times. There were sores on his beautiful face. A cut above his eye. I cried when I saw him. Saying anything was pointless. This I know, now. I was told so many times that this would be the case, but it had to be proven to me. Through trial, after trial, after painful trial.

This time when he called, it was he who requested another chance at treatment. He made the calls and arrangements. He got them his insurance information. He chose the location. Wasatch Recovery was also incredible. A month into treatment, we had a family weekend where guest speakers came from Washington to do an impact letter exercise. The program, called "Carefrontations," was taught by Jenny and Scott Graham. Scott was a former undercover vice/narcotics officer in West Hollywood, and had a wild story of addiction, jail, and recovery. The exercise was really one of the most difficult, yet moving, things that we had to do in all of this work toward recovery. Tyler and I both wrote letters, with some direction and guidance from the speakers. The next day, the letters were read to each other, in front of the entire group, each family sharing their own heart-wrenching, intimate stories of the devastation that their loved-one's addiction had created. It was an intervention, but with a very positive ending to each letter that was full of what our hopes for them were. It was so unbelievably draining that I practically collapsed as soon as I was home.

Letter from me to Tyler while he was at Wasatch

Dear Tyler,

I've written this letter to you because I am cautiously optimistic, and hopeful for you in regards to your recovery, but I'm also realistic that you could relapse sometime in the future.

You've had so many treatment attempts in the past three years, and I don't need to remind you of what they were. I feel like your "buy-in" of these attempts has varied, though I do feel that with each successive attempt, you have taken more responsibility for your own recovery. I feel as though you have started to become more and more responsible for your behavior over time, as your focus has shifted away from what others had and have done to you, and more to what your part in all of this is. I realize that the first attempt, when we had you kidnapped and sent to the wilderness,

Confessions of a Heroin Addict's Mother

was probably the most difficult for you to accept, and that being here at Wasatch today, which you arranged on your own, is most likely the most you have done toward "our" mutual recovery. I have wondered, in the past, if you were in recovery because it was a lot more comfortable than being homeless, or if inpatient was an attempt at avoiding the legal ramifications of your behavior, which are many. I do understand that you have not wanted to have your life completely dominated by your recovery, and that you regret that you can't have a "normal" life, like your friends, as long as recovery is your main focus. With this thinking, your addiction has completely dominated your life, and robbed you of anything that looks normal. I don't believe that this is what you wanted, or thought your life would look like.

Yet, your beautiful and caring soul was meant for greater things. I've seen how you touch people's lives. I've seen you take a homeless transgender kid under your wing because you were worried about what would happen to him on the block. You've told me about the kid from the homeless shelter, who was thrown out of his house for masturbation, who you counseled to go home and work things out with his parents. You didn't think he deserved to be homeless for that, and you feared for him in the shelter. He seemed so out of place and scared. And today, you told me about the kid that you saw get his 6 month sobriety chip, at an AA meeting that you went to while here at Wasatch last week. It was the same kid that you injected with Naloxone to save him when he was overdosing, downtown, last spring. Because of you, he lived. Because of you, he was able to get his 6 month chip, and have hope for his future. Your charming and loving spirit has touched more people than you can ever know. Your talent for art and music is a wonderful thing to witness. You have so much beauty inside you yet to share with this world. When you are not using, you are a delight to be around. I have savored the many wonderful experiences that we have had. Nobody gets my sense of humor or appreciation of things like you do. We think alike in so many ways, and I miss being able to connect with you on so many levels. I want to have experiences like we had on our road trip last year. It was one of the best times of my life. Reflecting, introspecting, meditating and exploring, while camping in the desert and freezing our asses off. Going wherever the road took us, stopping wherever we felt like. Talking, nonstop, for hours on end. That makes me want so badly for you

Chapter 12: Harm Reduction

to stay clean, so we can do these things again and again. Your mind is so sharp and observant, with an eye for justice, beauty, and design, when you are clean.

However, if you continue on the path that you have been on, I believe that you will continue to push away the possibility of having your family and friends in your life. Your handsome good looks could certainly decline. I see your health being in jeopardy. You have been lucky that your multiple near death experiences have not taken your life yet. I cannot see you even getting a job or a place to live if you are using, and will likely continue to be homeless. You will have legal issues that need to be resolved, most likely, including jail time when you get out of Wasatch, but they will be much worse if you continue to use. Five arrests this year won't look so good to a judge if they are trying to figure out whether or not you should go to jail on arrest number six. I hate to say that I have played your funeral over and over in my head. What would the obituary look like? Would I be honest in it? Would I say you died of an overdose? Which of your friends would come? What would I dress you in? Would it be "old" Tyler clothes like a soccer jersey or school uniform? Or would it be your badass street clothes? Would I dye your hair back to it's original dark chocolate brown? Would I cover your track marks? When I think about this, I'm just devastated. I feel like we would all be robbed of a clean and free Tyler bringing joy to our lives. I would be robbed of hearing you play your cello again. I would be robbed of possibly being a grandmother. I would be held in a suspended state of grief.

But, I can envision more with your life. I can see you clean, happy, and free. I have seen glimmers of hope through the last few years, and I truly believe that you want it to be different. I have never believed in fate until the last year or so. I just feel like your life has a greater purpose, that you were meant to be here, to live a wonderful and prosperous life, and to touch others in an impactful and positive way. To make a difference. You have the ability to restore your health. I believe in you. The cravings will certainly get easier. Your lust for better things in life will strengthen as you start finding joy in the things that you have been missing. Your love of yourself will grow as you reach goals and surpass roadblocks. I see you making a great father and becoming a wonderful spouse, because your

239

empathy and compassion for those suffering will grow. You CAN succeed in ways that you can't see now, in the height of your disease. You will need to create a plan for relapse. You need to be able to ask for help when you need it. We will always do whatever we can and are able to do to aid you in your recovery. I feel so hopeful when I think about this life for you. One of hope, joy and freedom. I love you so much!

Mom

He almost finished at Wasatch. After testing positive for a tiny amount of meth, but swearing up and down that it had to be the nasal inhaler that had an ingredient that can show up as meth on a drug test, he fought to contest his dismissal. I stayed out of it, not sure what to believe. Besides, he needed to learn to defend himself if he thought he was right, and learn a lesson about doing dumb-ass things like using that sort of inhaler. His pleas fell on deaf ears. The psychiatrist affiliated with Wasatch had heard enough excuses from addicts over the years that he wouldn't even consider Tyler's argument. The only problem was that he got thrown out the day before thirty-five family members and friends were to show up at my house for Thanksgiving dinner, and I was cooking most of the meal. I was completely stuck. Chris had to drive him all the way up to Oakley after I convinced Matt that we should let him stay, for at least Thanksgiving night. My brother and his wife were staying with us, and it would be good for Tyler to be around family. I didn't scold or lecture, I just concentrated on making the holiday as great as possible.

It was a glorious holiday. It was everything I wanted in hosting the party at my house. With three extra tables in the family room, the smoked turkey, and all of the young adult kids sitting at a table and laughing and joking with each other, I could think of no better day. It was a relief for my dad and step-mother to get a break from all of the preparations, and I felt like a generational torch had been passed my way. Weston made a spectacular pork roast, and both kitchens, upstairs and down, were cranking out amazing dishes with contributions from everyone. We would all try to forget that court would happen again in a few days. Tyler had broken his probation, and we heard there was a ten-thousand-dollar cash bench warrant out for his arrest from his probation officer. But right now, everything was right with the world. To learn to savor moments like this would be my salvation.

Tyler thought he could turn on his charm with the judge and explain why he missed months of drug testing. He had a notion that he could get in a couple weeks' worth of clean tests, and the rest would be forgiven. It didn't work. In addition, Chris had sent a letter to the judge, asking her to lock him up, in a completely desperate attempt to save him from himself. He asked her not to say that he had written the letter. I knew about the letter, but did not stop him. It was our strange way of letting each other take turns at taking care of business, while the other parent got a pass in our weird triangle of dysfunction. Chris's plan of staying anonymous backfired, as the prosecuting attorney read the letter aloud, announcing that it was from Tyler's father, and that she had never seen this happen before, where a parent implicated their own child. Six months in jail. They cuffed him and took him out. I sat there, numb, as he looked back at me in disbelief.

I didn't know where to go after that so I went to the bank to close his account for some reason. It had a negative balance so I wanted just to pay it off and close it. I guess just to feel like I was doing something, or to clean up another mess. I hate the small talk bullshit that the bank tellers engage in.

"What are you up to today?" What was I supposed to say?

"I watched my son get hauled off to jail today and now I'm here closing his bank account?"

This book started to be about how difficult my son's addiction has been in my life, but more and more, it has forced me to look at myself and my own recovery. It's the only thing that I have any control over. I sent what I had written of this book to Weston to review and give me his thoughts. It had been much too difficult for him to finish it. It was all too real to him. He told me that he thought the subject was a "tired trope," and he couldn't imagine what I could say about the matter that had not been said before by someone. I think he's right in some ways. But his pain probably comes from the nightmare that reading it brings back to him. Though our experience as parents of addicts is unique in many ways, there are universalities that most people can relate to who have addicted children, and perhaps, be comforted by the knowledge that they are not alone. This is why Al-Anon is so helpful to so many people. I see the desperate search for answers and comfort from a group of people with brutal, universally shared experiences. There is hope, if not answers, from the group, from those that understand our unique pain. From others I received more positive feedback on my book. Regardless of if I ever publish this, it has provided some clarity to me. For that, I am eternally grateful to myself for my efforts.

I continued my Al-Anon meetings as time has permitted, and came to realize the importance of that to me. I have continuously attended a Step Meeting with Al-Anon on Monday nights, which means we read in "Paths to Recovery," and go through each and every step, tradition, and concept. Al-Anon, much like AA, is organized around twelve steps.

Most people are somewhat familiar with these twelve steps, but not the twelve traditions or the twelve concepts. The traditions are more or less rules for conducting business as an organization. The concepts are organizational details. For the outsider, I'm assuming, and for me when I first walked into a meeting, it seemed like a lot of rules and mundane issues that take up too much time for study in a meeting. When I'm hurting, and struggling to pack a meeting into my busy schedule, it's difficult to muddle through things like the business of how a meeting is to be run, and how Al-Anon deals with organizational details and structure. The more I sit in the meetings however, the more I see purpose and connection. I find relevance to my life even in the concepts and traditions.

We were on concept five. The rights of appeal and petition that protect minorities and ensure that they be heard. We went through the reading first, then read the questions that were in conjunction with the reading, as we went around the table taking turns.

"Have you ever suggested to someone that they speak up when they don't believe they are being heard?" Earlier that day, I had received a call from my stepdad. He was really upset with my mother, and suggested that he thought that she might have a personality disorder, or some other mental health issue. I was surprised that he was just figuring that out. They had only been married for 18 months or so. I could totally understand and relate to him about my mom. For years, my siblings and I all treaded lightly around my mother, discussed her mental health when we got together, and genuinely wondered how we had made it through our childhood, as "normal" as we were. I had decided many years ago that I wasn't going to hinge my happiness on whether or not my mother was talking to me. I speak to her frequently now, and try not to let her drag me into whatever drama she is creating, savoring, or perpetuating. When we speak, I pretend that nothing is wrong between us, even if she has hung up in a previous conversation. I see her frequently when I travel to St. George, but it exhausts me. She has so much to be grateful for, but she is the most miserable person I have ever met. The views from her home, built like others in the neighborhood to blend in with the Southern Utah environment, are breathtaking. If I point things like that out, she just ignores me. There is no gray in her life, just black and white. There is no compromise. No empathy. We have never had a heart to heart conversation that I can remember. She interrupts, ridicules, and screams. She is never wrong, nobody else is ever right. I could go on...but why?

I really did feel bad for my stepdad. He is really a sort of likable guy, except for his propensity for talking about conservative politics, and debating. At least he will listen, and seems to have an open mind. I get the sense that he sincerely does want to know why I think the way I do, and he is not just looking to say "gotcha," in a debate. He adores Tyler, and reaches out to connect with him on a "grandfatherly" level, as well as from someone else who is in recovery, which he is. I think that his financial situation drove him toward my mom, who is fairly financially secure, and who has dangled her beautiful home and fancy cars in front of men who would not otherwise put up with her bullshit. I have spent my life trying to not be like her.

I suggested to my stepdad that he softly confront her about the need for therapy, or I could. He said that had been to a few sessions, and that she screamed and walked out of their last session, I imagine, as she does with doctors and lawyers, as well, that she has been unhappy with. He is afraid of what will happen if she even thinks that we have spoken. How could I ask him to confront her when I have never really been able to? Even about something as small as hitting me with the hairbrush if I made a peep that she was pulling my long hair too hard. Then there was that bigger thing. Getting molested by a missionary, and being told not to tell anyone. Making me feel dirty or guilty for something an eight-year-old could not have been at fault for.

Growing up, I was the quietly compliant child. The one that could be trusted to monitor the others if my parents left us alone. I had a lot of friends in Elkhart, Indiana, but we really were the outsiders, growing up Mormon in Catholic country, transplanted Westerners living in a painfully different Midwestern town. In high school, we were only to date other Mormon kids, and there was only one, unacceptable choice in my school. When I went out with friends, I would get physically sick to my stomach with anxiety about our plans. I frequently did not want to do whatever they were suggesting, but I never spoke up and told them otherwise. I was agreeable and friendly, but I wasn't one of the kids who rocked the boat or directed others. I had bouts of depression that would force me to stay alone in my room knitting, or doing some other quiet activity. I had a suicide attempt and ended up in the hospital for a couple of weeks. Being heard was not something that I felt like I deserved.

I had learned a number of coping mechanisms as a kid. We had this really cool English teacher that taught some kind of after school yoga class. This was in the late seventies, and she was the total hippie type. She was white, but wore an afro and seemed so different than the rest of the teachers. I don't remember why I took the class, but I loved it. I specifically remember meditating at the end of class and how great that felt. The breathing; the calming effect of just focusing on nothing. I would use the same breathing to calm my anxiety with friends. When I'd feel my stomach tighten up and start to get panicky, I would slow my breathing and focus the calm feeling toward the tight spot in my stomach. It totally worked then, and it still does now.

I had done alright in high school, but nothing terribly earth-shattering. I don't really remember my parents inquiring about our grades, or going to parent teacher conferences or anything. Maybe after my mom left, when being a mother to five kids born within six years of each other was just not doing it for her anymore, things like our education must have fallen through the cracks. Or maybe they went to the conferences and just didn't say anything that I remember. Or maybe I was doing fine enough. In any event, my academic career was unremarkable, from my parents' point of view. I don't remember them making a big deal out of going to college either. I just figured out on my own that college would be the next step after high school.

Chapter 12: Harm Reduction

When I was on my own, I discovered that I was much smarter than I had been led to believe. I started getting a real kick out of skewing the grading curve in a class because I scored so high. I sought out the recommendation of a school counselor to help me get into the "easy stats" class, because I had not excelled at math in high school (mostly because I wouldn't speak up if I didn't understand). She told me she signed me up for the "best" class, but she did not tell me that it was the most difficult one. This was a class that started with something like 350 students, but so many dropped it that there was usually something like eighty who finished the semester. I maintained the top score in the class, and became a tutor for it the following year.

I'm not trying to be pompous in talking about these things, just to point out that I was coming into my own self-confidence and finding out that I was intelligent, and that I had a voice. I had found that nobody would stick up for me if I couldn't stick up for myself. No longer a wallflower or a doormat. I had an opinion about things, I was fierce, and I wasn't going to be controlled, or just go along with the program. The next thirty years became a backlash to the first twenty. Possibly an overcorrection. I went from quiet and complacent, to loud and controlling. If I took charge of everything, I wouldn't be disappointed. None of this helped me deal with being a mother to an addict child. As much as I wanted to, and tried, I couldn't fix any of this. I could plan, beg, suggest, cajole, and guilt-trip, but I couldn't change anything but my expectations. I had to admit my helplessness. Step one in Al-Anon.

Jail
CHAPTER 13

Perhaps jail is what we all need. There is really nothing that I can do for Tyler, now. I can't rescue him, or interfere. There doesn't seem to be anyone that I can call when something is needed on Tyler's behalf. He claims that instead of providing dental work when you have dental problems, and he does, they simply extract a tooth. I asked him how he knows, and he said he heard it from a toothless inmate. He also says that someone who works in the kitchen saw that the potatoes they cook with say, "not for human consumption," on them. Maybe it's just jailhouse folklore. I don't know, and I can't find out. Even his pillow must be purchased at the commissary. The letter I sent him for Christmas got sent back. They told him that he got a letter that had five photographs instead of four, and the rule stated that only four were allowed. Of course I had carefully read the rules before I sent the letter, but two of the photos of his little cousin must have stuck together. Nothing can be forgiven or fudged. They couldn't just remove one picture and let him read his Christmas letter that I spent so much time writing. He simply couldn't have five cute baby pictures, only four. I saved the letter anyway. Maybe he can read it when he gets home.

Christmas 2017

Merry Christmas Tyler, December 23, 2017

I've written you so many letters over the last few years, and I find this one the most difficult yet. I wish so much that you could be enjoying the holiday with us this year, just as we enjoyed a rare holiday with you at Thanksgiving,

Chapter 13: Jail

because you were doing so much better. Your presence lights up the room, and I am still basking in the thankfulness and gratitude I felt with everyone here together at the house, having fun and enjoying the moment.

On the Solstice, a couple days ago, I thought again of the letter that I wrote you on the Solstice two years ago, when you were in the wilderness at Second Nature. A reminder that rebirth and renewal are possible. A focus on the coming year and all of the possibilities contained therein. You will probably get tired of hearing this from me, and everyone, but during this time of so little freedom, reflect on the things that you are grateful for. This has become my recent focus myself, and, to be honest, my salvation these days. The card that contains this letter was purchased a couple months ago, because I liked the saying on the front, "What You Think On Grows." I didn't know when I'd use it, but this seemed the perfect time. Think about all of the good things… the good friends…the people that have stuck by you, through thick and thin. You have so much going for you, when you look at it. "Think" on the positive and good. Drag yourself out of the darkness that has surrounded you for years. Meditate…exercise…read positive things…do yoga…meditate again.

I believe you and I have always had difficulty being alone with our thoughts. We fill empty space with anything that we can. As I sit in the waiting room waiting to see you here, I realize this very blatantly. There is no iPhone, no music, no magazines, no television. Facing your thoughts and reflecting for a half hour is so difficult, as I'm sure you are finding out, much more so than me. I'm trying to meditate during this time. One thing that I've found is that jail is the great equalizer. Any entitlement that you or I thought we had in life is gone. Nobody gets any special treatment. These people in the waiting room don't look like me, but we are suffering in the same way. Nobody gives a shit that you went to private school, or played the cello in the chamber orchestra. Consequences are consequences and eventually everyone must pay, you and me both.

You really have a lot of people that care about you. The true friends show up in the roughest of times. Jenny has reached out and really wants you to know how much she cares. Friends like April are hard to come by. Ben and Sarah sent me pictures of Wilder because they know how much you love your little cousin. When I was in high school, I had a serious bout of depression and I ended up in the hospital for a while. I knew who my true friends were. They were the ones who showed up when it was difficult. The ones that had to make a bit of an effort to see me, or show me that they cared. I'll always remember those friends. The ones that just show up because you have drugs, or for some other shallow reason, aren't in it for anyone but themselves. It's all about positive human connectivity and the comfort that well intentioned friends and family bring.

I hope that you get to do something relaxing and positive on Christmas. I got the sheet music for the Gabriel Faure "Elegie for Cello and Piano" that I told you I wanted to learn. I'll learn my part, and you can learn yours when you get out. It's so beautiful. As I'm writing this, I'm looking out on the soft snow falling. I can barely see the trees and horses across the pasture. So pretty! I thought about that Great Horned Owl you saw right before you went to jail, the same one I saw the other day, in the same place. It flew right over the hood of my truck. I've always seen owls as a sign of bad times to come. Maybe I've had it wrong all along. Maybe, in their wisdom, they are telling us that a learning experience is ahead. An opportunity to grow. I will try and change my perception of what I think of the owl, remember, "What you think on Grows."

Love Always,

Mom

We would all be punished and made to live by the rules. My contact is now limited to when he calls me and I accept the collect call on the account that I established, as well as twice a week visit time, when I can take the half a day out of my schedule to drive to Salt Lake and be put through the procedures that they require.

I brought the two Smith boys with me on a Wednesday visit. Nick, home from college, along with his younger brother Jonathan. They were friends from our Mayberry neighborhood, both doing well and thriving. Nick was living every musicians dream, going to Berklee College of Music in Boston, partly paid for with the proceeds of the house in California

Chapter 13: Jail

that I had cleaned out for them to sell. We had all done so much together. Perhaps we were at their house as much as we were home during the daytime hours. Tyler had spent so much time at their burger joint while I worked in the summer and he was off school. Days spent playing video games in the back office with the boys and eating burgers and fries.

The boys were having trouble finding the jail. I wasn't very specific about the instructions, but I figured they would map quest it or something. It's hard to miss; a huge, looming, windowless concrete building. They were a minute late for visiting, though the line was still forming to get a locker key to put your belongings in before going back to the second waiting room. The stern female guard just glared at me, her face unsmiling and cold.

"You'll have to wait until the next visit time." What could I do? The boys came in and Johnathan had forgotten his I.D.

"He can't come in then," she seemed to take pleasure in saying. Johnathan's middle school history teacher was there in the lobby and came up and gave him a big hug. I had asked the guard if he could vouch for his identity, and she didn't even answer me. Rules are rules, I guess. Tyler will need to learn to advocate for himself. Drive himself forward, and make whatever changes he needs to make, without me.

And so it goes. A different speed and rhythm to which to get accustomed. The quiet is deafening. The guilt over the relief that I'm now feeling with Tyler's incarceration has overtaken me. But I can now box up the random clothes, toiletries, books, and belongings spread between our basement, guest room, garage, my truck, and the storage unit. Get them all in one place for the first time in years. Boxed up and labeled for the future, hopefully to be unboxed in one stable place and kept there for a reasonable amount of time. I can stop worrying for a little while about where he is going to live next, or if I will get a call from the police, or worse, the morgue.

249

Burnt Toast

Little mishaps
A fender bender
Dealing with a customer's ridiculous, petty expectations
A hitch in the project
Burnt toast
A plant I forgot to water
Overheard talk about me, my child

All things that don't matter to me anymore

The only good outcome of all of this is perspective
I know a mother's hell
It's not burnt toast

Eva Summerhill

Poetry, recovery books, meditation. Whatever it takes to get some peace. I read in my Al-Anon daily reader, *One Day at a time in Al-Anon.*

"For though we are made especially for the sake of another, still each of us has his own tasks. Otherwise another's faults would harm me, which God has not willed in order that my happiness may not depend on another." Marcus Aurelius: *Meditations*, paraphrased

A couple days after Tyler went to jail, I impulsively went to the Best Friends Animal Rescue and adopted a kitten to fill the void. Not just any kitten. She had been found with her sister, abandoned from a very young age, and had been bottle fed and raised by foster humans. She would require a special diet for life and had a medical history packet an inch thick. I could pour all of my need to take care of something into this adorable furry black bundle. Something I couldn't harm by "over-mothering." I can see how people become cat ladies now. It's really hard to screw up a cat.

Home
CHAPTER 14

After jail there were months of inpatient and outpatient at Odyssey house, the rehab that was funded by the state. Probation and sober living. Counseling, and drug testing. There was an acceptance of this by Tyler, and by us. He had learned that there were consequences to stepping out of line, and that there were rules that just came along with the decisions that he had made previously. He stopped blaming us. We stopped blaming him. It seems that learning from the natural consequences had worked best after all.

We fell into a sort of normalcy when he lived at Odyssey House sober living. We let him make all of his appointments and become responsible for himself. We let him suffer the consequences when he would slip up and miss a meeting and get time added to his therapy end date. We let him find the job that he wanted, not one that we thought he should have. We let him own his successes, and failures.

Sometimes when we got together it was like the old days. He seemed to have an interest in living again. Not just living, but living fully. We could have conversations about things that he had a passion for. On a drive with him I brought up the Kingfisher bird I frequently saw on the telephone wire perched above the stream when I drove through Peoa. The little hunter looking for dinner in the water. I tried numerous times to photograph it but I couldn't park close enough without scaring it. We had a nice discussion about birds again. He may not have recognized the significance of this but I didn't miss it. I savored the moment. It was like a spark finally igniting the fire that you have needed to stay warm, after a long, long winter.

When I first heard of detachment in Al-Anon, I rejected it as being a tool I could adopt. I didn't understand it. I thought that detachment meant not thinking about or seeing something, or someone. To cut

251

Confessions of a Heroin Addict's Mother

someone out of your life. To forget completely about them. My whole life seemed to consist of places that I had taken difficult phone calls, or had stressful interactions with Tyler. There was no place that I could go, nothing that I could do, where I wouldn't be reminded in some way of his situation, our situation. A sort of PTSD. Panic would set in, memories flooding back to me. When I flipped through my phone, I would see countless contacts that related to Tyler's recovery. Going into the basement or my storage was always a reminder of the chaos, when I would see the boxes of residual items from some move or another. There was that place by the windows at the gym where I would go talk, so I could get privacy for the countless calls that happened when I was trying to get some exercise. How does one "detach" with all of these reminders of "what is?" What should I make of my feeling that my Higher Power resides in the connectedness between people, and animals? Is this "connectedness" making us sick? No, codependency is.

This poem is from a great article on detachment (*http://www.livestrong.com/article/14712-developing-detachment/#develop*).

"Letting Go"
- To "let go" does not mean to stop caring; it means I can't do it for someone else.
- To "let go" is not to cut myself off; it's the realization I can't control another.
- To "let go" is not to enable, but to allow learning from natural consequences.
- To "let go" is to admit powerlessness, which means the outcome is not in my hands.
- To "let go" is not to try to change or blame another; it's to make the most of myself.
- To "let go" is not to care for, but to care about.
- To "let go" is not to fix, but to be supportive.
- To "let go" is not to judge, but to allow another to be a human being.
- To "let go" is not to be in the middle arranging all the outcomes, but to allow others to affect their own destinies.
- To "let go" is not to be protective; it's to permit another to face reality.
- To "let go" is not to deny, but to accept.

Chapter 14: Home

- To "let go" is not to nag, scold or argue, but instead to search out my own shortcomings and correct them.
- To "let go" is not to criticize and regulate anybody, but to try to become what I dream I can be.
- To "let go" is not to adjust everything to my desires, but to take each day as it comes and cherish myself in it.
- To "let go" is to not regret the past, but to grow and live for the future.
- To "let go" is to fear less and love myself more.

I must practice detachment from an outcome in which I have no control, while connecting with that person with all of the love that is within me. This is the summation of all of my learning about addiction.

"Peace never visits the controller."
- *Karen Casey*, Let Go Now: Embracing Detachment -

Turning Point
CHAPTER 15

Turning Point is probably not really accurate. A proper diagnosis of Bipolar Disorder was certainly helpful. There wasn't one singular event where things started to improve, except maybe my realization that nothing I could do could fix this, and perhaps, my release of expectations. But those things were not singular instances. They were long fought battles with myself over time.

Life

I brought you into this world, but it is your job to live it
I can't do it for you
It is my responsibility to do that for myself now;
Live my own life, not yours

Eva Summerhill

I read, "Not to create a crisis; not to prevent a crisis if it is the natural course of events," in *Courage to Change*. Tyler had to be given the opportunity to have success at making the right decisions and realize that it was him that did that, and feel the pride which comes from accomplishment.

New Year's Eve. My resolutions this year are simple. In addition to losing the twelve or so pounds I have gained by not paying attention to myself, I resolve to learn to live with the calm. That is the goal now. To stop anticipating drama, so accustomed to it that I create it where it doesn't exist, just out of familiarity. To not be bored when there is not a crisis to attend to. To even welcome boredom. To progress in my life without guilt when Tyler is not progressing. To learn to love him in a different way. To come to realize that detachment does not mean to stop loving him, or to deny all contact, it means to not attach myself to an outcome over which

254

I have no control. To understand that the wake behind the boat, the past, isn't driving anything forward. It will dissipate and turn to calm again after the boat stops disrupting the water.

I read on a quote on Pinterest that I had seen in Al-Anon literature that says it perfectly: "An expectation is just a premeditated resentment." That he's at peace is all I really want. However he comes to it. It may not look like the life that I had expected for him, that we were trying to create for him. Long gone are the days that I lament over the different paths that we had all taken. I now appreciate the path we are all on together, staying in our own lanes, and I respect him enough to allow his decisions to be his alone. In this way, he can enjoy his victories as his own, and learn from his mistakes. Don't get me wrong, I still love him with all of my heart, maybe even more now. I still offer my advice which he can take or leave. I still help him when he asks for it, and I feel that what he is asking of me is something he is really not capable of doing on his own. He's still only twenty, after all. Learning about himself and exploring his emotions, and learning to think about the outcomes of his decisions has been a long journey for him, and he's getting there.

February 14, 2017 was his first court date. Now, February 14, 2019 will be the second audition for the *High School Musical* series. My son possibly in a Disney show! I can hardly believe it. We laughed because at outpatient they always called him *Breakfast Club*, after the Judd Nelson character John Bender in the classic eighties movie that explored high school relationships and pressures. John Bender was that kid who got a carton of cigarettes from his folks for Christmas: "Smoke up Johnny!" Tyler wondered if they were planning to cast him in a "bad boy" role if he got the part. I'm glad we could laugh about it now. Now that he has been clean for over a year, and has a gratifying job at Nordstrom in the young men's department, where he is usually in the top of the department in sales. Over the last five years, he had very little to pride himself in, until I let him muddle through things on his own and discover his capabilities. He has created in himself a person he can be proud of. He may decide to go to school when he's ready. He'll figure that out if and when the time is right. It's not my place to push it at him, only to support his decision and help where I can.

When he first got set up with a modeling agency, he sent me a picture of his mugshot and then, his modeling headshot. As if I needed a pictorial example of how far he has come.

"I think I have to learn everything the hard way," he had told me in a reflective conversation we had while driving from an audition. In that moment, I was able to really relate to him, this young man, my boy.

"Yes, we both do. I'm proud of you son."

We enjoyed a relatively peaceful year and a half or so, until the next relapse. We all must now strive to implement what we have learned in our previous trials, and work toward finding peace and joy, in whatever places that we can. My wish is that you, the reader, may also find peace and joy in your life, and perhaps learn from our journey, so that your load might be a little lighter.

Credits

From the book *The Four Agreements* © 1997, Miguel Angel Ruiz, M.D. Reprinted by permission of Amber-Allen Publishing, Inc. All rights reserved.

Excerpts from *Man's Search for Meaning* by Viktor E. Frankl. Copyright 2006, Beacon Press. All right reserved. Used by permission.

Excerpt from "The New Macho" Copyright 2010 by Boysen Hodgson of "The Mankind Project" Used by kind permission.

"Let God and Let Go" from *One Day At A Time In Al-Anon*, Copyright 1968, 1972, 2000, by Al-Anon Family Group Headquarters, Inc. Reprinted by permission of Al-Anon Family Group Headquarters, Inc.

"All Things Considered" on National Public Radio "Most Medicaid Patients Can't Get Advanced Hep C Drugs" - Jake Harper December 27, 2015

"Carefrontations" by Jenny & Scott Graham.

Excerpts from *Paths to Recovery*, Copyright 1997, by Al-Anon Family Group Headquarters, Inc. Reprinted by permission of Al-Anon Family Group Headquarters, Inc.

"Letting Go" - *http://www.livestrong.com/ Article/14712-developing-detachment/#develop)*

Confessions of a Heroin Addict's Mother

"Not to prevent a crisis if it is in the natural course of events." - from *Courage to Change*, Copyright 1992, by Al-Anon Family Group Headquarters, Inc. Reprinted by permission of Al-Anon Family Group Headquarters, Inc.

"An expectation is a premeditated resentment" - from *Courage to Change*, Copyright 1992, by Al-Anon Family Group Headquarters, Inc. Reprinted by permission of Al-Anon Family Group Headquarters, Inc.

O'Brien, Barbara. "Why do Buddhists Avoid Attachment?" Learn Religions, Apr. 17, 2019, learn *religions.com/ why-do-buddhists-avoid-attachment-449714*

Living Life from *facebook.com* "Detachment is not always...."

"Open Letter From the Alcoholic," excerpt from "Courage to Change," copyright 1992, by Al-Anon Family Group Headquarters, Inc. Reprinted by permission of Al-Anon Family Group Headquarters, Inc. Permission to reprint this excerpt does not mean that Al Anon Family Group Headquarters, Inc. has reviewed or approved the contents of this publication, or that Al Anon Family Group Headquarters, Inc. necessarily agrees with the views expressed herein. Al Anon is a program of recovery for families and friends of alcoholics-use of this excerpt in any non Al-Anon context does not imply endorsement or affiliation by Al Anon.

"Grief" by Gwen Flowers. Used by permission.

Hari, Johann. (Date) Everything You Know About Addiction Is Wrong. [Video File] Retrieved from *http//www.ted.com.rest_of_URL*.

Alexander, B.K., Coambs, R.B., and Hadaway, P.F. (1978). "The Effect of Housing and Gender on Morphine Self-Administration in Rats"

Centers for Disease Control and Prevention, Overdose Deaths, *https:// www.cdc.gov/drugoverdose/data/statedeaths.html*

Acknowledgments

My gratitude pours out for the many who have helped me and my family on this difficult journey. Many connections with amazing individuals have been made that I would not have met, were it not for this trial. My editor, Nella Holden, and my publisher, Katie Mullaly of Surrogate Press, came to the book side of this journey with immense support and patience as I relived my struggles to get my insights into a format that I hope will be helpful to others.

Many people in Al-Anon and other support groups have helped me understand so much about myself and addiction. In the spirit of anonymity, I won't mention names as you know who you are. The counselors and therapists for myself and my family where especially helpful. Devon Glissmeyer, Sari Souter, Chris Robertson, James Meyer, Alema Harrington, Kristi Johnson, Shannon Boxley, and Ramona Sierra all offered support for which I'm grateful.

Many treatment programs have helped in one way or another and were indispensable for "our" recovery, especially: Second Nature, Brighton Recovery, DaySpring, Odyssey House, Phoenix Recovery, Highland Ridge, Carefrontations with Jenny and Scott Graham, and Wasatch Recovery.

Tyler may not have made it out alive without the harm reduction and recovery community including: One Voice Recovery, Utah Naloxone, USARA, Fit To Recover, and those involved with these groups who spend countless hours helping those who struggle with addiction as well as those who love them. Warriors in this effort who have touched our lives include, Jen "Naloxone" Plumb, Patrick Rezak, McCall Christensen, Ed Schwartz, Bryer Bagwell, Xander Gordon, Randall Carlisle, Ann Lobos, and so many more.

259

I want to thank the friends who have offered support, advice, a shoulder to cry on, or a much-needed hug. I love you Stanna Frampton-Coury, Linda Steadman, Cathleen Imo, Stacey Lynn Kratz, Mel Menlove, Joanna Bastian, Michael Kirklen, and Curt Wallin. I want to thank those who were patient with me when I was not as emotionally available to them as I should have been while I struggled, especially my family.

But mostly, I want to thank the strangers. The people who prayed with Tyler in the park when he was down. The ones to which true empathy flows to those who hurt. You all make recovery possible.

About the Author

Eva Summerhill lives in a cabin the mountains of Utah with an old Jack Russell Terrier and a mean rescue cat, named Eva. She borrowed the cat's name and her tenacity to write this difficult, honest memoir.

In pouring her soul into searching for answers to help her addicted son, Eva started journaling. She started looking at those writings, along with letters and other correspondence, and decided that a compilation of these works might give suffering parents some insight, and spare them some of the crushing pain.

Before she became and "accidental" writer, Eva had done everything from general contracting to teaching music, and a few random things in between. When she isn't working on recovery advocacy within her family and community, she is passionate about playing outside, gardening, cooking, painting, working on her cabin, and trekking in Europe. She loves spending time with her two wonderful sons and extended family.

Visit her website at *evasummerhill.com* to sign up for her mailing list, and for information and recovery resources.

Made in the USA
Monee, IL
01 February 2021